50 STEPS TO IMPROVING YOUR Grammar

Study Book

Chris Sowton

Garnet EDUCATION

Published by
Garnet Publishing Ltd
8 Southern Court
South Street
Reading RG1 4QS, UK
www.garneteducation.com

ISBN: 978 1 78260 222 4

British Library Cataloguing-in-Publication Data
A catalogue record for this book is available from the British Library.

Production

Project manager:	Alan Dury
Editorial team:	Alan Dury, Chris Little
Design & layout:	Neil Collier, Simon Ellway, Bob House, Madeleine Maddock
Photography:	iStockphoto

Printed and bound in Lebanon by International Press: interpress@int-press.com

Dedication

This book is dedicated to the people of Nepal, who on 25th April and 12th May 2015 experienced two terrible earthquakes, which killed nearly 10,000 people. Having set up the charity Global Action Nepal (www.nepalaction.global) and lived for many years there, I believe that it is crucial that those who died and those who are trying to rebuild society are not forgotten.

Chris Sowton

Acknowledgements

Page 11. Extract by Roald Dahl from *Someone Like You*. Reproduced with kind permission of Penguin Books.

Page 27. Extract by CS Lewis © CS Lewis Pte Ltd.

Page 51. Stephen Fry quotation from an interview in the *Radio Times*, July 2010. Reprinted with kind permission of Stephen Fry.

Page 79. Clifton Fadiman quotation reprinted with permission from *Reader's Digest* © 1956 by The Reader's Digest Association, Inc.

Page 175. Kurt Vonnegut excerpt from *A Man Without a Country* © 2010 by Kurt Vonnegut. Reprinted with permission of The Permissions Company, Inc., on behalf of Seven Stories Press: www.sevenstories.com.

Contents

Introduction

> *'I will not go down to posterity talking bad grammar.'*
>
> **Benjamin Disraeli (1804–1881)**
> *UK Prime Minister 1868 and 1874–1880*

Overview of this book

50 Steps to Improving Your Grammar is different to the grammar books which you may have read before. Many grammar books are dense and inaccessible, with long, complicated explanations. The idea of reading one of these books is unexciting. *50 Steps to Improving Your Grammar* builds on the approach used in *50 Steps to Improving Your Academic Writing*: the key information for each topic is presented in a simple, concise format, and is accompanied by activities which help you to practise and consolidate what you have learnt. By breaking down the key areas of English grammar into short steps, the book makes grammar accessible and helps you to structure and focus your own learning.

Structure of the book

The 50 steps in this book are divided into ten units (A–J), each of which contains five steps. Each unit has a different focus, and together the units deal with the major areas of English grammar. Once you have completed the 50 steps, you will understand why grammar is important, know how to use the different word classes and have a clearer idea of the grammar to use in different situations. The ten units of the book are listed below. The individual steps can be found in the *Contents* on pages 3–4.

Unit A What is grammar?
Unit B Nouns and pronouns
Unit C Verbs
Unit D Adjectives and adverbs
Unit E Conjunctions, prepositions and determiners
Unit F Sentence structure
Unit G Grammar for specific purposes
Unit H Grammatical precision
Unit I Punctuation and spelling
Unit J Academic grammar

Structure of each step

Each step is made up of four pages and follows the same pattern, which is as follows.

A. Reflection (½ page)
This section evaluates your existing understanding of the topic through targeted questions.

B. Contextualization (½ page)
This section demonstrates the topic's relevance and importance by presenting the learning point in context.

C. Explanation (2 pages)

This section explains the topic in detail by answering the specific questions posed in Parts A and B. The structure of each step is interrogative: it asks a series of questions, and then answers them. In Part C, you will also come across a number of special features designed to increase your understanding of the subject matter. These include the following.

- *Glossary link*
  This shows you that a word or phrase is found in the *Glossary*. Glossary links are highlighted in SMALL CAPITALS. The *Glossary*, on page 227, provides clear definitions of the grammatical terms used in the text.
- *Example sentence from Parts A and B*
  Sentences from Parts A and B are often examined in more detail in Part C. They are highlighted in green.
- *Link to another step*
  Arrows are used with step numbers (▶Step 17) to refer to places in the book where a particular topic is discussed in detail.
- *Summary box*
  Each Part C concludes with a summary of the step in three points.

D. Activation (1 page)

This section helps you to apply what you have learnt through a range of focused activities. The answers to the questions posed in Part D of each step can be found in the *Answers* section on page 207.

The English used in this book

Where there are important grammatical differences between them, British English (BrE) and American English (AmE) are compared. The book itself is written in British English.

How to use this book

Each step should take you 45–60 minutes to complete: 10–15 minutes for Parts A and B, 20–25 minutes for Part C and 15–20 minutes for Part D. Exactly how long you spend will depend on the precise details of the step and your existing level of knowledge.

The structure of the book means that you can decide how best to use it. If you are already aware of your areas of weakness in grammar, then you should focus on the particular steps which apply. Each step is stand-alone, and will make sense if you look at it in isolation. If, however, you feel you need more consistent support, it will benefit you to follow the book through from beginning to end.

However you use this book, it is important that you try to apply what you learn as much as you possibly can. Grammar is not something theoretical which you can just learn for tests and then forget. To improve the quality of your speaking and writing in English, you must constantly try to apply the knowledge and skills you gain.

If you have any questions or comments about this book, or about grammar in general, please feel free to contact me via Twitter @GarnetEducation using the hashtag #50steps.

Chris Sowton
March 2016

What is grammar for and why is it important?

'Proper words in proper places, make the true definition of a style.'

Jonathan Swift (1667–1745)
Irish satirist and poet

A Reflection

Why did you buy this book? Explain your reasons in the box below.

B Contextualization

In 1979, William Safire wrote his 'Fumblerules of Grammar'. Fifteen of these 'rules' are given below. They show some of the most common grammatical mistakes in English.

Read the 'rules' and identify the grammar problem in each case. Think about whether you make any of these mistakes in your own speaking or writing.

1. Avoid run-on sentences they are hard to read.
2. Don't use no double negatives.
3. Verbs has to agree with their subjects.
4. Use the semicolon properly, always use it where it is appropriate; and never where it isn't.
5. Reserve the apostrophe for it's proper use and omit it when its not needed.
6. No sentence fragments.
7. Avoid commas, that are not necessary.
8. A writer must not shift your point of view.
9. Don't overuse exclamation marks!!!
10. Avoid un-necessary hyphens.
11. Write all adverbial forms correct.
12. Don't use contractions in formal writing.
13. Everyone should be careful to use a singular pronoun with singular nouns in their writing.
14. One-word sentences? Eliminate.
15. capitalize every sentence and remember to always end it with a full stop

Write each number from the list above in the appropriate column below, according to the type of mistake which is being made.

Using the incorrect form of the word	Using an incorrect sentence structure	Using punctuation incorrectly	Using poor style
3	6	1	2

C Explanation

Why did you buy this book?

People want to learn English for many reasons. You may be studying English at school or university; you may need it in your work or for day-to-day conversations. Indeed, you may need it for a combination of these reasons. Whatever the reason, it is very useful to know what you want to learn from the beginning, as you will be more motivated. If you are motivated, you are likely to learn more and become better at using English grammar.

This book will help you to develop your grammar by:

- building on what you already know
- focusing on the most important areas of grammar in English
- checking your understanding of these key areas with clear activities and exercises
- showing you that English grammar is not as difficult as you might think

Why is grammar important?

Many people find grammar difficult and confusing. Since you have bought this book, you may find this too! Even if you do find grammar hard, it is still important for improving your English. Three key reasons why are as follows.

1. **Good grammar helps make your meaning clear.** If your writing contains grammatical mistakes, it may be hard to understand what you mean. Small grammatical mistakes can have a significant impact on your meaning. This is particularly important in English, where the majority of people who use the language are not **NATIVE SPEAKERS**. The possibility of misunderstanding is therefore higher.
2. **Good grammar helps you look professional.** Good grammar helps to create a good impression. People can react negatively to speech or writing which has many grammatical mistakes. If you want to use your English to impress people, you need good grammar.
3. **Good grammar means that people take you more seriously.** If you make grammatical mistakes when you say something, people may assume that what you say is not worth listening to. People may think this when you have something important to say!

What are some common grammatical problems, and how will this book address them?

William Safire's list of grammatical 'rules' highlights some of the main types of grammatical problem which students of English face. The purpose of this book is to help you solve these and many other problems. The 15 specific problems identified can be categorized as follows:

Using the incorrect form of the word	Using an incorrect sentence structure	Using punctuation incorrectly	Using poor style
3, 11, 13	6, 14	1, 4, 5, 7, 10, 15	2, 8, 9, 12

The 'Fumblerules' are corrected (corrections highlighted in yellow) in the table opposite. An explanation of each problem is given, and links to the various steps in which the issue is discussed are provided. Note that in some cases more than one correction is possible.

Rule	Correction	Explanation
1	Avoid run-on sentences. They are hard to read.	A **FULL STOP** is used to separate the **SENTENCES**. A **SEMICOLON** could also have been used (▶Steps 41, 43).
	Avoid run-on sentences because they are hard to read.	**CONJUNCTIONS** can also be used to link **CLAUSES** together (▶Step 21).
2	Don't use any double negatives.	Where there is already a **NEGATIVE**, you do not need another. Use a positive form instead (▶Step 34).
	Use only a single negative.	Alternatively, rewrite the sentence without using negatives.
3	Verbs have to agree with their subjects.	The **SUBJECT** is plural, so the **AUXILIARY VERB** should also be plural (▶Step 36).
4	Use the semicolon properly; always use it where it is appropriate, and never where it isn't.	A semicolon separates **INDEPENDENT CLAUSES**. It is more like a full stop than a **COMMA** (▶Steps 41, 43).
5	Reserve the apostrophe for its proper use and omit it when it's not needed.	**APOSTROPHES** are used to show missing letters and for possession. The first *its* is a possessive **PRONOUN**; the second is the contracted form of *it is* (▶Step 41).
6	There should be no sentence fragments.	Every sentence needs a subject and a verb (▶Step 29).
7	Avoid commas that are not necessary.	Commas are commonly misused, even by native speakers (▶Step 42).
8	A writer must not shift his or her point of view.	Consistency is important. Here, *writer* is 3rd person, and so the pronoun should also be 3rd person (▶Step 7).
9	Don't overuse exclamation marks!	One **EXCLAMATION MARK** is sufficient in almost every situation.
10	Avoid unnecessary hyphens.	There are rules about **HYPHENS**, and when/when not to use them (▶Step 44).
11	Write all adverbial forms correctly.	**ADJECTIVE** and **ADVERB** forms are sometimes confused. Generally, adverbs end in *~ly* (▶Steps 16, 17).
12	Do not use contractions in formal writing.	**CONTRACTIONS** (using an apostrophe to show a missing letter) are a feature of informal grammar (▶Step 5).
13	Everyone should be careful to use a singular pronoun with singular nouns in his or her writing.	Agreement between pronouns is important. Nowadays, the original sentence (using *their* to mean *his or her*) is more acceptable, since non-gender specific pronouns are more commonly used.
14	Eliminate one-word sentences.	Every sentence needs a subject and a verb (▶Step 29).
15	Capitalize every sentence and remember to always end it with a full stop.	It is important to know when to use **CAPITAL LETTERS** and when to use lower-case letters (▶Step 41).

Summary

1. It is important for you to think about why you want/need to learn grammar.
2. Grammar is important because it helps make your meaning clear, helps you look professional and means that people take you seriously.
3. Four key grammar areas to learn about are form, sentence structure, punctuation and style.

D Activation

1. **Complete and comprehend.**
   Why is grammar important? Summarize in your own words.

2. **Check your understanding.**
   Sentences a–e contain mistakes. Match them up with the feedback given in 1–5.

a. No verb, no sentence.

b. Don't use run-on sentences separate them using punctuation.

c. The use of negative forms doesn't make your English any clearer.

d. The use of a long noun phrase at the start of a sentence is confusing.

e. Don't use informal grammar in written English!

1. This is a run-on sentence. This means that two sentences are incorrectly combined as one.

2. It can be confusing to overuse negative forms. Use positive forms where possible.

3. Putting the long noun phrase later in the sentence will make it easier to understand.

4. Contractions and exclamation marks are considered to be informal.

5. This is a sentence fragment, meaning that it is not complete.

3. **Create your own.**
   Rewrite the sentences above in a more appropriate, grammatically correct way.

a.	*Every sentence must contain a verb.*
b.	
c.	
d.	
e.	

What are word classes?

'Then suddenly, he was struck by a powerful but simple little truth, and it was this: that English grammar is governed by rules that are almost mathematical in their strictness!'

Roald Dahl (1916–1990)
British novelist and short story writer

A Reflection

Rearrange the following words so that the sentence makes sense.

English it relatively has because easy of clear is rules The grammar

B Contextualization

Read the following passage. It contains examples of all the word classes of English. Two examples of each word class are shown in the table. Find at least three additional words in each group.

Many books about grammar have been published. Although some of them are very clear and easy to follow, many are really difficult to understand. Therefore, many students are bored or scared by grammar. The purpose of *50 Steps to Improving Your Grammar* is to change this. I hope it succeeds, because grammar is important.

Each of the steps has four parts: *Reflection* (where you hopefully identify what you already know about the subject), *Contextualization* (where you see that grammar point in context), *Explanation* (where the main points of the step are clearly outlined and explained) and *Activation* (where you practise the points learnt).

Word class	Examples
Noun	books, grammar
Verb	have, published
Adjective	clear, easy
Adverb	very, really
Pronoun	them, you
Preposition	about, of
Conjunction	although, therefore
Determiner	many, the

C Explanation

What are word classes?

Word classes (also called 'parts of speech') are the basic bricks of language. Each word class has a specific job. For your English to make sense, you need to understand each word's function, and how word classes interact. If you do not know what a word should be doing, you will probably not use it correctly.

In English, there are eight main word classes. The sentence below, from Part A, contains each of the classes.

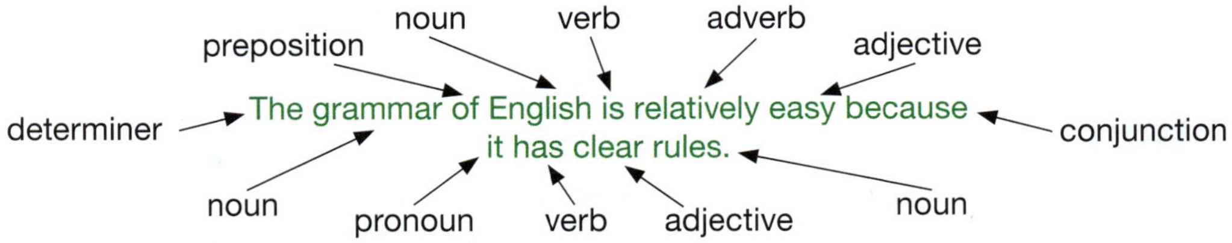

The table below shows the functions of these word classes, and provides further examples from Part B. (**Note:** not every word from the text is included.)

Word class	Text examples	Function
Noun	*books, grammar, students*	A noun is a person, place or thing. It may also refer to ideas, feelings, qualities, events and organizations.
Verb	*have, published, are*	A verb is a 'doing' or 'action' word. It often describes what happens in a sentence.
Adjective	*clear, easy, difficult*	An adjective describes/modifies nouns and pronouns.
Adverb	*very, really, already*	An adverb describes/modifies verbs (as well as adjectives and other adverbs).
Pronoun	*them, you, it*	A pronoun replaces/represents a noun.
Preposition	*about, of, to*	A preposition shows the relationship (e.g., in terms of place or time) between other word classes, most often between nouns and verbs.
Conjunction	*although, therefore, or*	A conjunction shows the relationship between clauses (e.g., time, cause and effect, transition).
Determiner	*many, the, each*	A determiner provides more information about nouns and noun phrases.

What is the difference between open and closed word classes?

The word classes noted above can be divided into two major types, namely **OPEN** (or **LEXICAL**) and **CLOSED** (or **FUNCTIONAL**). Each of these word classes is looked at in more detail in other steps. Word classes which are open are nouns (▶Steps 6–10), verbs (▶Steps 11–15) and adjectives and adverbs (▶Steps 16–20). Word classes which are closed are pronouns (▶Step 7), conjunctions (▶Step 21), prepositions (▶Step 22) and determiners (▶Steps 23–25). The two main differences between the two groups are as follows.

- There are a fixed number of words in closed classes. This means that once you know the prepositions, conjunctions, determiners and pronouns of English, you never have to learn any more! However, there are new open class words being invented all the time. (See ▶Step 6 for recent nouns and ▶Step 11 for recent verbs.)
- Closed class words do not describe anything unless they are related to an open class word. For example, *in*, *on* and *at* do not describe times or places by themselves; they only do this when used in phrases such as *in London*, *on time* or *at school*.

Can a word be in more than one class?

Yes, particularly with nouns and verbs. Many common words can be both nouns and verbs, for example, *answer*, *break*, *cook*, *email*, *face*, *laugh*, *miss*, *order*, *run*, *set*, *train* and *visit*. Some words may also be in more than one closed class, or even be in an open as well as a closed class. For example, *each* can be an adverb (*They cost $20 each*) and a determiner (*Each day I learn more*). *On* can be a preposition (*The TV is on the table*), an adverb (*Turn on the TV*) or an adjective (*Your favourite TV show is on*).

Word roots
There may be more than one type of word in each class which has the same **ROOT**. For example, both *cook* and *cooker* are nouns: the former means a person who makes food, whereas the latter refers to the machine in which food is cooked.

How can a word change class?

Noun	Verb	Adjective	Adverb
clarity	clear/clarify	clear	clearly
depth	deepen	deep	deeply
help	help	helpful	helpfully
sadness	sadden	sad	sadly
success	succeed	successful	successfully

Many words belong to groups of words which share the same root. One root can be used to make different words which belong to different word classes. Understanding the relationship between these words can be extremely useful for building your vocabulary and avoiding mistakes. The table shows some common examples. Knowing what **SUFFIXES** are usually found in each class can help with word building. Common suffixes for each of the open word classes include:

- **Nouns:** *~er* (*worker*), *~tion/~sion* (*creation*, *inclusion*), *~ance/~ence (attendance, dependence)*
- **Verbs:** *~en* (*shorten*), *~fy* (*simplify*), *~ise/~ize* (*legalise/legalize*)
- **Adjectives:** *~al* (*central*), *~ent* (*different*), *~ful* (*beautiful*), *~ous* (*famous*)
- **Adverbs:** *~ly* (*clearly*)

Summary
1. There are eight main word classes in English. Four are open class (noun, verb, adjective, adverb) and four are closed class (preposition, conjunction, determiner, pronoun).
2. Open class (lexical/content) words carry the main meaning of the sentence, and closed class (functional/grammar) words show the relationship between them.
3. Understanding what suffixes can be used with each word class can increase your accuracy.

D Activation

1. **Complete and comprehend.**

   a. **What are the main differences between open and closed word classes? Answer in 20 words or fewer.**

   ____

   ____

   b. **Write the name of a word class in the following gaps.**

   1. An ______________ adds information to nouns or pronouns.

   2. A ______________ shows the relationship between different word classes, usually nouns or verbs.

   3. A ______________ shows the relationship between clauses.

   4. A ______________ replaces a noun.

   5. An ______________ generally provides more information about a verb.

   6. A ______________ indicates the action in a sentence.

2. **Check your understanding.**
   What class are the following words in? Use a dictionary if necessary.
   Note: some words may be in more than one class.

Word	Class(es)	Word	Class(es)
computer		development	
justify		around	
fasten		while	
fast		some	

3. **Create your own.**
   Answer the following questions. Use a dictionary if necessary.

   a. What is the verb form of *computer*? ______________________

   b. What is the adjective form of *colour*? ______________________

   c. What is the name of the person whose job is cleaning? ______________________

   d. What are the noun and verb forms of *special*? ______________________ and ______________________

   e. What is the noun form of *refuse*? ______________________

   f. What is the adjective form of *misery*? ______________________

   g. What is the adverb form of *obvious*? ______________________

   h. What is the adverb form of *clear*? ______________________

What grammar should I learn and how should I learn it?

'Knowing about grammar offers a window into the human mind and into our amazingly complex mental capacity!'

Brock Haussamen (1945–)
American writer and social activist

A Reflection

Do you agree or disagree with the following quotations?

I should use the kind of grammar found in books.

I should learn to use the grammar native speakers use.

Making mistakes is a natural part of learning grammar.

Which of the following sentences would you be more likely to say?

1. **a.** Have you seen my phone? **b.** Did you see my phone?
2. **a.** My team are winning. **b.** My team is winning.
3. **a.** They've gotten a new car. **b.** They have got a new car.
4. **a.** I'll be home at the weekend. **b.** I'll be home on the weekend.

B Contextualization

Each sentence has different grammar from its pair. Identify how the meanings differ.

Sentence 1	Sentence 2	Difference in meaning
Sam likes football.	*Sam liked football.*	Sentence 1: Sam's current feeling. Sentence 2: how Sam used to feel.
He's leaving tonight.	*He may be leaving tonight.*	
You're silly.	*You're being silly.*	
Do you have a paper?	*Do you have paper?*	

All the grammar (function) words in the following sentences have been removed. What do you think the correct sentence is?

Example: Bus come I late work. Because the bus didn't come, I was late for work.

1. We saw dog. ________________
2. She left you came. ________________

C Explanation

What difference does grammar make to a sentence?

Without grammar, our sentences would not make any sense. If we understood some of the words, we might be able to get a **general** understanding of what was being said, but not a **detailed** one. As the quotation at the beginning of this step suggests, one of the things that makes us human is the ability to use complex grammar.

When sentences lack grammar words, it is sometimes possible to understand their meaning. It is possible to guess the meaning of the example *Bus come I late work*. However, we could easily use other grammar words to interpret the meaning of the sentence in a different way, for example: *Although the bus didn't come, I wasn't late for work*. We could also put a range of grammatical words in the other sentences to express very different meanings.

We saw dog. →	*We saw a dog.*	→ The listener does not know which dog.
	We saw the dog.	→ The listener knows which dog is meant.
	We saw that dog.	→ The listener knows which dog is meant. The speaker adds significant emphasis.
She left you came. →	*She left when you came.*	→ The leaving/coming occurred at the same time, but are not necessarily causally related.
	She left after you came.	→ The leaving happened after the coming, but they are not necessarily causally related.
	She left because you came.	→ The leaving/coming are causally linked.

The sentences in the table in Part B show just how important grammar is. In each case, the two sentences have almost the same grammar. However, the small differences significantly change the meaning and emphasis of each sentence. This can be called the BUTTERFLY EFFECT. Just as one small flap of a butterfly's wings can cause a storm, one small grammatical change can significantly alter the meaning of a sentence.

Sentence 1	Sentence 2	Difference in meaning
He's leaving tonight.	*He may be leaving tonight.*	Sentence 1: this is definitely happening – there is a specific plan for him to leave tonight. Sentence 2: it is only a possibility. The MODAL VERB *may* (▶Step 31) changes the meaning.
You're silly.	*You're being silly.*	Sentence 1: talks about a permanent fact. (*You are silly all the time.*) Sentence 2: the silliness is only temporary. (*You are not always silly, but you are at the moment.*)
Do you have a paper?	*Do you have paper?*	Sentence 1: the noun *paper* is COUNTABLE – it is used as an abbreviation for *newspaper*. Sentence 2: *paper* (i.e., what you write on) is UNCOUNTABLE.

What kind of English grammar should I learn and how should I learn it?

'I should use the kind of grammar found in books.'

There are two ways in which people view grammar. One group believes that there is a set of specific rules and principles (found in books) which people should follow at all times. Another group believes that language changes over time, and that people should use the kind of grammar which people actually use (found in real life).

This book believes that whilst it is very important to understand the basic rules and 'building blocks' of a language, the whole point of learning grammar is so that you can be understood. Therefore, the grammar in this book reflects the kind of language people are actually using in day-to-day life.

'I should learn to use the grammar native speakers use.'

The first question to ask here would be: *What kind of* NATIVE SPEAKER? Whilst there are many different varieties of English (e.g., British English, American English, Australian English, Indian English), most of their differences are in vocabulary and pronunciation rather than grammar. This said, there are a few noticeable grammatical differences between the two varieties of English which are most commonly taught in the classroom, namely British English (BrE) and American English (AmE). Four such differences are highlighted below.

Grammatical area of difference	British English examples	American English examples
In AmE, the present perfect (▶Step 14) is not commonly used – the past simple is used instead.	*Have you seen my phone?*	*Did you see my phone?*
In AmE, COLLECTIVE NOUNS (nouns referring to groups of people or things) are grammatically singular. In BrE, they can be singular or plural.	*My team is/are winning.*	*My team is winning.*
Past simple and past participle verb forms may differ between BrE and AmE.	*dive-dived-dived* *get-got-got*	*dive-dove-dived* *get-got-gotten*
The use of prepositions differs between BrE and AmE in particular phrases.	*I'll be home at the weekend.*	*I'll be home on the weekend.*

'Making mistakes is a natural part of learning grammar.'

Students of English often get concerned about the number of mistakes they make. However, in the same way that you made mistakes when you learnt your mother tongue, you will also make them when learning another language. It does not matter if you make mistakes, so long as you learn from them. It is important not to get worried or upset if you make mistakes – if you do, the speed at which you learn English will decrease.

Summary

1. Very small changes in grammar can have a significant impact on the whole sentence.
2. You will make mistakes when learning grammar. As long as you learn from your mistakes, this is fine!
3. Although there are some grammatical differences between different varieties of English, they are not that significant.

D Activation

1. **Complete and comprehend.**

   Match each person a–e to the correct sentence 1–5.

a
I now work in an office, but back in 2013 I was a barista.

b
I am bored in my current job. I'd enjoy serving customers and selling coffee.

c
I work in an office. I like going to cafés.

d
They really liked my interview and offered me a job. I start tomorrow.

e
So that's two coffees, a sandwich and a bottle of water?

1	2	3	4	5
He does not work in a café.	She's going to work in a café.	She's working in a café.	She worked in a café.	He'd like to work in a café.
______	______	______	______	______

2. **Check your understanding.**

   Match the grammatical structures and meaning to the correct sentence 1–5 from Exercise 1.

   a. The past simple talks about events which occurred in the past, and are now finished.

   b. The modal verb indicates a desire or wish.

   c. The negative word implies the opposite meaning, and the present simple a current fact.

   d. The auxiliary verb shows that there is a specific plan/intention.

   e. The present continuous describes something which is unfinished.

   1. He does not work in a café.

   2. She's going to work in a café.

   3. She's working in a café.

   4. She worked in a café.

   5. He'd like to work in a café.

3. **Create your own.**

   The box below contains open class words. Add as many different combinations of grammar words as you can to make different sentences.

answer	phone	ring

Example: I answered the phone because it was ringing.

Sentence a: ____________________

Sentence b: ____________________

Sentence c: ____________________

Is the grammar of my own language similar to English?

STEP 4

'The greater part of the world's troubles are due to questions of grammar.'

Michel de Montaigne (1533–1592)
French essayist

A Reflection

Complete the following questionnaire about your own language. Try to explain your answers in as much detail as possible. Use the *Glossary* at the back of the book if you are unsure about the meaning of any of the words used.

Questions about my language	My response
1. What is the normal word order in a sentence?	1.
2. Is your language inflected? (Do any words in your language change form?)	2.
3. How are nouns made plural?	3.
4. Are articles used?	4.
5. Are there irregular verbs? If so, are they common?	5.
6. How many different grammatical forms of the verb *eat* are there?	6.

B Contextualization

Now imagine you are completing the same questionnaire for English. For each question in Part A, choose the correct answer from the options below.

1.	subject-verb-object	subject-object-verb	verb-subject-object
2.	Yes, commonly.	No, not at all.	To some extent, e.g., for plurals and some verb forms.
3.	Add ~*s*.	Put a word like *two* or *many* before the noun.	Repeat the word.
4.	Yes, frequently.	Yes, occasionally.	No, not at all.
5.	No, all the verbs are regular.	Only a few verbs are irregular, but they are used very frequently.	Many verbs are irregular.
6.	Many	Five	One

C Explanation

Why are you asking me about my own language? I thought this was supposed to be a book about English grammar?

Don't worry. This *is* a book about English grammar. However, a better understanding of your own language, and how it is similar to or different from English, can help you to avoid mistakes. Below are some common mistakes made by speakers of five languages and the reasons for these mistakes. Even if your own language is not represented here, you may have similar problems.

Chinese uses a different word order for questions.

Korean uses word classes differently.

There is only one present tense in Arabic.

Word order is more flexible in Spanish.

There are no articles in Japanese.

It can be very difficult to get rid of some of these problems. The reason for this is that they have become fossilized (see **FOSSILIZATION**). This means that the mistake has been made so many times that it has become normal. Indeed, many students avoid working on these problems because they are so difficult to eradicate. However, by ignoring them, you are restricting your ability to use English properly.

Therefore, it is important that you try to identify the problems which may be caused by your mother tongue and that you actively try to address these problems. Do not ignore them – they will not go away!

Your mother tongue and English

Just as you can experience grammatical difficulties because of the differences between English and your mother tongue, you may also experience problems in other areas, such as vocabulary and pronunciation.

- In **vocabulary**, you may discover false friends – words which look very similar to a word in your own language, but which have a different meaning.
- In **pronunciation**, there may be certain phonemes (sounds) which exist in English, but which do not exist in your mother tongue.

What are the major differences between English grammar and the grammar of my own language?

Don't worry if you find some of the language used in the six points below difficult to understand: the steps in this book address these points in more detail. Follow the references in brackets to find out more about a particular point. Of course, these six points do not cover all aspects of English. However, they do show some of the main areas where there are differences between English and other languages.

1. **English WORD ORDER is usually subject-verb-object.**
   1. Who does the action (**SUBJECT**). 2. What the action is (**VERB**). 3. Who the recipient of the action is (**OBJECT**). This can be reversed when using the passive voice (▶Step 15), where the order becomes object-verb-subject.

2. **English is not a particularly INFLECTED language.**
   This means that English words do not generally change form. (There are a few exceptions, for example **PLURALS**, 3rd person *~s*, past simple *~ed* and **PRESENT PARTICIPLE** *~ing.*) In English, relationships between words are shown through **FUNCTIONAL WORDS** such as **PRONOUNS** (▶Step 7), **PREPOSITIONS** (▶Step 22) and **DETERMINERS** (▶Step 23).

3. **Plurals in English are formed by adding *~s/~es* to the singular form of the noun.**
   Depending on the noun, you may also need to change some of the letters at the end of the base form (▶Step 45).

4. **ARTICLES (*the/a/an*) are used very frequently in English.**
   Articles are a kind of **DETERMINER** (▶Step 23). Articles add information about **NOUNS**, indicating whether the content is known or unknown.

5. **IRREGULAR VERBS are very commonly used in English.**
   It is estimated that although only three per cent of English verbs are irregular, they account for 70 per cent of use. The ten most commonly used verbs in English are all irregular: *be, have, do, say, make, go, take, come, see* and *get.*

6. **The verb system in English is quite easy to understand.**
   There are only ever five ways of referring to a verb. For the verb *eat*, there is the base form (*eat*), the 3rd person singular form (*eats*), the past simple form (*ate*), the past participle form (*eaten*) and the present participle (*eating*). As ▶Steps 11–15 show, the English verb system is regular and easy to follow.

Top tip
To understand what specific grammatical problems you might have because of your own language, search the internet for the following phrase: 'grammatical differences between English and <your language>'.

Summary
1. Thinking about your own language can help you to identify why you make particular mistakes in English.
2. Some grammatical problems may be very hard to get rid of because you have been making them for such a long time.
3. Some of the major areas to consider when comparing English with your own language are: word order, inflection, pluralization of nouns, use of articles and the verb system.

D Activation

1. **Complete and comprehend.**

   Complete the following description of English with relevant words and phrases.

   a. The usual word order of English is ________________________. This can be reversed when using the ________________________ voice.

   b. In general, English is not an inflected language, although the addition of ______ to the end of nouns to make plurals or ______ to put verbs into the past simple are examples of inflection.

   c. Although only about three per cent of English verbs are ________________________, this group includes some of the most common verbs. Three common examples are ______, ______ and ______.

   d. The verb system in English is simpler than in many languages. There are only ever ______ ways to write a verb. The forms of *eat*, for example, are ________, ________, ________, ________ and ________.

2. **Check your understanding.**

   Identify the kind of mistake which is being made in each of these sentences. Correct them as necessary.

Original sentence	Mistake	Corrected version
a. The boy the ball kicked.	*word order*	*The boy kicked the ball.*
b. I went to the London last year.		
c. He falled over in the street.		
d. You like playing football?		
e. I am helping to my mother.		

3. **Create your own.**

   What are three major grammatical differences between English and your mother tongue? Refer to this step or search in a book or online to answer this question.

   a. ____

   ____

   b. ____

   ____

   c. ____

   ____

How are formal and informal grammar different?

'All styles are good except the boring kind.'

Voltaire (1694–1778)
French philosopher, playwright and historian

A Reflection

Look at the following pairs of sentences. Which would be more likely to appear in spoken English (S), and which in written English (W)?

I didn't know that.	W	Didn't know that.	S
You've met before, probably.	______	You've probably met before.	______
She's gonna be late.	______	She's going to be late.	______
Anyway, what d'you think?	______	What do you think?	______

Which of the following do you think is more likely to be the genuine text message? Why?

1. Are we going to meet later? I would like to see you. However, I understand you could be busy.

2. Are we gonna meet later I'd like 2 c u but think u cd be busy.

Which of the following is more likely to be the genuine complaint letter? Why?

1. Dear Sir/Madam,
I have a problem with one of your products. In brief, I took it home and it subsequently broke.

2. Hiya. A problem. Your product – no good! Basically, I got it. Then it broke.

B Contextualization

Look at the two passages below. Text 1 uses the normal rules of English grammar, whilst text 2 uses 'international English'. Consider some of the topics in the box.

Note: all of these terms can be found in the *Glossary* at the back of the book.

verb forms plurals agreement determiners

1. I have been to New York before. There were so many people there. We saw the Statue of Liberty and the Empire State Building. My sister now lives there.

2. I went to New York before. There were so many peoples there. We saw Statue of Liberty and Empire State Building. My sister now live there.

C Explanation

What are the major differences between informal and formal grammar?

As the texts in Part A show, there is a significant difference in the type of grammar which is expected in informal and formal circumstances. Informal grammar is more commonly used in speaking and informal writing (e.g., text messages, emails to friends, tweets, Facebook posts), whereas formal grammar is used in written texts such as essays and letters. Generally speaking, you should use grammar which is suitable to the circumstances. As such, the formal grammar of text message 1 is inappropriate. The grammar of text message 2 is more suitable. Similarly, the grammar in complaint letter 2 is too informal; letter 1 is more appropriate.

Formal grammar is not necessarily better – or worse – than informal grammar. The most important thing is the **GENRE** of a text: when people receive a text message from a friend, for example, they do not expect it to be written in a very formal way.

The table below highlights some of the key differences between the kinds of grammar usual in informal and formal English.

Grammar in informal English	Grammar in formal English
At times, grammar words may be left out, especially when the meaning is clear from the context, e.g., *(I) didn't know that*, *(It/That) sounds interesting*. In speaking, people also have the opportunity to ask questions and get clarification.	All grammar words should be included. It is not appropriate to leave out any grammar words. In writing, people only have one chance to make their meaning clear: there is no opportunity for clarification. Therefore, the grammar must be accurate.
Phrases (▶Step 27) can exist by themselves. There is no need for every utterance to have a subject and a verb.	Full sentences are needed, using a subject and a verb. If either is missing, the sentence is not complete.
There is a greater tolerance/acceptance of grammatical mistakes, e.g., *Shes gonna be late.*	There is less tolerance of grammatical mistakes. Sentences are expected to be grammatically correct.
'Discourse markers', are used to move between different topics. Such words include *anyway*, *right*, *okay*, *I see*, *I mean*, *mind you*, *well*, *right*, *you know*, *like*, *actually*, *basically*, *what's more*, *so* and *now*.	These words are not used. In formal writing, a **TOPIC SENTENCE** (the first sentence in each paragraph) indicate a change in topic. When topics are linked, more formal conjunctions are used (▶Step 21).
In speaking, there is no punctuation. Turn taking shows when one sentence has finished and another begins. Changes in voice and intonation can also show the relationship between sentences. In writing, punctuation such as commas and full stops are not necessarily used.	Punctuation is important, since it shows the relationship between clauses and between sentences. Without punctuation, the meaning may be less clear.

Top tip

When writing on a computer, ensure that you use all the software available to improve the accuracy of your written grammar. Most programmes will have a spellchecker, which can help you avoid making unnecessary spelling mistakes. In addition, many programmes will also identify where you may have made certain types of grammatical mistake.

What is 'international English'?

'International English', which is also known as 'global English', 'world English' and 'Globish', has become increasingly common worldwide in recent years. Supporters of international English argue that because most people who use English are actually non-native speakers, certain mistakes should be more widely accepted. Language is seen as a combination of vocabulary and basic grammar.

Some of the areas in which there may be greater tolerance of mistakes include the following.

Verbs

- Both **REGULAR** and **IRREGULAR** endings can be used with irregular verbs to make past **VERB FORMS**, e.g., *kept* and *keeped* are both correct.
- Verb forms other than the present continuous can be used to talk about current activity, as long as time words like *now* or *currently* are also used.

Plurals

- **UNCOUNTABLE NOUNS** can be pluralized in the same way as **COUNTABLE NOUNS**: *There were so many peoples there*.

Agreement

- 3rd person singular in the present simple does not take ~*s*: *My sister now live there*.

Determiners

- **ARTICLES** are not commonly used: *We saw Statue of Liberty and Empire State Building*.

Top tip

If you are ever unsure which form to use, use the more formal form. It is better to be too formal than too informal.

Summary

1. The kind of grammar used in formal and informal English differs in a few key areas.
2. It is important to use the correct type of grammar in the correct situation.
3. International English has lower standards of grammar, but as a system it is not generally accepted yet. If in doubt, use more formal grammar.

D Activation

1. **Complete and comprehend.**

   Answer the following questions. Answer as concisely as possible.

a. What is genre and why is it important?	
b. Why can you leave out some grammar words in spoken English?	
c. What is a discourse marker?	
d. How can computer software help your grammar?	
e. What is international English?	

2. **Check your understanding.**

   Are the following examples of informal or formal grammar? Do you think they are more likely to be spoken or written?

a. Yeah, thought it was gr8.

c. Dear Sir, please let me reply to your letter of the 18th.

b. Definitely, she'll like it.

d. The key focus of my presentation is going to be Europe.

a. informal – written	**c.**
b.	**d.**

3. **Create your own.**

   Rewrite each of the sentences above. If it is an example of informal grammar, turn it into formal grammar. If it is formal, turn it into informal.

Sentence	Rewritten version
a.	Yes, I thought it was great.
b.	
c.	
d.	

What are nouns and how do they work in English?

'Never use abstract nouns when concrete ones will do. If you mean "More people died", don't say "Mortality rose".'

C. S. Lewis (1898–1963)
Irish novelist and literary critic

A Reflection

A noun can be described as a word which refers to people, places or things.

Read the following passage and underline all the nouns you find.

The United Kingdom is composed of four separate parts, namely England, Scotland, Wales and Northern Ireland. Its capital is London and the Head of State (and the Governor of the Church of England) is Queen Elizabeth II, who lives in Buckingham Palace. Today, the Queen has little real power. She cannot make laws; that is the work and responsibility of the Houses of Parliament. The most important person in Parliament is the Prime Minister.

B Contextualization

Match the groups of nouns 1–6 to the category a–f which they belong to.

1. London, Queen Elizabeth II, Buckingham Palace
2. power, work, responsibility
3. government, governor
4. part, government, work
5. queen, law, head
6. Head of State, most important person

a. some of the most common nouns in the English language
b. proper nouns (i.e., the names of specific people or places)
c. countable nouns (i.e., nouns which can be pluralized)
d. uncountable nouns (i.e., nouns which cannot be pluralized)
e. nouns which come from the same root
f. noun phrases

C Explanation

What are ten key facts about nouns in English?

1. **Nouns refer to people, places and things.**

   Nouns are the word class which includes:

   - People: *Queen Elizabeth II, the Prime Minister*
   - Places: *United Kingdom, London*
   - Things: *government, head, responsibility*

2. **Nouns are content words and an open class.**

   Nouns are content words: without them, a sentence does not refer to anything. They are also an open class, which means that new nouns are being created on a regular basis (see the Grammar box for three recent examples). Indeed, there are more nouns than any other type of word.

> **Three recent nouns**
>
> **approximeeting:** a rough arrangement to meet, which is then finalized by mobile phone.
>
> **digital afterlife:** what remains of a person's online life after they die.
>
> **olinguito:** the name given to a newly discovered mammal, living in the forests of South America.

3. **When writing any sentence, we must use a noun.**

   There are two things every sentence needs: a noun and a verb – the 'doer' (SUBJECT) and the 'thing which is done'. If your sentence doesn't contain a noun, then it is not a sentence!

4. **About 15 per cent of words used in spoken English are nouns.**

   Although DETERMINERS (▶Step 23) and other FUNCTIONAL WORDS are more frequently used in English, the most commonly used CONTENT WORDS are nouns. In spoken English, they constitute about 15 per cent of spoken words. In academic writing, this figure doubles. A very high percentage of noun usage is restricted to the 25 most common nouns. According to the *Oxford English Dictionary*, these are as follows: *time*, *person*, *year*, *way*, *day*, *thing*, *man*, *world*, *life*, *hand*, *part*, *child*, *eye*, *woman*, *place*, *work*, *week*, *case*, *point*, *government*, *company*, *number*, *group*, *problem* and *fact*.

5. **One noun can have many different meanings.**

   When using a noun, it is important that you use it in the right SENSE. For example, here are three of the different ways in which the word *bank* can be used.

   - *I need to go to the bank later.* (= a place where you keep money)
   - *Be careful you don't fall down the bank.* (= a slope going down to a river)
   - *It's going to rain – look at that bank of black clouds.* (= a group, a pile)

6. **More than one noun may come from the same word family.**

   The same word root can produce multiple nouns. For example, *government* (the system) and *governor* (the person who governs) are in the same family.

7. **Nouns in English do not have a gender.**

   In many languages, nouns can be masculine or feminine; some languages also have a neuter gender. In such languages, the articles take the gender of the nouns they precede. This is not the case in English, where the only articles are *the*, *a* and *an* (▶Steps 24 and 25). The gendered pronouns *he* and *she* are used for male and female people, and *it* is used for almost everything else (▶Step 7).

8. **It is possible to make new nouns from other word classes.**
   In some languages this is not possible, but English is quite flexible.
   - For verbs, add *~ing* to turn the verb into a **GERUND** (a noun that looks like a verb): *Winning is my life. Eating is my hobby.*
   - With adjectives, add suffixes such as *~ce* (*importance*, *violence*), *~ity* (*popularity*, *regularity*), *~ness* (*happiness*, *laziness*) and *~y* (*difficulty*, *honesty*).
   - You can also place *the* before an adjective to make it a noun: *I feel sorry for the poor and the unhappy*.

9. **Nouns are often combined with other words to make noun phrases.**
   At a basic level, this might mean placing an adjective before a noun (*most important person*), or combining two nouns together with *of* to show possession (*Head of State*). This is more common in formal types of speaking and writing, where you may be talking about more complex ideas. Noun phrases are the specific focus of ▶Steps 9 and 10.

10. **Generally speaking, nouns are not capitalized.**
    In some languages, all nouns have a capital letter. This is not the case in English, where only proper nouns are capitalized. Common nouns only have a capital letter when they appear at the beginning of a sentence or in a title (▶Step 41).

What are the different categories of nouns?

It is important to know what category or categories a noun falls into as this will affect the grammatical structure of your sentence. For example, if a noun is uncountable, it will generally not have an article; if it is compound, it is necessary to think about how you join the parts together. The main ways that nouns can be categorized are as follows.

- **Common noun:** a general class of person, place or thing – the most frequently used type of noun (*part, government, head*)
- **Proper noun:** the specific name of a person, place or thing (*London, Queen Elizabeth II, Buckingham Palace*)
- **Countable noun:** a noun which can be counted – it can be pluralized or have a number put before it (*queen, law, head*)
- **Uncountable noun:** a noun which cannot be counted – also known as a mass noun (*part, work, responsibility*)
- **Compound noun:** a noun made up of two or more words. There are three ways of making compound nouns, namely:
  - Joining two separate nouns together (*basketball*)
  - Placing the words next to each other, with a space in between (*unemployment benefit*)
  - Putting a hyphen between two nouns (*mind-reader*)
- **CONCRETE NOUN:** a noun which exists physically and can be seen, heard, felt, smelt or heard (*table*, *cat*)
- **ABSTRACT NOUN:** a noun with no physical reality – a concept or quality (*love*, *hope*)

Summary
1. Nouns are the most commonly used content words in English.
2. Nouns have no gender in English.
3. Nouns can be categorized in many different ways; the grammar you use will be affected by the kind of noun you are using.

D Activation

1. **Complete and comprehend.**

   Are the following statements about nouns in English true or false? If they are false, correct them accordingly.

Statement	True / False
a. Nouns are functional words and a closed class.	
b. It is necessary to include a noun in every sentence.	
c. Nouns only ever have one sense.	
d. Nouns have no gender.	
e. Nouns are never capitalized.	

2. **Check your understanding.**

   Use a dictionary to answer these questions.

   a. What other nouns are in the same family as *child*? Try to find at least three examples.

   b. Identify three different senses of the noun *set*.

   c. What are the noun forms of the following adjectives: *modest*, *patient*, *formal*, *careless*?

   d. Some nouns can be used in both a countable and uncountable way. Can you name any?

3. **Create your own.**

   Rewrite the sentences by transforming the nouns.

   a. She was happy when she was a child.

   She had a happy childhood.

   b. Rich people are getting richer.

   c. I spoke to the person who works at reception.

   d. He was very ill.

What are pronouns and how do they work in English?

STEP 7

'Through the You, a person becomes I.'

Martin Buber (1878–1965)
Austrian-born philosopher

A Reflection

The pronouns in the following sentences have been underlined. Look at how they are used. When you have done this, write a one-sentence definition of their function.

- I cut the paper with the scissors.
- Everyone came.
- Somebody should help.
- The manager himself wrote to me.
- Whose is this pen? Is it yours?
- The bag is hers.
- This is not good enough.
- You must not get help from anybody. You must do it yourselves.
- That is the car I want to own. One day it will be mine!
- Who won the game?
- The robot can teach itself.
- Those are the men who I saw.
- Did we win? Was it us?
- Nobody cares.
- Which is your favourite?
- Anything could happen.
- Here's the book that I wanted.
- Did you help them?
- These should be sent first.
- One should do the right thing.
- The pen which you need is there.
- What is the capital of France?

In English, pronouns …

B Contextualization

Describe what each of the following groups of pronouns has in common.

Groups of pronouns	What do they have in common?
I, you, we	All are subject personal pronouns
I, mine, me	
me, us, them	
this, that, these, those	
myself, yourselves, itself	
yours, hers, mine	
who, which, that	
everyone, anything, somebody, nobody	
what, which, whose, who	

C Explanation

What is the purpose of pronouns in English?

The main function of a PRONOUN in English is to replace a noun. Using pronouns will make your English both easier to follow and less repetitive. Repeating the same nouns in a text again and again makes it boring and difficult to read. Therefore, using pronouns is an efficient way of simplifying and clarifying your speaking or writing. Some learners find pronouns difficult because of the differences between English and their mother tongue. Some languages do not use pronouns. Instead, the same role is performed by, for example, changing the endings of words.

What different types of pronouns are there in English?

The five most common types of pronouns used in English are **personal** pronouns, **relative** pronouns, **demonstrative** pronouns, **indefinite** pronouns and **interrogative** pronouns. Details of each of these types are outlined below.

1. **Personal pronouns**

   Personal pronouns are in the 1st (*I*), 2nd (*you*) or 3rd (*he/she/it*) person. Personal pronouns can be placed in four categories, namely **subject**, **object**, **possessive** and **reflexive**.

   - **Subject:** the pronoun is in the subject position (i.e., before the verb): ***I*** *cut the paper with the scissors.*
   - **Object:** the pronoun is in the object position (i.e., after the verb): *Was it* ***us****?*
   - **Possessive:** the pronoun indicates ownership: *The bag is* ***hers****.*
   - **Reflexive:** the object of the verb is the same as the subject: *The robot can teach* ***itself****.* These pronouns are also used for emphasis after a subject or object: *The manager* ***himself*** *wrote to me.*

   The following table presents a list of all the personal pronouns used in English.

Subject pronoun	Object pronoun	Possessive pronoun	Reflexive pronoun
I	*me*	*mine*	*myself*
you	*you*	*yours*	*yourself/yourselves*
he	*him*	*his*	*himself*
she	*her*	*hers*	*herself*
it	*it*	*its*	*itself*
we	*us*	*ours*	*ourselves*
they	*them*	*theirs*	*themselves*

Three key facts about personal pronouns

- In English, there is no distinction between 'polite/formal' and 'friendly/informal' forms of the second person pronoun: *you/yours/yourself/yourselves* are always used.
- The group of words often known as possessive adjectives (*my*, *your*, *his*, *her*, *its*, *our*, *their*, *whose*) are not pronouns. The reason for this is that they do not actually replace words, and must be followed by a noun (▶Step 23). Possessive pronouns, however, can stand by themselves.
- When using personal pronouns, ensure that they are close to the nouns they refer to. Otherwise, their meaning might not be clear.

2. **Relative pronouns**

The relative pronouns are *who*, *whom*, *which*, *that* and *whose*. Their job is to provide more information about the noun which comes before. See ▶Step 28.

3. **Demonstrative pronouns**

The four main demonstrative pronouns in English are *this* and *these* (used to refer to things which are near in either space or time) and *that* and *those* (used to refer to things which are further away in space or time). Note that these words are also used as determiners (▶Step 23). When they are used as demonstrative pronouns, however, they do not precede nouns, because they act as nouns themselves.

- ***This** is not good enough. / **These** should be sent first.* (close to the speaker)
- ***That** is the car I want to own. / **Those** are the men I saw.* (distant from the speaker)

4. **Indefinite pronouns**

Indefinite pronouns are used to refer to people or things when the details are unknown or unclear. The suffixes *~body and ~one* are used for people, and *~thing* for objects.

- *Everybody/everyone* = all people. *Everything* = all things. ***Everyone** came.*
- *Anybody/anyone* = it doesn't matter who does it. *Anything* = it doesn't matter, or it isn't known, what the thing or object is. ***Anything** could happen.*
- *Somebody/someone* = an unspecified person. *Something* = an unspecified thing or object. ***Somebody** should help.*
- *Nobody/no one* = no person. *Nothing* = no things or objects. ***Nobody** cares.*
- *One* is a more formal indefinite pronoun meaning 'anybody including the speaker'. It can be used as a synonym for *I/me*. ***One** should do the right thing.*

Three key facts about indefinite pronouns

- Indefinite pronouns should be followed by a singular verb: *Everything is ready.*
- A possessive can be formed by adding *'s*: *Someone's phone is ringing.*
- When using *nobody/no one/nothing*, no additional negative word is needed.

5. **Interrogative pronouns**

These pronouns are used in questions when the information is unknown (▶Step 35).

- *What* is used in general questions: ***What** is the capital of France?*
- *Who* is used when asking about a person/people: ***Who** won the game?*
- *Which* is used where there are limited choices: ***Which** is your favourite?*
- *Whose* is used when asking who owns something: ***Whose** is this pen?*

Summary

1. Pronouns refer back to, and replace, nouns. Good use of pronouns can make your speaking/writing clearer.
2. There are five main types of pronouns in English: personal, relative, demonstrative, indefinite and interrogative.
3. You should be extra careful about using pronouns if they are not used in your mother tongue.

D Activation

1. **Complete and comprehend.**

   a. **Explain, in your own words, the purpose of pronouns in English.**

   b. **Complete the table with the correct personal pronouns.**

Subject pronoun	Object pronoun	Possessive pronoun	Reflexive pronoun
I			myself
	you		
		his	
she			
			itself
		ours	
	them		

2. **Check your understanding.**
   Complete the sentences with an appropriate pronoun.

   a. It's the nicest house we've seen. Shall we buy ____________?

   b. Julia just called to say ____________ would be late.

   c. I haven't seen Terry for years. I'm not sure that I'll recognize ____________.

   d. Don't touch that. It's ____________. I bought it ages ago and it's very precious.

   e. We've only got ____________ to blame. We didn't prepare well enough.

3. **Create your own.**
   Rewrite the following text using pronouns wherever appropriate.

The World Cup is a football tournament. The football tournament is played every four years. The football tournament was first played in 1930. Brazil are the most successful side, having won the World Cup five times. Italy have won the World Cup four times. The fact Brazil and Italy have won nine times in total is amazing, since other countries have only won the World Cup 11 times in total.

What are countable and uncountable nouns?

STEP 8

'How do I love thee? Let me count the ways.'

Elizabeth Barrett Browning (1806–1861)
English poet

A Reflection

Study the following nouns. Look up any unknown words in an English–English dictionary.

~~apple~~ ~~flour~~ flower information water equipment television chair reason air

Now write the words in the appropriate part of the table below.

A number can come before the noun	A number cannot come before the noun
apple	*flour*

B Contextualization

Look at the pairs of sentences below. In some pairs, both sentences are correct; in others, only one of the sentences is possible. Put a tick ✓ next to those which are correct and a cross ✗ next to those which are wrong. Justify your answer in each case.

1. a. How many apples were on the tree? ✓	**b.** How much apples were on the tree? ✗
Justification: *Apples is a countable noun: a number can come before it. The word many can come before countable nouns, but much cannot, so (b) is incorrect.*	
2. a. How many water were in the pool? ____	**b.** How much water was in the pool? ____
Justification:	
3. a. There were some apples in the tree. ____	**b.** There was some water in the pool. ____
Justification:	
4. a. I have been to the UK three times. ____	**b.** I don't have much time right now. ____
Justification:	
5. a. How many fruits did you buy? ____	**b.** How many apples did you buy? ____
Justification:	
6. a. How much coffee would you like? ____	**b.** How many coffees would you like? ____
Justification:	

C Explanation

What is the difference between countable and uncountable nouns?

In many languages, there is no distinction between **COUNTABLE** and **UNCOUNTABLE NOUNS.** This means that it is possible to put a number before any noun. In English, however, there are some nouns where this is not possible. Such nouns are called uncountable and are a common source of confusion for learners. The list in Part A can be divided as follows.

- Countable: *apple, flower, chair, reason, television*
- Uncountable: *flour, information, water, equipment, air*

Some of these uncountable nouns might be countable in your own language. *Information* and *equipment*, for example, are countable in many languages. In your mother tongue, therefore, you might be able to say *I used five equipments at the gym*. In English, this is not possible. Instead, you must say *I used some equipment at the gym* or, alternatively, *I used five pieces of equipment at the gym*.

If you are unsure whether a noun is countable or not, ask yourself:

- Can I write a number before the noun?
- Can I pluralize the noun?

If you answer *yes* in both cases, the noun is countable.

What quantity words can be used with uncountable and countable nouns?

QUANTIFIERS such as *much*, *many* and *some* are commonly used with both countable and uncountable nouns. It is important to know grammatically which kinds of word these quantifiers can be combined with. Quantifiers are a type of **DETERMINER** (see ▶Step 23 for more details). A few are presented below, with examples.

Quantifiers which can be used only with countable nouns:

none of, a couple of, (a) few, several, a number of, many

✓ *How many apples were on the tree?* ✗ *How many water were in the pool?*

Quantifiers which can be used only with uncountable nouns:

no, not much, little, a little, a bit of, much, a great deal of

✓ *How much water was in the pool?* ✗ *How much apples were on the tree?*

Quantifiers which can be used either with uncountable or countable nouns:

a lack of, some, a lot of/lots of, plenty of, all of

✓ *There were some apples in the tree.* ✓ *There was some water in the pool.*

Note that when quantifiers are used with a countable noun, the verb is 3rd person plural, but when they are used with an uncountable noun, the verb is 3rd person singular.

Can some nouns be both countable and uncountable?

The answer to this question is *yes*. In English, many words can have different **SENSES**. For example, in Part B, both sentences 4a and 4b are correct, because a different meaning of *time* is being used in each. In 4a, *time* is being used as a countable noun to mean an occurrence of a particular event. In 4b, *time* is being used in a more general, philosophical way. Used in this way, it is an uncountable noun. Other common nouns which can be countable or uncountable include: *damage(s)*, *expense(s)*, *light(s)*, *noise(s)*, *paper(s)*, *room(s)*, *sport(s)* and *work(s)*. When using such nouns, consider exactly which use you are employing.

What do I do if I want to pluralize an uncountable noun?

Look again at sentences 5a and 5b in Part B. While 5b is correct, since *apple* is a countable noun, 5a is incorrect, since *fruit* is uncountable, and so cannot be pluralized. So what would you do if you wanted to talk about fruit in general? The solution is to add one of the many phrases in English which can be put in front of uncountable nouns to make them countable.

- *How many **pieces of** fruit did you buy?*

By doing this, you are adding a general, countable noun (*piece*) which can be pluralized. *Fruit* can then remain in its uncountable form. Other common phrases which perform a similar job are *types of* and *kinds of*. These phrases can be used with many uncountable nouns.

The key reason for adding such a phrase is to avoid the confusion which can come from using quantity words. For example, in response to the question *Would you like some sugar in your tea?*, the answer *Yes, please, I'll have **some** sugar* is not very specific. The listener's and speaker's understanding of the word *some* may be very different. To avoid confusion, the speaker might say *one* or *two spoons of sugar*.

There are also several specific phrases which can be used for particular uncountable nouns, as shown in the Grammar box. Some of these expressions have a very general meaning and can be used with many uncountable nouns: *grams of* can be used with anything which can be weighed (sugar, cheese, flour) and *bottles of* with anything which can be drunk.

Phrases that change uncountable nouns into countable nouns

- cups/glasses of water
- litres of air
- litres/gallons of petrol/oil
- bottles/glasses of water
- slices/grams of cheese
- pieces/sheets of paper
- megabytes of data
- items of furniture
- grains of sand
- teaspoons of salt/pepper/sugar

One final point is that in spoken English, **NATIVE SPEAKERS** may leave out these phrases. Sentence 6b, for example, does not make sense grammatically since *cups of* is missing before *coffee*, which is an uncountable noun. However, the sentence would be clearly understood by the listener.

Summary

1. Do not be influenced by your mother tongue as there are often large differences in concepts of countability between languages.
2. Ask yourself *Can I write a number before the noun?* and *Can I pluralize the noun?* to see if a noun is countable.
3. Use quantifiers carefully – don't just think about language; think about the grammar too.

D Activation

1. **Complete and comprehend.**

   What were these nouns examples of in Part C?

Nouns	Examples of
a. *equipment, information*	
b. *time, damage, noise*	
c. *coffee(s)*	

2. **Check your understanding.**

   Complete the following paragraph using each phrase from the box only once.

some	types of	not much
two or three teaspoons of	many	lots of

I like ____________________ different foods from all over the world, although I prefer the food of ____________________ countries more than others. In particular, I like Italian food, especially pasta. There are two ____________________ pasta which I really love: spaghetti and fusilli. When I don't have ____________________ work to do, I like to cook, although my wife thinks I use too much salt – but I only put in ____________________ it. That's ____________________.

3. **Create your own.**

   a. Turn the countable words/phrases into uncountable phrases.

   1. How many pieces of equipment are in your gym?

      ____

   2. Could you give me five sheets of paper, please?

      ____

   b. Turn the uncountable words/phrases into countable phrases.

   1. She drank a lot of water.

      ____

   2. How much air can you hold in your lungs?

      ____

How can I premodify nouns to make more complex noun phrases?

STEP 9

'Out of intense complexities intense simplicities emerge.'

Winston Churchill (1874–1965)
UK Prime Minister 1940–1945 and 1951–1955

A Reflection

Read the following passage. Underline any phrases which contain words which come before a noun, providing more information about it. There are 14 phrases in all.

The interesting points of the government's budget were as follows:

- Married couples to benefit from increased allowances.
- More money for retired people.
- Reduced salaries for government workers.
- Lower taxes on swimming pools and running machines, to encourage healthier lifestyles.
- A new tax on bank accounts.

B Contextualization

If you are unclear about some of the language used in this exercise, check in the *Glossary* at the back of the book.

Match each of the noun phrases from the text above to the structures outlined below. The numbers in brackets show how many phrases fit into each category.

Structure	Examples
noun + noun (2)	*government workers*
past participle + noun (4)	*retired people*
gerund + noun (2)	
determiner + adjective + noun (2)	
comparative adjective + noun (3)	
determiner + possessive noun + noun (1)	

C Explanation

What is a noun phrase?

A **NOUN PHRASE** is a group of words which acts as one unit, in which a noun is the most important word. Noun phrases are important because by adding more information before and after the noun, we can be much more specific. The text in the box on the right shows this clearly. The information before each noun has been removed. The removed information is represented by the Ø symbol. The difference is clear: the text lacks very important information!

> The Ø points of the Ø budget were as follows:
>
> - Ø couples to benefit from Ø allowances.
> - Ø money for Ø people.
> - Ø salaries for Ø workers.
> - Ø taxes on Ø pools and Ø machines, to encourage Ø lifestyles.
> - A Ø tax on Ø accounts.

How can I create noun phrases?

The two ways of making a noun into a noun phrase are to add information before it (premodification) and after it (postmodification). The rest of this step focuses on premodification, while postmodification is the focus of ▶Step 10.

Creating noun phrases may seem hard. To make it easier, think of it like blowing up a balloon. You start with the main noun, and gradually add information to it, making it more complex. People often try to create the whole noun phrase in one go, resulting in phrases which make no sense.

When you are thinking about what information to add to a noun to make it more complex, it can be useful to ask yourself a series of questions. By doing this, you can establish what kind of grammatical structure is required to add the information. The table below gives an example of this process, using the sentence *In the park, I saw a dog.*

Question about noun	Grammatical structure needed	Noun phrase
Who did the dog belong to?	Add possessive before noun	… **my neighbour's** dog
What did the dog look like?	Add adjective(s) before noun	… my neighbour's **small**, **black** dog
What was the dog doing?	Add present participle before noun	… my neighbour's small, black, **barking** dog
Where was the dog?	Add prepositional phrase after noun	… my neighbour's small, black, barking dog **in the bushes**
What was the dog doing in the bushes?	Add relative clause after noun	… my neighbour's small, black, barking dog **which was getting its ball** in the bushes

This final noun phrase acts as one idea, and can be broken down as follows.

> [my neighbour's] [small, black,] [barking] [**dog**] [which was getting its ball] [in the bushes]
>
> [my neighbour's] ↑ possessive noun
> [small, black,] ↑ adjectives
> [barking] ↑ present participle
> [**dog**] ↑ NOUN
> [which was getting its ball] ↑ relative clause
> [in the bushes] ↑ prepositional phrase

What are five main ways to premodify a noun?

1. **Use an adjective** (*a **new** tax*)

   The most basic way to add information to a noun is to use an ADJECTIVE (▶Step 16). It is possible to use more than one adjective per noun, but they must follow a specific order (▶Step 19). Adjectives can also appear in COMPARATIVE (***lower** taxes*) and SUPERLATIVE forms.

2. **Use a past participle** (***married** couples, **increased** allowances*)

   The PAST PARTICIPLE (~*ed* form) can work like an adjective. In the examples above, *married couples* is a neater way of saying *couples who are married*. Likewise, *increased allowances* means *allowances which have been increased*. Other past participles, along with nouns they could modify, include: ***broken** (window)*, ***burst** (pipe)*, ***frightened** (animal)*, ***frozen** (pond)*, ***injured** (player)*, ***married** (man/woman)*, ***reduced** (fee)*, ***retired** (teacher)*, ***rotten** (food)*, ***worried** (parents)*. Some past participles can only be used when combined with an adverb, for example, ***recently sold** car.*

3. **Use a present participle** (***interesting** points*)

   The PRESENT PARTICIPLE (~*ing* form) can be used as a premodifier when it refers to a permanent quality or characteristic. Some of these participles have degrees of comparison, or can have an intensifier put before them. Examples include: ***boiling/freezing** (point)*, ***disappointing** (news)*, ***relaxing** (afternoon)*, ***satisfying** (job)*, ***sleeping** (baby)*. See ▶Step 20 for more information about ~*ing* and ~*ed* participles being used as adjectives.

4. **Use another noun** (***bank** accounts, **government** workers*)

   Nouns can be placed before other nouns to provide more information about them. This structure is often used to say that the main noun is part of the noun which comes before. For example, *car window* = *window which is part of a car*. Two specific examples of this type of structure are given below.

   - **Gerunds** (***running** machines, **swimming** pools*)

     GERUNDS have the same form as the present participle. Imagine the phrase *which is used for* is between the gerund and the noun in the opposite order (i.e., *running machine* means *machine which is used for running*). Other common noun phrases of this type include: ***chewing** gum*, ***dining** room*, ***ironing** board*, ***walking** stick*.

   - **Nouns which are used as materials**

     When describing the material an object is made of, the material can be placed before the object. For example: ***gold** watch*, ***rubber** tyre*, ***stone** floor.*

5. **Use a possessive phrase** (***the government's** budget*)

   Phrases which indicate the ownership of the noun can also be used as premodifiers. Generally speaking, the 'owner' is followed by *'s*. Sometimes, a possessive adjective (e.g., *my*, *your*, *her*) may be used (▶Steps 7, 23).

Summary

1. Noun phrases can be created by adding information either before the noun (premodification) or after it (postmodification).
2. When you are creating a noun phrase, do it piece by piece – do not try to write it in one go.
3. There are five main ways to premodify a noun, namely by using adjectives, past participles, present participles, other nouns and possessive phrases.

D Activation

1. **Complete and comprehend.**

   What are the five main ways of premodifying a noun in English? Complete the table below with as much information as you can recall.

Strategy	Explanation	Examples
	• Put it before a noun. • If using more than one, think about order. • Comparative/superlative forms also possible.	
Use a past participle		
		disappointing (news), sleeping (baby)
Use another noun		
Use a possessive phrase		

2. **Check your understanding.**

   Look at the following phrases and identify each of the parts.

   a. large red car = adjective + adjective + noun

   b. frozen swimming pool = ______

   c. worrying global situation = ______

   d. water's boiling point = ______

   e. my aunt's recently sold house = ______

3. **Create your own.**

   Describe the following pictures using the words in the box below.

happy	bicycle	injured	gold	couple	badly	back
married	wheel	beautiful	clock	football player		

a ______

a ______

a ______

a ______

STEP 10

How can I postmodify nouns to make more complex noun phrases?

'If it doesn't turn out right, we can modify it as we go along.'

Franklin D. Roosevelt (1882–1945)
32nd President of the United States

A Reflection

Many noun phrases can be made by joining nouns together with *of*. Create noun phrases using *of* by combining the nouns in the box below. Use determiners where necessary.

~~top~~	many floors	coffee	eldest	litre	building	water	history
my brothers	tennis	cup	~~mountain~~	group	game	friends	London

1. the top of the mountain
2. ______
3. ______
4. ______
5. ______
6. ______
7. ______
8. ______

B Contextualization

Match the following examples of postmodification to the description.

The **owner of the restaurant** spoke to me.	noun + adjective
Put it on the **table in the kitchen**.	noun + relative clause
The **phone that I got last month** is broken.	noun + present participle
I saw the **man talking** in the restaurant.	noun + prepositional phrase
I'd like **some food to eat**.	noun + infinitive
There was **food aplenty** at the party.	noun + *of* + noun

You should have identified one relative pronoun above (*that*). A list of other words which can be used as relative pronouns is below. What do they refer to?

who	people	*which*		*that*	
whose		*whom*		*what*	
where		*when*		*why*	

C Explanation

What are five main ways to postmodify a noun?

1. Combine with another phrase.

NOUN PHRASES can be combined with other types of phrases (▶Step 27) to form bigger and more complex noun phrases. Very often, a noun phrase will be combined with a prepositional phrase (e.g., *in the kitchen*), as in the following example: *Put it on* ***the table in the kitchen*** (= the table which is found in the kitchen, rather than another table in a different room).

Of is frequently used to link two nouns together. Some of the main instances in which this structure is used are given below.

- Ownership or possession: *the owner of the restaurant*
- To show group membership: *the eldest of my brothers*
- To link a part to a whole: *the top of the mountain*
- To talk about quantity: *a litre of water*
- For containers: *a cup of coffee*
- After group nouns: *a group of friends*
- To talk about qualities: *a building of many floors*
- General phrases which do not fit other models: *a game of tennis, the history of London*

> **Using *of***
> Sometimes these nouns can be placed next to each other. For example, we do not say *the centre of the city*, but rather *the city centre*.

2. Use a relative clause.

A RELATIVE CLAUSE is a common type of DEPENDENT CLAUSE. It can be used to add detailed information about a noun phrase which comes before it. Relative clauses are introduced by a RELATIVE PRONOUN. The following words can act as relative pronouns in English: *that*, *which*, *who*, *whose*, *whom*, *what*, *where*, *when*, *why*. They can be used in the following ways.

- ***Which/that*** are used for things and objects: *The phone that I got last month is broken. That* is more common than *which*, but there are some circumstances where it is not possible to use *that*, e.g., NON-DEFINING RELATIVE CLAUSES: *London, which is the capital of the UK, has eight million inhabitants*.
- ***Who/whom/whose*** are used for people. *Who* can be used for either the subject or object of the sentence, whilst *whom* can only be used with the object: *The person who I saw at the bank was your brother. Is that the teacher whom you were talking about? Whose* is used to indicate possession: *She's the friend whose bike I borrowed.*
- ***Where*** is used for a place: *We're moving to the small village where I grew up.*
- ***When*** is used for a time: *Do you remember the day when we met?*
- ***What*** is used to mean 'the thing(s) that': *Take what you want.*
- ***Why*** is used for a reason: *I don't know the reason why we came!*

> **Use of relative pronouns**
> - When these are used with the object, they can be left out, e.g., *the computer ~~that~~ I bought, the person ~~who~~ I saw at the bank.*
> - *Whom* is not very commonly used, even by native speakers. Whilst correct, it is better to use *who* in less formal English.

More specific information about the different types of relative clauses (defining/non-defining) can be found in ▶Step 28.

3. **Use a participle phrase (~*ing* or ~*ed* clause).**
   Participle clauses can postmodify nouns as well as premodifying them (▶Step 9). These participle clauses would generally be followed by another phrase, such as a PREPOSITIONAL PHRASE or ADVERB PHRASE.
   - Present participle: *I saw the **man talking** in the restaurant.*
   - Past participle: *The **food cooked** last night was terrible!*

4. **Use an infinitive.**
   An infinitive form of a verb may come after a noun. The infinitive may be in the ACTIVE VOICE (*I'd like some food **to eat***) or the PASSIVE (*What is the question **to be discussed**?*).

5. **Use an adjective or adverb phrase.**
   Although adjectives almost always go before the noun they describe, they can occasionally go after the noun as well. For example: *There was **food aplenty** at the party.*

Can nouns be both premodified and postmodified?

Yes, but they can be tricky to write. Such complex phrases are common in formal writing, especially academic writing, and can be very useful for clearly expressing your point of view. If you do premodify and postmodify a noun, you must ensure the resulting phrase is clear. For example, you could premodify the phrase *a group of friends* to *a **large** group of friends* and then postmodify to *a large group of friends **who have known each other a long time***.

What are five key things to remember when using noun phrases?

1. **Think about language as a series of phrases, not as individual words.** This can improve the quality of your speech or writing. Many grammatical problems come from thinking about language as a series of words with no connection to each other.

2. **Think about whether a determiner is needed (▶Step 23).** Most noun phrases require a determiner (e.g., an article) before them. Because they are small words, DETERMINERS are often forgotten, but they are necessary if your English is to make sense.

3. **Don't make noun phrases too long.** If your noun phrases are too long, they will be difficult to follow and understand. Make them complex, but not complicated.

4. **Noun phrases are more common in written than in spoken English.** This is not to say you should not use them in spoken English, but because of their complexity, they can sometimes be difficult to understand.

5. **COLLOCATION is important.** It is important to think about which words go together in order to make your writing sound more like that of a native speaker.

Summary
1. There are five main ways to postmodify a noun, namely: combine with another phrase, use a relative clause, use a participle phrase, use an infinitive and use an adjective or adverb phrase.
2. Nouns can be premodified and postmodified; this is especially common in formal or academic writing.
3. Ensure that you consider whether a determiner is needed for the noun phrase.

D Activation

1. **Complete and comprehend.**

Complete the following sentences using the words in the box below.

things	places	which	times	reasons	complex	long	passive	that

a. *Which/that* are used to refer to __________. __________ is more common than __________.

b. *Where*, *when* and *why* can be used in relative clauses. They refer respectively to __________, __________ and __________.

c. When using an infinitive after a noun, it may be in the active or __________ voice.

d. If your noun phrases are too __________, they will be difficult to follow and understand. Make them __________, but not complicated.

2. **Check your understanding.**

a. **Complete the noun phrases using the words in the box below.**

written by my father	different	in the corner	of the cinema
to help me learn English	whose books are on the table		

1. Can you see that picture ____________________?
2. This weekend I'd like to go somewhere ____________________.
3. I don't like this seat. I'd like to talk to the manager ____________________.
4. Do you know ____________________?
5. This is a book ____________________.
6. I received an email ____________________.

b. **What is the structure of each of the postmodified noun phrases you have created?**

1.	4.
2.	5.
3.	6.

3. **Create your own.**

Write three sentences which include noun phrases with both premodified and postmodified information.

a.	
b.	
c.	

What are verbs and how are they used in English?

'Nothing is improbable until it moves into the past tense.'

George Ade (1866–1944)
American novelist, journalist and playwright

A Reflection

A verb can be described as a word or phrase that describes an action, condition or experience.

Read the following conversation and underline all the verbs you find.

Tom: Have you been on holiday this year?
Sam: Yes, I visited Spain in June.
Tom: Whereabouts did you go?
Sam: After we'd spent two days in Madrid, we took the train to Barcelona. It was fantastic.
Tom: Would you go again?
Sam: Yes, it was such a great experience. I've been thinking about it all the time since we arrived back. I'm planning to go next year. I'll definitely return to Barcelona.

What are all the different ways of writing the following verbs?

To walk: walk, walks, walked, walking
To go: go, goes, went, gone, going
To eat: ______
To look: ______

B Contextualization

Write the words in the box under the correct heading in the table. Use the *Glossary* at the back of the book to help you.

~~past~~ ~~continuous~~ future present participle perfect continuous ~~base form~~ present simple perfect present simple 3rd person singular past simple past participle

Tenses (when something happens)	Aspects (how something happens)	Ways of expressing a verb
past	continuous	base form

C Explanation

What are ten key facts about verbs in English?

The following ten facts are some of the most important things you need to know about using **VERBS** in English. Many of these points are discussed in more detail in the rest of this unit (▶Steps 12–15).

1. **Verbs are CONTENT WORDS, and an OPEN WORD CLASS.**
As content words, verbs carry meaning in the sentence. They are an open class, which means that new verbs are being created on a regular basis (see the Grammar box for three recent examples).

2. **When writing any SENTENCE, we must use a verb.**
There are two things every sentence needs: a **NOUN** and a verb – the door (subject) and the thing which is done. If your sentence doesn't contain a verb, then it is not a sentence! When proofreading, it is important to check that each sentence contains a verb.

> **Three recent verbs**
>
> **self-interrupt**: to stop working briefly and check email/social media
> **teletreat**: to provide medical advice remotely, via computer
> **squee**: to squeal in delight or excitement

3. **About 15 per cent of words in English are verbs.**
There are tens of thousands of verbs in English, but many of these verbs are either very rare or obsolete (no longer used). A very high percentage of verb usage is restricted to the most common 25 verbs. According to the *Oxford English Dictionary*, these are as follows: *be*, *have*, *do*, *say*, *get*, *make*, *go*, *know*, *take*, *see*, *come*, *think*, *look*, *want*, *give*, *use*, *find*, *tell*, *ask*, *work*, *seem*, *feel*, *try*, *leave*, *call*. Notice how all of these words have only one **SYLLABLE**!

4. **Some verbs can also be found in other WORD CLASSES.**
Most commonly, words which are verbs can also appear as nouns. From the list above, for example, we could write the following pairs of sentences.

As verb	As noun
Come on, let's play. You can **go** first.	Come on, let's play. It's your **go**.
Have you been **working**?	Have you been doing your **work**?
I'll **call** you later.	I'll give you a **call** later.

5. **English verbs are not heavily inflected (see INFLECTION).**
Many languages are inflected, meaning that letters are added to the beginning, middle or end of verbs to change their meaning. English, however, does not have much inflection. Instead, it uses **AUXILIARY VERBS** (▶Step 12). The only inflection in English regular verbs is as follows.
   - to form the 3rd person of the present simple (+ ~*s*)
   - to form a past simple form or past participle (+ ~*ed*)
   - to form the present participle or a gerund (+ ~*ing*)

6. **When deciding which verb form to use, we must decide when the action happens. This is known as TENSE.**
There are three ways of expressing when something happens.

- **PAST** (what has happened)
- **PRESENT** (what is happening now, or what generally happens)
- **FUTURE** (what is going to/will happen)

More information about tense can be found in ▶Step 13.

> **Note**
> Sometimes the word *tense* is used to refer to, e.g., the past simple or present continuous. This book will use the phrase *verb form* instead. *Tense* refers only to the idea of time.

7. **When deciding which verb form to use, we must decide how the action happens. This is known as ASPECT.**
There are four ways of expressing how something happens.

- **CONTINUOUS** (unfinished activity)
- **SIMPLE** (finished activity)
- **PERFECT** (activity before a point in time)
- **PERFECT CONTINUOUS** (unfinished activity before a point in time)

More information about aspect can be found in ▶Step 13.

8. **There are five ways of expressing a verb in English.**
In some languages, there are hundreds of ways of expressing a verb. In English, there are generally only ever five.

- **BASE FORM** (*look*, *eat*)
- present simple 3rd person singular (*looks*, *eats*)
- past simple form (*looked*, *ate*)
- **PAST PARTICIPLE** (*looked*, *eaten*)
- **PRESENT PARTICIPLE** (*looking*, *eating*)

> **Note**
> There are just a few verbs which are expressed in more than five ways. The most common is the verb *be*. It is special because it doesn't use the base form for the present simple 1st and 2nd persons. Instead, it uses *am* and *are*. It also has two past simple forms (*was*, *were*).

9. **When using verbs, ensure you know why you are using them.**
Verbs can be used in different ways for different purposes.
Examples for the present simple and present continuous forms of *help* are given here.

- Positive: *You help. You are helping.*
- Negative: *You do not help. You are not helping.*
- Question: *Do you help? Are you helping?*
- Negative question: *Do you not help? Are you not helping?*

10. **Many English verbs are formed by adding PREFIXES and SUFFIXES to nouns and ADJECTIVES.**
+ ~*ise* (BrE) / ~*ize* (AmE): *modernise/modernize, realise/realize*
+ ~*fy* / ~*ify*: *clarify, notify, simplify*
+ ~*en*: *darken, deepen, frighten, shorten*

Summary
1. Verbs are content words, making up about 15 per cent of English words.
2. Every sentence must contain a verb; otherwise it is not a sentence.
3. There are only five ways of expressing a verb in English, which is fewer than in most languages.

D Activation

1. **Complete and comprehend.**

   a. **Complete the following gaps to accurately describe the English verb system.**

   1. There are three ways of expressing when something happens: the ____________, ____________ and ____________.

   2. There are four ways of expressing how something happens: the ____________, ____________, ____________ and ____________.

   b. **Complete the table. It shows the five ways of expressing verbs in English.**

Base form	Present simple 3rd person singular	Past simple	Past participle	Present participle
call		called		calling
	gives		given	
		wanted		
use				
				trying
	tells			

2. **Check your understanding.**
   In each sentence, identify the type of mistake which was made and correct it.

Sentence	Type of mistake
He ~~maked~~ made a cake for my birthday. I ~~eated~~ ate too much though.	Confusion between regular and irregular verbs
He think about football all the time.	
You were travelling all day tomorrow, so go to bed now.	
I am being forty years old.	

3. **Create your own.**
   Using the verb *go*, write four example sentences as indicated.

Positive:	
Negative:	
Question:	
Negative question:	

What different types of verb are there?

> *'We are not nouns, we are verbs ... I think you can be imprisoned if you think of yourself as a noun.'*
>
> **Stephen Fry (1957–)**
> ***English actor, writer and presenter***

A Reflection

Look at the following pairs of sentences. Read each one carefully and tick the one which is correct.

1. She should.	☐	She should sleep.	☐
2. She sent.	☐	She sent an email.	☐
3. She owns a dog.	☐	She is owning a dog.	☐
4. My friend builded his own house.	☐	My friend built his own house.	☐

B Contextualization

Each piece of feedback below relates to one of the incorrect sentences above. Write each incorrect sentence in the appropriate place.

- Because of their meaning, and the activity they describe, some verbs in English very rarely take the continuous aspect. These stative verbs generally appear in the simple or perfect aspect.

  ____

- An irregular verb has had its past simple formed according to the rule of regular verbs. It is important to learn which verbs are regular and which are irregular.

  ____

- Some verbs in English are transitive, meaning that they require a direct object. Without a direct object, they do not make sense.

  ____

- There is a subject and an auxiliary verb only. While this is sometimes possible, it does not make sense here. An auxiliary verb is usually combined with a main verb.

  ____

C Explanation

What is the difference between main and auxiliary verbs?

She should sleep. ✓ *She should.* ✗

The **MAIN VERB** of a sentence is the verb which tells you the main information – the main thing which is happening. In the example, *sleep* is the main verb and *should* is the **AUXILIARY VERB**. Auxiliary verbs add meaning to, or alter the meaning of, the main verb. For example, *She sleeps* just describes a situation, but *She should sleep* is a recommendation. Auxiliary verbs cannot be used by themselves: they must be combined with a main verb. For example, *She should* is not grammatically correct as a sentence (although it is sometimes used as a sentence informally). Below are six main ways in which auxiliary verbs can be used.

1. **To show ASPECT (▶Step 13)**
   - *be* is used to form the **CONTINUOUS ASPECT**: *We **are** going. We **were** talking*.
   - *have* is used to form the **PERFECT ASPECT**: *She **has** visited the USA. I realized she **hadn't** taken her coat.*
2. **To form questions (▶Step 35)**
   - *do*, *be* and *have* can all be used in questions: ***Did** she go? **Are** we leaving? **Has** she arrived?*
3. **To show VOICE (▶Step 15)**
   - *be* is used to make **PASSIVE** forms: *He **was** given the news.*
4. **To form NEGATIVES (▶Step 34)**
   - *do* can be combined with *not*: *He **doesn't** talk. They **didn't** tell me.*
5. **For emphasis (▶Step 39)**
   - *do* can increase the power of a verb: *I **did** tell her.*
6. **To show MODALITY (▶Step 31)**
   - A range of **MODAL VERBS** (*would, should, can, could, may, might, must, will, shall, ought*) can alter the meaning of the main verb in areas such as degree of certainty or obligation: *I can swim*. *She must go*. *They may come*.

Key facts about auxiliaries

- They always precede the main verb.
- More than one can precede a main verb: *She was being told.*
- They can be used without a main verb if the meaning is clear: *Are you going? I might (go).*

What is the difference between transitive and intransitive verbs?

She sent an email. ✓ *She sent.* ✗

Some verbs in English must be followed by an **OBJECT**. We call these verbs **TRANSITIVE**. Without a **NOUN** or **NOUN PHRASE** acting as a **DIRECT OBJECT**, they do not make sense. *Send* is a common transitive verb. In the example, it does not make sense to just say *She sent* – what did she send? Other common transitive verbs include *bring*, *buy*, *get*, *give*, *make*, *take* and *write*.

Other verbs are **INTRANSITIVE**, meaning that they cannot be followed by a direct object. Common intransitive verbs include *cough*, *die*, *dream*, *go*, *sit*, *sneeze*, *sleep*, *fall*, *run*, *rise* and *cry*. Intransitive verbs can be followed by an **INDIRECT OBJECT**, as in *I sat on a chair* or *I slept in a bed*.

Note: many verbs are transitive when they are used in one way, but intransitive when they are used in another way. For example, *play* is usually transitive, as in *Every Thursday, I play football.* However, it can be intransitive, as in *Children love to play.*

What is the difference between stative and dynamic verbs?

She owns a dog. ✓ *She is owning a dog.* ✗

Some verbs hardly ever appear in the continuous aspect. These are known as **STATIVE VERBS.** This is because it is not possible to think about them as being 'unfinished' or 'temporary'. Example 3 in Part A shows this clearly. In English, the verb *own* means something permanent, i.e., a state: you either own a dog, or you do not own a dog. The statement of ownership does not make sense if you talk about it as if it is temporary. There are several other verbs which fall into this category, including the following categories.

- 'Knowledge' and 'opinion' verbs: *agree*, *believe*, *doubt*, *guess*, *know*, *mean*, *remember*
- 'Feeling' and 'emotion' verbs: *dislike*, *hate*, *like*, *love*, *prefer*, *want*, *wish*
- 'Relation' verbs: *contain*, *consist of*

DYNAMIC VERBS, by contrast, often appear in the continuous aspect. These verbs often refer to physical or mental actions. Examples include *buy*, *decide*, *go*, *leave*, *read*, *think* and *write*.

What is the difference between regular and irregular verbs?

My friend built his own house. ✓ *My friend builded his own house.* ✗

Most verbs in English are **REGULAR**. That is, to form their **PAST TENSE** and **PAST PARTICIPLE** forms, you need to add the **SUFFIX** *~ed* onto the **INFINITIVE** (e.g., *walk/walked/walked*, *deliver/delivered/delivered*). However, even though only three per cent of English verbs are **IRREGULAR**, about 70 per cent of verbs actually spoken or written are irregular. Indeed, the ten most common verbs in English are all irregular (*be*, *have*, *do*, *say*, *make*, *go*, *take*, *come*, *see*, *get*). Their irregular forms are given in the Grammar box.

Common irregular verbs in English

Base form	Past simple	Past participle
be	was/were	been
come	came	come
do	did	done
get	got	got
go	went	gone
have	had	had
make	made	made
say	said	said
see	saw	seen
take	took	taken

Summary

1. Using a verb correctly requires knowing how it works grammatically.
2. Key questions you should ask to understand a verb include: *Is it regular or irregular? Is it transitive, intransitive or both? Is it stative or dynamic?*
3. Ensure you use the correct auxiliary verb with the main verb, in order to say exactly what you want to.

D Activation

1. Complete and comprehend.
Write brief definitions of the terms.

Term	Definition
Auxiliary verb	
Transitive verb	
Stative verb	
Irregular verb	

2. Check your understanding.

a. Look up the following verbs in a dictionary, and tick the appropriate columns. Remember: some verbs can have both transitive and intransitive meanings.

Verb	Regular	Irregular	Transitive	Intransitive
eat				
go				
look				
run				
die				

b. Complete each gap with an appropriate form of the verb given in brackets. Note that you may also need to add negatives and adverbs.

My friend Alan ____________________ (*learn*) English for five years. Although he ____________________ (*like*) learning English, he ____________________ (*prefer*) watching TV. He ____ (*work*) hard enough. As a result, I think he ____________________ (*fail*) his exams next year.

3. Create your own.
Write sentences following the instructions.

Instruction	Example
a. Use *do* as an auxiliary verb	*I do believe you!*
b. Use a modal auxiliary	
c. Use more than one auxiliary verb	
d. Use *dislike* as a stative verb	
e. Use an intransitive verb followed by an indirect object	

What is meant by tense and aspect?

STEP 13

'I see the past, present and future existing all at once before me.'

William Blake (1757–1827)
English poet and painter

A Reflection

The following sentences all refer to the English verb system. All of these points have been discussed in either ▶Step 11 or ▶Step 12.

Complete the sentences with the correct number.

- There are ______ tenses (when the verb happens).
- There are ______ aspects (how the verb happens).
- There are ______ ways of expressing a verb.

B Contextualization

The sentences in each pair are either in the same tense, or have the same aspect. Identify which. Then identify the word from the box which describes the tense or aspect used. Looking back at ▶Step 11 or ▶Step 12 may help you.

perfect past perfect continuous future ~~continuous~~ simple

Pair of sentences	Same tense or aspect?	What tense or aspect?
1. They **were playing** all yesterday afternoon. Right now, it **is raining** very heavily.	aspect	continuous
2. They **played** the game last night. It finished 0–0. It **rains** all the time in London!		
3. At 3 p.m. this afternoon, I'**ll be washing** my car. I **will wash** your car tomorrow.		
4. They played against Manchester United after they **had played** Chelsea. They **had been playing** football for two hours before the rain came.		
5. It **has rained** every day for the past week. By 7 p.m., I **will have washed** all the cars.		
6. It **has been raining** since 7 o'clock. At 7 p.m., I **will have been washing** cars for eight hours.		

C Explanation

Why are you telling me about tense and aspect?

When you hear verbs being described as past simple or present perfect, do you know what these words mean? The way we describe a verb is very important, and directly relates to how the verb is being used. A good understanding of how verbs work will decrease the number of errors you make.

The English verb system is often thought to be difficult, illogical and hard to understand. This is unfortunate, and also inaccurate. The English verb system is actually quite logical, and much simpler than the verb systems of many languages.

There are only 12 ways to express verbs in English: each of three **TENSES** (**PAST**, **PRESENT** and **FUTURE**) can be expressed in each of the four **ASPECTS** (**CONTINUOUS**, **SIMPLE**, **PERFECT** and **PERFECT CONTINUOUS**). The diagram below shows this.

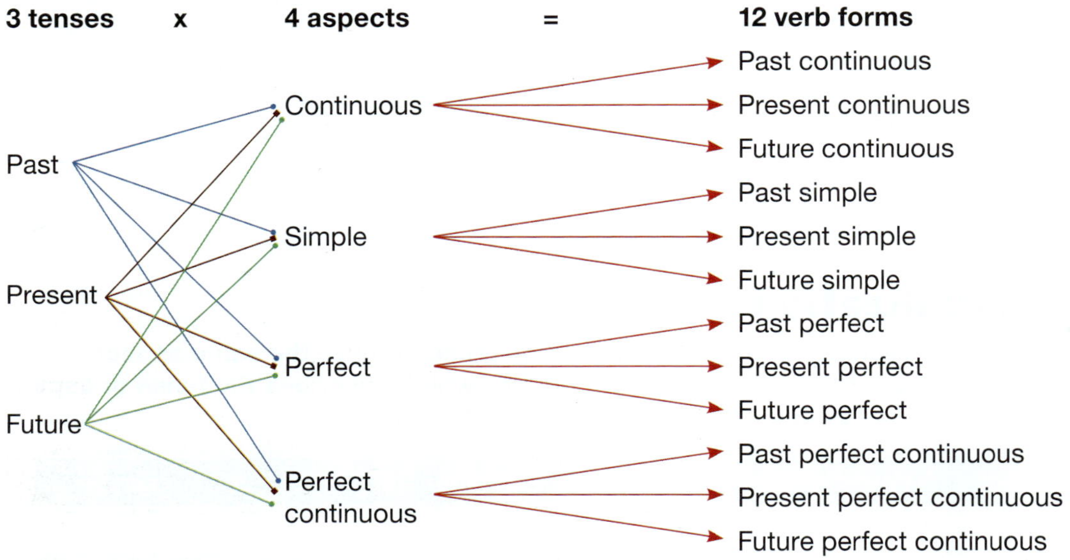

What are the tenses and aspects of English?

Answers to Part B table

2. aspect – simple **3.** tense – future **4.** tense – past **5.** aspect – perfect **6.** aspect – perfect continuous

The first part of the question is the easier to answer: the three tenses are the past, the present and the future. But although tense refers to time, the name of the tense does not always tell you when the action takes place. This is particularly true for present forms. For example, the present simple can be used to describe things which are true over an extended period of time in the past, present and future. Past and future tenses, however, almost always refer to things which have already finished and which have yet to begin.

The aspect of a verb refers to whether an action is unfinished or completed. Therefore, the aspect indicates very important information about the verb. Each aspect has its own function, which stays the same regardless of the tense it is combined with. For example, the continuous aspect indicates unfinished activity in any of the three tenses.

The information on the next page provides example sentences and explanations.

The **continuous aspect** is used to describe **unfinished activity**.

They **were playing** all yesterday afternoon.	Right now, it **is raining** very heavily.	At 3 p.m. this afternoon, **I'll be washing** my car.
At the time the speaker is talking about (yesterday afternoon), the action was unfinished (even though in reality it has finished).	At the time the speaker is talking about (now), the action is unfinished.	At the time the speaker is talking about (3 p.m. this afternoon), the action is unfinished (even though in reality it has not yet started).

The **simple aspect** is used to describe **states and events** which are considered to be **completed**.

They **played** the game last night. It finished 0–0.	It **rains** all the time in London!	I **will wash** your car tomorrow.
The game is complete, and occurred at a specific point in time.	The speaker is talking about a series of complete actions which surround the present.	The speaker is predicting a future event.

The **perfect aspect** is used to describe **what happens before a point in time**. It talks about not only when an action began, but when it was completed.

They played against Manchester United after they **had played** Chelsea.	It **has rained** every day for the past week.	By 7 p.m., I **will have washed** all the cars.
The speaker is talking about a past event which finished before another past event.	The speaker is referring to events which began before the present and which are now completed, but which have a connection to the present.	The speaker is saying that something will have finished before a point in the future (even though it has not yet started).

The **perfect continuous aspect** is a combination of the perfect and continuous aspects. It is therefore used to describe **unfinished activity before a point in time**.

They **had been playing** football for two hours before the rain came.	It **has been raining** since 7 o'clock.	At 7 p.m., I **will have been washing** cars for eight hours.
The speaker is talking about an activity which was unfinished at a specific point in the past and which occurred before another past event.	The speaker is saying that an activity began in the past, and is unfinished at the moment of speaking (and the activity will probably continue).	The speaker is saying that before a specific point in the future, an event will have started, but it will not be complete.

Summary

1. There are three tenses and four aspects in English, making a total of 12 verb forms.
2. The three tenses are the past, the present and the future.
3. The four aspects are the continuous, the simple, the perfect and the perfect continuous.

D Activation

1. **Complete and comprehend.**
   Complete the following statements in as much detail as possible.

The continuous aspect is used to describe …	
The simple aspect is used to describe …	
The perfect aspect is used to describe …	
The perfect continuous aspect is used to describe …	

2. **Check your understanding.**
   What verb form would you need if you wanted to describe …
   a. what you are doing at the moment?
   present continuous
   b. an event that finished before another event in the past?
   ______
   c. an event which will be unfinished at a point in the future?
   ______
   d. an event which started in the past, but which is still unfinished in the present?
   ______
   e. an event which will have finished before a point in the future?
   ______

3. **Create your own.**
   Write a sentence using each of the following verb forms.

a. Present continuous	*At the moment, I am learning about how to use verb forms in English.*
b. Past simple	
c. Present perfect	
d. Future continuous	

Which verb form do I use?

STEP 14

'Existence really is an imperfect tense that never becomes a present.'

Friedrich Nietzsche (1844–1900)
German philosopher and classical scholar

A Reflection

For each sentence, tick the tense and aspect the verb is in.

Sentence	Tense			Aspect			
	Pa	Pr	F	S	C	P	PC
New York **is** in the USA.		✓		✓			
My parents **went** yesterday.							
By next year, I **will have got** a new job.							
They**'re talking** to him.							
When you arrive, **I'll be cooking** dinner.							
Had she **studied** English before she moved to London?							
They**'ll arrive** this evening.							
I've been learning English for six years.							
Were you **working** at 9 o'clock this morning?							
I **have been** to France many times.							
By 6 p.m. tonight, **I'll have been working** for three hours!							
He**'d been working** hard before he was fired.							

Tense: Pa = past, Pr = present, F = future. Aspect: S = simple, C = continuous, P = perfect, PC = perfect continuous

Which three verb forms are used most and least commonly in English?

Three most common verb forms	Three least common verb forms
1.	**1.**
2.	**2.**
3.	**3.**

B Contextualization

Look at the time phrases. Match them to the definitions.

1. yesterday 2. next year 3. when 4. after 5. for six years 6. for a long time

A specific point in the past ____

A specific point in the future ____

Specific duration ____

General duration ____

Indicates two things are happening at the same time ____

Indicates one event happens later than another event ____

C Explanation

What are the most commonly used verb forms in English?

The frequency with which a verb form is used will depend on why and where you are using English, and who you are speaking to. In spoken English, we are likely to use the present continuous; in academic writing, the present simple; in novels, the past perfect. The diagram below shows how frequently the 12 verb forms are used overall.

past simple, present simple, present perfect	**Most common forms**
future simple, past continuous, present continuous	↕
future continuous, past perfect, present perfect continuous	
future perfect, future perfect continuous, past perfect continuous	**Least common forms**

How, specifically, are the 12 verb forms of English used?

The table below provides a more detailed overview of the specific functions of English verb forms. It provides additional information to the core principles outlined in ▶Step 13. Note that the table only includes the ACTIVE VOICE: the PASSIVE VOICE is discussed in ▶Step 15.

The table also includes a list of relevant TIME WORDS – words which are commonly used with specific verb forms. For example, *at the moment*, *now* and *currently* are often used with the present continuous, since they all refer to things which are incomplete. Time words can be categorized as follows.

Three top tips for using verbs

1. Be consistent. Do not jump between verb forms unnecessarily.
2. When deciding which verb forms you need, think about all the events/actions in the sentence, and how they relate to each other in time.
3. Consider how verb forms work with each other. For example, the past simple is often used with the past perfect/past continuous.

- ADVERBS/ADVERB PHRASES (▶Step 17): *historically*, *regularly*, *currently*
- PREPOSITIONAL PHRASES (▶Step 22): *in the past, by next week, at the moment*
- CONJUNCTIONS (▶Step 21): *when*, *while*
- NOUNS/NOUN PHRASES (▶Steps 6–10): *yesterday*, *today*, *three weeks ago*

Example sentences	Functions	Related time words
Past simple: base form + *~ed* / irregular		
My parents **went** yesterday.	To show a single action started and finished at a specific point in the past	*yesterday, two days ago, four weeks ago, in 1977, historically, in the past*
Sue **lived** in London for three years.	To show something happened in the past for a period of time	
She **was** happy as a child.	To show past habits, truths or facts	
Present simple: base form + *~s*/*~es* in the 3rd person / irregular		
New York **is** in the USA.	To state general truths or facts	*generally, regularly, usually, always, never, every day/ week/month/year*
Most Americans **speak** English.	To make generalizations	
She **goes** to school every day.	To describe repeated actions	
I **leave** tomorrow at 8 o'clock.	To show a planned future action or event	*next week, tonight*

Future simple: *will* + base form		
They**'ll arrive** this evening.	To predict a future event or state	*tomorrow, in three years' time, next week/month*
Will you **help** me do this?	To show or request a voluntary action	
Past continuous: *was/were* + present participle		
Were you **working** at 9 o'clock this morning?	To indicate an unfinished action at a particular point in the past	*between 2010 and 2012, from 9 o'clock to 10 o'clock, when, while* see past simple
I **was writing** an email when the computer crashed.	To show an action was interrupted in the past, usually not for a long time	
Present continuous: *am/is/are* + present participle		
They**'re talking** to him.	To indicate an unfinished action	*at the moment, now, currently, at present, at this time*
I**'m working** on it now.	To show you are in the middle of doing something	
I**'m doing** lots of overtime these days.	To discuss things that are generally true at the moment	*today, nowadays, this week/month/year*
She**'s visiting** her aunt tomorrow.	(Possible) future action/event	see future simple
Future continuous: *will* or *am/is/are going to be* + present participle		
When you arrive, I**'ll be cooking** dinner.	To predict what you will be doing at a particular point in the future	*probably, possibly* see future simple
Past perfect: *had* + past participle		
Had she **studied** English before she moved to London?	To talk about actions or events that took place before another past event	*after, before, until, already … by*
Present perfect: *have/has* + past participle		
I **have been** to France many times.	To show (an) event(s) took place in the past, but not at a specific time	*since, for, until now, just, in the last year, recently, lately, already, yet*
She **has grown** recently.	To talk about changes over time	
I**'ve had** a headache all day.	To show that actions/events which began in the past have continued until now	
Future perfect: *will have* or *am/is/are going to have* + past participle		
By next year, I **will have got** a new job.	To show an action or event will be completed by a point in the future	*by next year, by the time, within five years*
Past perfect continuous: *had been* + present participle		
He**'d been working** hard before he was fired.	To indicate an unfinished action which took place before another past point	see past perfect
Present perfect continuous: *have/has been* + present participle		
I**'ve been learning** English for six years.	To show that actions/events which began in the past are still incomplete	see present perfect
What **have** you **been doing**?	To talk about recent events or actions	
Future perfect continuous: *will have been* or *am/is/are going to have been* + present participle		
By 6 p.m. tonight, I**'ll have been working** for three hours!	To show that at a point in the future, an action or event will be incomplete	see future simple and future perfect

Summary

1. Focus mainly on the most common verb forms: past simple, present simple and present perfect.
2. Ensure you know the specific grammatical construction of each verb form.
3. Know which time words commonly go with each verb form.

D Activation

1. **Complete and comprehend.**

   Which verb forms are required to express the following? Also make a note of any time words which may be commonly used.

Function	Verb form	Time words
a. To show past habits, truths or facts	past simple	yesterday, in 1977, last week
b. To describe repeated actions		
c. To show that past actions are still unfinished		
d. To discuss things that are generally true at the moment		
e. To show or request a voluntary action		
f. To indicate simultaneous actions in the past		

2. **Check your understanding.**

   What is the difference in meaning between the sentences in each pair?

   a. Sue lived in London for three years. / Sue has lived in London for three years.

   ____

   b. They'll arrive sometime this evening. / By 10 p.m. tonight, they'll have arrived.

   ____

   c. She studied English when she moved to London. / She had studied English before she moved to London.

   ____

3. **Create your own.**

   Complete each sentence with an appropriate form of the verb in brackets. Sometimes more than one answer may be possible.

   a. At the moment, I ______________ (*travel*) to London by train.

   b. The essay ______________ (*finish*) by tomorrow.

   c. I ______________ (*sit*) on the sofa when my dog ______________ (*jump*) on me.

   d. Her plane ______________ (*leave*) at 10 a.m. tomorrow. Hopefully she ______________ (*get back*) home by midnight.

What are the active and passive voices?

'The whole of nature ... is a conjugation of the verb to eat, in the active and passive.'

William Ralph Inge (1860–1954)
English writer and Dean of St Paul's Cathedral

A Reflection

Which of the following represents the normal order of words in English? Is this the same as in your language?

1. subject-verb-object (SVO)
2. object-verb-subject (OVS)
3. subject-object-verb (SOV)

What is the difference in emphasis in each pair of sentences?

1. I made a mistake. / Mistakes were made.
2. She'll be playing football tomorrow. / Football will be being played tomorrow.
3. I was given a birthday present. / I was given a birthday present by my parents.

B Contextualization

Compare the following pairs of sentences. The sentences in the first column are in the active, whereas the sentences in the second column are in the passive. In each case, explain why you might choose to use the passive sentence.

Active	Passive	Specific reason used
The Swiss speak German, French and Italian.	German, French and Italian are spoken in Switzerland.	*The writer wants to emphasize the object rather than the subject.*
Somebody has stolen my car.	My car has been stolen.	
She discovered her company was paying her less than men in the same position.	She discovered she was being paid less than men in the same position.	
The people on the bus who are late for work are shouting at the driver.	The driver is being shouted at by the people on the bus who are late for work.	

C Explanation

What is the passive voice and when is it used in English?

> **Note**
>
> Since the majority of English sentences use the verb in the active, if you use the passive too often, your language may sound a bit strange and, possibly, a little bit boring.

The **WORD ORDER** which the majority of English **SENTENCES** follow is **SVO** (▶Unit A). Many major world languages, such as Chinese, French, Spanish, Portuguese and Thai, also predominantly use this word order. However, many other languages, such as Japanese and Turkish, have an SOV structure. Knowing what order your language follows can help you form the passive more accurately in English.

In English, the **PASSIVE VOICE** is used when the SVO word order is reversed to become OV(S). The **SUBJECT** is in brackets here because it is not always necessary to include it in a sentence.

There are four main reasons the passive might be used. These are outlined below.

1. **The object is to be emphasized.**

   German, French and Italian are spoken in Switzerland.

   There may be occasions where you need to emphasize the **OBJECT** of the sentence rather than the **AGENT**. In this example, the writer wants to stress the languages rather than the country, and so reverses the order of the sentence.

2. **The agent is not known or unimportant.**

   My car has been stolen.

   In this situation, you might not know or care who stole the car. What is important is the fact that it is no longer there! Wherever possible, in English, it is best to avoid vague subjects like *somebody*, *people*, *person*, *everybody* and *anybody*. The passive can also be used to actually avoid identifying responsibility, as in *Mistakes were made.*

3. **The agent is obvious.**

   She discovered she was being paid less than men in the same position.

   In certain circumstances, it is clear from the context who the subject is. When this is the case, it is best not to use the subject. This means we can avoid repetition.

4. **The subject is very long.**

   The driver is being shouted at by the people on the bus who are late for work.

   In this sentence, the subject and the object are both important. Although it might seem more natural to use the normal SVO order, doing so makes the sentence difficult to understand. When the long subject (*people on the bus who are late for work*) comes first, you have to remember a lot of information before getting to the verb. Putting the object (*the driver*) at the beginning makes the sentence easier to understand.

What types of verbs can be put into the passive voice?

As discussed previously, verbs can be divided into those which are **TRANSITIVE** and those which are **INTRANSITIVE** (▶Step 12). Transitive verbs (e.g., *give*, *write*) are those which have direct objects. Since using the passive requires putting a direct object before the verb, only transitive verbs can be used in the passive. Intransitive verbs (e.g., *arrive*, *sleep*) do not have an object, and therefore cannot be put into the passive.

How do I form the passive?

The passive is formed by using *be* as an **AUXILIARY VERB** (▶Step 12), followed by the past participle form (pp) of the **MAIN VERB**. A table of the most commonly used passive forms is given below.

Reminder

- To make the past participle of a **REGULAR VERB**, you add *~ed* to the infinitive: ***looked***, ***walked***, ***worked***.
- The past participles of **IRREGULAR VERBS** must be learnt separately. Past participles commonly used in the passive include: ***bought*** *(buy)*, ***broken*** *(break)*, ***built*** *(build)*, ***caught*** *(catch)*, ***chosen*** *(choose)*, ***drunk*** *(drink)*, ***eaten*** *(eat)*, ***given*** *(give)*, ***gone*** *(go)*, ***known*** *(know)*, ***left*** *(leave)*, ***made*** *(make)*, ***read*** *(read)*, ***said*** *(say)*, ***seen*** *(see)*, ***sent*** *(send)*, ***taught*** *(teach)*, ***thought*** *(think)*, ***told*** *(tell)*, ***won*** *(win)*.

Verb form	Construction	Example
Present simple	*am/is/are* + pp	English **is spoken** here.
Present continuous	*am/is/are being* + pp	Lunch **is being** eaten.
Present perfect	*has/have been* + pp	He**'s been** fired.
Past simple	*was/were* + pp	Mistakes **were made**.
Past continuous	*was/were being* + pp	The meal **was being served** when I arrived.
Past perfect	*had been* + pp	The meat **had been cooked** for too long.
Future simple	*will be* + pp	The work **will be finished** by 5 o'clock.
Future perfect	*will have been* + pp	The phones **will have** already **been sold**.
Infinitive	*am/is/are to be* + pp	We **are to be invited** to the party.

Although other verb forms can be put into the passive, this is not common in English since they do not sound right. The future continuous passive, for example, can be very awkward, as in *Football will be being played tomorrow*. Also note that **PHRASAL VERBS** can be used in the passive, so long as they are transitive: *He was looked after by his daughter for many years*.

When do I need *by* + subject?

When using the passive, there are two options about what to do with the subject. You can either leave it out entirely (*I was given a birthday present*) or you can use the *by* + subject structure after the verb (*I was given a birthday present by my parents*).

Summary

1. There two voices in English: the active and the passive. The active is used more frequently, and follows the word order subject-verb-object. The passive follows the word order object-verb-(*by* + subject).
2. The passive is used in particular situations, such as when the subject is less important than the object, unknown, obvious or too long.
3. The passive is formed by using *be* as an auxiliary verb, followed by the past participle form of the main verb.

D Activation

1. **Complete and comprehend.**

   What are the main reasons for using the passive in English?

   - ______________________________
   - ______________________________
   - ______________________________
   - ______________________________

2. **Check your understanding.**

   Read the following pairs of sentences and decide whether the active or passive form would be more appropriate. In each pair, the active form is given first.

   a. A builder built the house in 1890. / The house was built in 1890.
   b. We'll help you later on. / You will be helped later on.
   c. A repairman is repairing the road. / The road is being repaired.
   d. Finally, the government passed the laws. / Finally, the laws were passed.
   e. Cheesemakers make cheese through the UK. / Cheese is made throughout the UK.

3. **Create your own.**

   Read the notes below about the artist Pablo Picasso. When you have done this, write five sentences about his life using the passive voice.

   - Pablo Picasso (1881–1973)
   - Inventor of Cubism
   - 2 marriages – Olga Khokhlova and Jacqueline Roque
   - Spent lots of time in Paris in his early life
   - Many galleries around the world have his paintings

a.	
b.	
c.	
d.	
e.	

What are adjectives and how can I use them?

'As to the adjective: when in doubt, strike it out.'

Mark Twain (1835–1910)
American writer

A Reflection

An adjective is a word which adds meaning to a noun or pronoun.

Read through the passage below and underline the adjectives.

Adjectives are an important group of words in English. They are useful because they can make your meaning stronger, so that your writing will be more interesting to read. Adjectives can help you to be clear about what you want to say. However, if you use too many adjectives, it may be difficult to understand your point.

Adjectives can often be recognized by their suffixes. Some common adjectival suffixes are listed below. Try to think of at least one adjective which has each suffix.

~able *reasonable*	~ed	~ic	~ive
~al	~ent	~ile	~less
~ant	~esque	~ing	~ous
~ary	~ful	~ish	~y

B Contextualization

Look at the six sentences below. In each case, identify the problem and correct it.

Sentence	Problem
1. The Taj Mahal is a ~~building beautiful~~. *beautiful building*	*In English, adjectives generally come before the noun.*
2. The Parthenon is an old, interesting building.	
3. The Empire State Building is very interested.	
4. The Great Pyramid of Giza is very enormous.	
5. The Great Wall of China is more long than Hadrian's Wall.	
6. Egypt has many ancients buildings.	

C Explanation

What are adjectives and how should they be used?

ADJECTIVES are an important **WORD CLASS** in English. Their job is to add meaning to **NOUNS** and **PRONOUNS**. They are usually found immediately before the noun or pronoun which they modify. When using adjectives, ensure that they really do add to what you have written. Do not just add them because you think they sound nice. The passage from Part A is shown below with the adjectives underlined.

> Adjectives are an <u>important</u> group of words in English. They are <u>useful</u> because they can make your meaning <u>stronger</u>, so that your writing will be more <u>interesting</u> to read. Adjectives can help you to be <u>clear</u> about what you want to say. However, if you use too <u>many</u> adjectives, it may be <u>difficult</u> to understand your point.

What are the most common adjectives in English?

The table below gives 100 of the most commonly used adjectives in English.

100 common adjectives in English						
afraid	closed	expensive	hard	many	rich	tiny
alive	cold	fake	heavy	mean	right	tired
angry	cool	false	high	near	sad	together
annoyed	dangerous	far	hot	new	safe	true
annoying	dark	fast	huge	next	same	ugly
apart	dead	few	interesting	nice	short	warm
bad	different	fine	large	noisy	slow	weak
beautiful	done	finished	last	old	small	wet
big	dry	first	late	open	soft	wrong
boring	dull	flat	lazy	ordinary	special	young
broken	early	free	light	poor	strange	
busy	easy	full	little	pretty	strong	
cheap	empty	good	long	quick	sure	
clear	excited	great	low	ready	surprised	
close	exciting	happy	lucky	real	tall	

How can suffixes help you to recognize/create adjectives?

It is often easy to identify a word as an adjective by looking at its **SUFFIX** (the group of letters at the end of a word). Suffixes can be added to nouns and **VERBS** to make adjectives. Common suffixes which can be added to nouns to make adjectives include:

- **~al** (*accidental*)
- **~ary** (*customary*)
- **~esque** (*picturesque*)
- **~ful** (*truthful*)
- **~ic** (*athletic*)
- **~ile** (*infantile*)
- **~ish** (*childish*)
- **~less** (*clueless*)
- **~ous** (*dangerous*)
- **~y** (*healthy*)

Common suffixes which can be added to verbs to make adjectives include:

- **~able** (*expandable*)
- **~ant** (*pleasant*)
- **~ed** (*relaxed*)
- **~ent** (*different*)
- **~ing** (*relaxing*)
- **~ive** (*effective*)

What are the main rules for using adjectives in English?

Refer to the answers you gave in Part B to check your understanding of how to use adjectives. The following general rules apply. The separate steps in this unit which talk about these issues in more detail are identified in brackets afterwards.

Rule 1: Adjectives generally come before the noun/pronoun they describe (▶Step 19).

The Taj Mahal is a ~~building beautiful.~~

beautiful building.

Rule 2: When more than one adjective is used, they come in a specific order (▶Step 19).

The Parthenon is an ~~old, interesting~~ building.

interesting, old

Rule 3: Adjectives do not have to 'agree' with nouns in English.

Egypt has many ~~ancients~~ buildings.

ancient

In some languages, the form of the adjective changes according to the noun with which it appears. For example, if the noun is **PLURAL**, then an *s* might be added to the end of the adjective. This does **not** happen in English. Also, nouns in English do not have a **GENDER**, as they do in some languages, so there are no masculine or feminine adjectives.

What common problems are there when using adjectives?

Again, refer to the answers you gave in Part B.

Problem 1: Using the wrong form of an adjective (▶Step 20).

The Empire State Building is very ~~interested~~.

interesting.

Adjectives can be formed using the **PRESENT PARTICIPLE** (*~ing*) and **PAST PARTICIPLE** (*~ed*) forms. These two forms have distinct meanings, and are commonly confused.

Problem 2: Using the wrong form of a comparative or superlative adjective (▶Step 18).

The Great Wall of China is ~~more long~~ than Hadrian's Wall.

longer

There is a specific set of rules which governs how you make the **COMPARATIVE** and **SUPERLATIVE** forms of adjectives. Generally speaking, for one- or two-syllable adjectives, *~er* is added to make comparatives and *~est* to make superlatives, whereas for adjectives with three or more syllables, the *more/most* + adjective structure is used.

Problem 3: Not recognizing that some adjectives are ungradeable (▶Step 20).

The Great Pyramid of Giza is ~~very~~ enormous.

Certain adjectives cannot be preceded by words like *very* or *quite*. Here, the **GRADEABLE** equivalent to *enormous* would be *large*: you can say *very large*, but not *very enormous*.

Summary

1. The job of an adjective is to add meaning to nouns and pronouns.
2. Knowledge of suffixes (e.g., *~al*, *~ful*, *~ic*) can help you learn and remember adjectives.
3. Three key rules for using adjectives are: they come before nouns; they must come in a specific order when more than one is used; they do not agree with nouns.

D Activation

1. **Complete and comprehend.**

   Complete each sentence with the appropriate choice from the brackets.

   a. Adjectives are used to describe ______________________ (*nouns / pronouns / nouns and pronouns*).

   b. The form of an adjective ______________________ (*sometimes / never / always*) changes depending on whether the noun is singular/plural or masculine/feminine.

   c. The form of the adjective which ends ~*er* is known as the ______________________ (*comparative / superlative*).

   d. Adjectives like ______________________ (*large / enormous*) can be called 'gradeable' because you can put words like *very* and *quite* before them.

2. **Check your understanding.**

   a. **What are the adjective forms of these nouns and verbs? Use a dictionary if you need to. Note: in some cases, more than one adjective may exist.**

Nouns	Adjectives	Verbs	Adjectives
artist	artistic	comfort	
centre		create	
day		expect	
skill		permit	
sun		urge	

   b. **Look up the following suffixes in a dictionary or online, and state what they indicate.**

~able	can be done	~ful	
~al		~ish	
~esque		~less	

3. **Create your own.**

   Choose five adjectives from the list you created in 2a. above, and write a sentence showing the meaning of each.

   Example: My friend is very artistic. He is always drawing or going to exhibitions.

   a. ______________________

   b. ______________________

   c. ______________________

   d. ______________________

   e. ______________________

What are adverbs and how can I use them?

'I'm glad you like adverbs – I adore them; they are the only qualifications I really much respect.'

Henry James (1843–1916)
American–English novelist and literary critic

A Reflection

An adverb can be described as a word that gives more information about a verb, adjective, phrase, or another adverb.

Read the passage below and underline the adverbs.

Learners of English often have difficulty with adverbs, finding it hard to use them correctly. There are many reasons for this. One reason is that many languages use adverbs differently to English. Additionally, learners are frequently confused about where to put an adverb in a sentence. Finally, it is important to note that adverbs should only be used when they genuinely add meaning to a text.

Many adverbs in English end with the suffix *~ly*. Write down as many such adverbs as you can think of in the box below.

B Contextualization

Say what the sentence would mean if the adverb was not included.

1. She ran **slowly** so that her son could overtake her and win.

   Without the adverb, the sentence makes no sense.

2. I will **probably** be late.

3. It was **extremely** hot when we went on holiday.

4. She was **absolutely** certain about her answer.

5. He is the best candidate for the job because he is **highly** educated.

C Explanation

What is an adverb?

ADVERBS are an extremely difficult **PART OF SPEECH** to define. Although the definition given on the previous page is correct, it does not quite capture the complexity of how adverbs are used. Whilst it is clear how to use **ADJECTIVES**, adverbs are a more difficult category of words to understand. However, as the passage below shows, they are an important and frequently used part of speech. Therefore, it is important to know how to use them.

> Learners of English often have difficulty with adverbs, finding it hard to use them correctly. There are many reasons for this. One reason is that many languages use adverbs differently to English. Additionally, learners are frequently confused about where to put an adverb in a sentence. Finally, it is important to note that adverbs should only be used when they genuinely add meaning to a text.

What difference does an adverb make to a sentence?

Adverbs can alter the meaning of a sentence quite radically, as the table below shows.

Sentence	What difference does the adverb make?
1. She ran **slowly** so that her son could overtake her and win.	Without the adverb, the sentence makes no sense.
2. I will **probably** be late.	The adverb weakens the certainty of the statement.
3. It was **extremely** hot when we went on holiday.	The adverb intensifies the meaning of the adjective. It may also signify a negative tone.
4. She was **absolutely** certain about her answer.	The adverb places extra emphasis on the adjective.
5. He is the best candidate for the job because he is **highly** educated.	Without the adverb, the sentence would have a very different meaning. The adverb allows the speaker to identify a specific quality.

In what situations are adverbs generally used?

Adverbs can be divided into several categories according to the situations in which they are generally used. The main categories are the following.

- **Place:** where something happens: *there*, *here*, *downstairs*
- **Time:** when something happens: *recently*, *afterwards*, *tomorrow*
- **Manner:** how something happens: *well, quickly, accurately*
- **Degree:** to what extent something happens: *very*, *really*, *so*
- **Frequency:** how often something happens: *sometimes*, *generally*, *always*

An adverb's position in a sentence can vary depending on what category it belongs to, and what its specific function is. This is investigated in more detail in ▶Step 18.

How are adverbs formed?

The majority of adverbs in English are formed by adding the suffix *~ly* to an adjective. The table below presents 100 of the most commonly used adverbs which follow this pattern.

100 common adverbs in English which have the suffix *~ly*				
absolutely	constantly	genuinely	occasionally	slowly
actively	correctly	gradually	only	smoothly
actually	currently	happily	originally	specifically
additionally	deeply	hardly	particularly	strictly
adequately	definitely	hopefully	perfectly	strongly
aggressively	directly	immediately	possibly	stupidly
anxiously	disappointingly	independently	practically	subsequently
apparently	easily	individually	previously	successfully
appropriately	effectively	instantly	privately	successively
approximately	equally	jointly	probably	surely
badly	essentially	largely	publicly	surprisingly
barely	ethically	lazily	quickly	suspiciously
basically	eventually	locally	really	totally
briefly	exactly	mainly	recently	undoubtedly
carefully	extremely	morally	regularly	urgently
clearly	falsely	naturally	respectively	usually
closely	finally	necessarily	significantly	virtually
completely	firstly/secondly	newly	similarly	visibly
confidently	fundamentally	normally	simply	widely
consequently	generally	objectively	slightly	wrongly

However, not all adverbs end with *~ly*, and not all words which end with *~ly* are adverbs! Common adverbs which do not end with *~ly* include *about*, *around*, *as*, *fast*, *hard*, *just*, *not*, *often*, *seldom*, *so*, *too*, *very* and *well*. Common words which end in *~ly* but which are adjectives rather than adverbs include *friendly*, *lovely*, *silly*, *timely* and *ugly*. **Note:** some words can be used as both adjectives and adverbs. Common examples include *daily, early, likely* and *only*.

How and when should I use adverbs?

When used well, adverbs can add important and sophisticated meaning to an academic text. However, when used poorly, they can reduce the quality and impact of your writing. Try only to use adverbs when they genuinely add value to your writing. When they do not, remove them.

Top tip

Be careful not to use an adjective when you need an adverb. This is a common mistake made by learners.

✘ *She hit the tennis shot perfect.*

✔ *She hit the tennis shot perfectly.*

✔ *She hit a perfect tennis shot.*

Summary

1. Adverbs mostly modify the meaning of verbs, but also adjectives and other adverbs.
2. The five main categories of adverbs are: place, time, manner, degree and frequency.
3. Very often, adverbs are formed by adding the suffix *~ly* to adjectives.

D Activation

1. **Complete and comprehend.**

   Complete each sentence with an appropriate word or phrase from the brackets.

   a. Adverbs can modify ____________________ (*verbs / adjectives / other adverbs / all of the above*).

   b. Adverbs ____________________ end with the suffix *~ly* (*always / generally / occasionally*).

   c. The position of adverbs in a sentence is ____________________ (*unimportant / important*).

2. **Check your understanding.**

   a. **Rewrite the following sentences using the adverb in brackets.**

   1. Her train left at 12:00. She arrived at 11:59. (*just*)

      She arrived just in time for her train.

   2. I agree with you a lot about this issue. (*strongly*)

      ____

   3. The cost was in the region of $100. (*about*)

      ____

   4. You have to apply by yourself. (*independently*)

      ____

   b. **Fill in each gap with an appropriate adverb from the table on page 73.**

   Note: in some cases, more than one option may be possible.

   1. She occasionally plays football – perhaps two or three times a month.
   2. Although he is quite overweight, he is ____________ fast.
   3. Our teacher ____________ said we should read Chapter 7. Don't you remember?
   4. I saw her very ____________ – a week ago, at most.

3. **Create your own.**

   Choose three adverbs from the table on page 73, and write sentences showing the meaning of each.

   Example: There were disappointingly few people in class today. Only seven turned up.

   a. ____________________

   b. ____________________

   c. ____________________

What are comparatives and superlatives?

'I am the last and highest court of appeal in detection.'

Sherlock Holmes
character created by **Arthur Conan Doyle (1859–1930)**
Scottish writer

A Reflection

A comparative is the form of an adjective or adverb that shows a difference in amount, quantity, degree or quality, e.g., *larger*, *less interesting*. The superlative form demonstrates that no object has a higher degree or quantity, e.g., *the largest*, *the most interesting*.

Read through the passage below. Underline those adjectives or adverbs which you think are comparative or superlative forms.

Probably the most difficult aspect of using superlatives correctly is understanding the grammatical rules involved. At first, they are not easy to remember, but with practice, the process becomes much simpler. You will be able to more effectively understand these forms with careful study. One final point to make is that the most common mistake in using superlatives is to forget to use *the*. Your English will be better if you can use these forms correctly!

B Contextualization

Read the following sentences. Then complete the table which follows in order to make the rules for forming comparative and superlative adjectives.

1. Ben is definitely **taller than** Imran. Ben is **the tallest** student in the class.
2. This is **the hottest** day of the year. It's **hotter** in London than in New Delhi.
3. Saul is **the most ambitious** person in my office. He has become **more ambitious** the longer he has been here.
4. Although a blue whale is **larger** than an elephant, an elephant is **the largest** land animal.
5. Eating chocolate makes me **the happiest** person in the world! Nothing makes me **happier**.

Word	Comparative form	Superlative form
tall	*add ~er*	*add ~est*
large		
hot		
happy		
ambitious		

C **Explanation**

How do I form comparative and superlative adjectives?

The ability to compare and contrast is extremely important in all languages. In English, the **COMPARATIVE** form is used to compare two people or things, whereas the **SUPERLATIVE** compares one person or thing with every other member of a group.

Comparative: *Ben is definitely **taller than** Imran.* (Only Ben and Imran are compared.)

Superlative: *Ben is **the tallest** student in the class.* (Ben is compared against the whole class.)

The comparatives and superlatives in the passage from Part A are underlined below.

> Probably the most difficult aspect of using superlatives correctly is understanding the grammatical rules involved. At first, they are not easy to remember, but with practice, the process becomes much simpler. You will be able to more effectively understand these forms with careful study. One final point to make is that the most common mistake in using superlatives is to forget to use *the*. Your English will be better if you can use these forms correctly!

This table gives an outline of the rules for forming comparative and superlative adjectives. Remember that comparatives are followed by *than* and superlatives are preceded by *the*.

Number of syllables	Ending	Example adjectives	How to form a comparative	How to form a superlative
1	–	tall, cold	add ~*er*	add ~*est*
1	VOWEL + CONSONANT	hot, fat	double consonant, add ~*er*	double consonant, add ~*est*
1 or 2	*e*	large, simple	drop *e*, add ~*er*	drop *e*, add ~*est*
2	*y*	happy, sunny	change *y* to *i*, add ~*er*	change *y* to *i*, add ~*est*
2	not *y*	boring, special	*more*/*less* + adjective	*most*/*least* + adjective
3 or more	–	ambitious, optimistic	*more*/*less* + adjective	*most*/*least* + adjective

Some common two-syllable adjectives can be modified in two different ways: the ~*er*/~*est* suffixes can be added, or *more*/*most* can be used. One example is *clever*. The examples below would all be acceptable in English.

✓ *Who is cleverer? Who is the cleverest?*

✓ *Who is more clever? Who is the most clever?*

Other adjectives on which either system can be imposed include *common*, *likely*, *pleasant*, *polite*, *quiet*, *stupid*, *sure*, *subtle* and *simple*. There is not universal agreement about which system should be used.

Irregular adjective forms

Adjective	Comparative	Superlative
good	better	best
bad	worse	worst
far	further	furthest
little	less	least

What if I want to compare things which are similar?

The most common way of doing this is to use *as* + adjective/adverb + *as*.

- Ben is **as tall as** Imran.
- My team played **as badly as** yours.

Top tip

Beware double comparatives.
For example: *Eggs are ~~more~~ **cheaper** than bread.*

How do I form comparative and superlative adverbs?

There are three main categories that adverbs can be divided into when forming their comparative and superlative forms. Each type follows its own pattern, as outlined below.

1. **~*ly* adverbs**

   ~*ly* adverbs take their comparative and superlative forms in the same way as three-syllable adjectives, namely with the addition of *more* and *most*.

   - She ran **slowly** so that her son could overtake her and win.
   - She ran **more slowly than** her son so that he could overtake her and win.
   - Of all the competitors, she ran **the most slowly**.

2. **Adverbs with only one syllable**

   Adverbs with one syllable take their comparative and superlative forms in the same way as adjectives with one syllable, namely with the addition of ~*er* and ~*est*.

   - Terry ran **fast**.
   - Terry ran **faster than** his mother.
   - Terry was **the fastest** of all the children.

   Other examples of adverbs of this type include *close*, *deep*, *hard*, *late*, *long*, *low*, *near*, *slow*, *soon* and *straight*.

3. **Irregular adverbs**

   The following adverbs are irregular and take the indicated comparative and superlative forms.

Adverb	Comparative	Superlative
well	better	best
badly	worse	worst
far	further	furthest
little	less	least

- Although Bob hit the ball **well**, Rod hit it **better**. However, Rob hit it **best** of all.

How do I increase the impact of comparative adverbs?

When using comparative adverbs, it is sometimes useful to be able to express the degree to which the two things are different. **INTENSIFIERS** can be used to strengthen the meaning of an adverb, as in *Rod hit the ball **much** better than Bob*. Other common intensifiers in English include *far*, *significantly*, *considerably*, *(quite) a lot*, *a great deal* and *a fair bit*. There is also a group of words which weaken the meaning of the adverb, as in *Rod hit the ball **slightly** better than Bob*. Other such words in English include *a bit* and *a little*.

Summary

1. The comparative form is used to compare two people or things, whereas the superlative compares one person or thing with every other member of a group.
2. There is a set of rules for forming the comparative and superlative forms of adjectives based on the number of syllables in the adjective.
3. The majority of comparative and superlative adverbs are formed by using *more* and *most*.

D Activation

1. **Complete and comprehend.**

   Complete the following table with information about how the comparative and superlative forms of adjectives are formed.

Description of adjective	Comparative	Superlative
one syllable		
one syllable, ending with vowel + consonant		
one or two syllables, ending with *e*		
two syllables, ending with *y*		
two syllables, not ending with *y*		
three syllables		

2. **Check your understanding.**

   Look at the information. Say whether the statements which follow are true or false.

Weather today around the world					
London	Riyadh	Buenos Aires	Rome	Paris	Moscow

25°C	35°C	7°C	15°C	23°C	7°C

   a. London is significantly hotter than Paris **True / False**
   b. It is as cold in Moscow as in Buenos Aires. **True / False**
   c. The sun is shining most brightly in Riyadh. **True / False**
   d. It is much sunnier in Paris than in Rome. **True / False**

3. **Create your own.**

   Complete the following sentences in an appropriate way using a comparative or superlative adjective or adverb form.

   a. The Empire State Building is taller than the Eiffel Tower.
   b. The United States of America ______
   c. London ______
   d. My best friend ______
   e. Football ______

Where in a sentence should adjectives and adverbs be positioned?

'The adjective is the banana peel of the parts of speech.'

Clifton Fadiman (1904–1999)
American cultural and literary critic

A Reflection

Read the three sentences. In each case, the same adverb is used, but in a different position. Consider the specific meaning of each sentence.

I have visited Spain only.
I have only visited Spain.
Only I have visited Spain.

Now read the questions below. Each of the sentences above answers one of these questions. Match the questions with the answers.

Has anyone else in your family visited Spain?
Have you ever been to Europe?
Have you ever lived in Spain?

B Contextualization

Look at the following groups of sentences. In each case, decide which sentence has the adjectives in the correct order.

1. **a.** It's an interesting, new concept.
   b. It's a new, interesting concept.
2. **a.** I love the beautiful, tall, old buildings in New York.
   b. I love the old, tall, beautiful buildings in New York.
   c. I love the tall, beautiful, old buildings in New York.
3. **a.** That's her cotton, warm sleeping bag.
   b. That's her warm, cotton sleeping bag.
   c. That's her sleeping, cotton warm bag.
4. **a.** The university bought grey six computer screens.
   b. The university bought grey computer six screens.
   c. The university bought six grey computer screens.

C Explanation

Why does adverb position matter?

In some languages, it does not matter where the **ADVERB** is positioned in a **SENTENCE**. In English, however, the position of the adverb is important. As the example sentences in Part A show, the position of *only* can completely change the emphasis of the sentence. Thus, in each response, *only* is put in a different position according to the specific meaning intended. In each case, the word being modified by *only* appears in bold.

- *Have you ever been to Europe? I have visited* ***Spain*** *only.*
  Meaning: I have not been to any other countries.
- *Have you ever lived in Spain? I have only* ***visited*** *Spain.*
  Meaning: I only stayed there for a short period of time.
- *Has anyone else in your family visited Spain? Only* ***I*** *have visited Spain.*
  Meaning: nobody else has, just me.

Where can adverbs be positioned?

There are three main positions for adverbs in a sentence.

1. Initial position (before the subject)
2. **MID POSITION** (between the subject and the verb, or after *be* when it is the main verb)
3. End position (after the direct object, at the end of a clause)

What follows is a guide to where adverbs can go. As ▶Step 18 made clear, adverbs are very tricky **PARTS OF SPEECH**. This guide does not have to be followed strictly, but it is a useful starting point. Depending on the specific emphasis of the sentence, the order might be changed.

Initial position[1]	Mid position[3]	End position
• **Linking adverbs** *next, however, subsequently* • **Comment/viewpoint adverbs[2]** *luckily, hopefully, frankly*	• **Adverbs of frequency** *often, rarely, sometimes, never* • **Adverbs of certainty** *probably, certainly, possibly*	• **Adverbs of manner** *correctly, carefully, angrily* • **Adverbs of place** *downstairs, south, elsewhere* • **Adverbs of time[4]** *tomorrow, yesterday, today*

Notes

[1] Such adverbs are almost always followed by a comma.

[2] These adverbs tell you the opinion of the speaker/writer about the whole sentence.

[3] When *be* is the main verb, these adverbs come afterwards. When an auxiliary verb is used, they come between it and the main verb.

- *She never comes to class.*
- *She is never here.*
- *She will never pass the course.*

[4] If you do not want to put emphasis on the time, place the adverb at the beginning of the sentence (e.g., *Yesterday, I ...*).

What about adjectives? Where do they go?

In English, adjectives almost always come before the noun they describe or modify. For example: *a green book*, *a square room*, *cold weather*. There are different rules, however, for different adjectives. Some adjectives can only come before the nouns they describe (**ATTRIBUTIVE-ONLY ADJECTIVES**), whereas others can only come afterwards (**PREDICATIVE-ONLY ADJECTIVES**). The box on the right lists some of the most common adjectives in these categories.

Attributive-only adjectives
absolute, atomic, complete, countless, digital, eastern, entire, existing, indoor, introductory, main, maximum, occasional, outright, perfect, positive, pure, real, true, uneasy, utter

Predicative-only adjectives
afraid, alone, asleep, awake, aware, due, ill, ready, sorry, sure, upset

When do adjectives come after the noun?

There are three occasions when adjectives are more likely to appear after the noun.

1. With 'condition' verbs	**2.** Modifying a **PRONOUN**	**3.** Combined with a **SUPERLATIVE ADJECTIVE**
Some adjectives describe 'condition'. Often verbs such as *be*, *fed*, *sound*, *become*, *get*, *look*, *seem* and *smell* are used. *He is **tall**. She felt **sleepy**.*	*Everyone **present** liked it. Those **responsible** will be punished.*	*Drive home by the **shortest** route **possible**. It was the **best** seat **available**.*

How can I use more than one adjective with a noun/pronoun?

Up to three adjectives can describe a noun. There is a generally accepted order outlined in the table below. Remember that commas are usually necessary between adjectives.

Determiner, enumerator	Opinion, general quality	Appearance	Age	Colour	Origin, material	Noun used as adjective
a the their six	bad beautiful good interesting	large square tall vast	new old recent young	blue grey orange red	English foreign cotton stone	sleeping football computer campus

Using this table, we can create the following phrases (see Part B).

- **1a:** *It's an interesting new concept.* (determiner-opinion-age)
- **2a:** *I love the beautiful, tall, old buildings in New York.* (determiner-opinion-appearance-age)
- **3b:** *That's her warm, cotton sleeping bag.* (determiner-general quality-material-noun used as adjective)
- **4c:** *The university bought six grey computer screens.* (enumerator-colour-noun used as adjective)

Summary
1. Adverb position is important: adverbs can go in initial, mid or end positions.
2. Adjectives usually go before a noun, but in some situations can go afterwards.
3. If there is more than one adjective before a noun, they must come in a certain order.

D Activation

1. Complete and comprehend.

Look at the adverbs in the word box below. Write them in the appropriate column of the table to show where they would generally appear in a sentence.

ideally seldom consequently ~~honestly~~ definitely lazily
weekly obviously similarly inside tonight backwards

Initial position	Mid position	End position
		honestly

2. Check your understanding.

Rewrite each sentence so that the highlighted adverb is in the correct position.

a. We had enough money **luckily** to get a taxi.

____

b. **Upstairs** we are getting a new carpet.

____

c. I am going to the party tonight **probably**.

____

d. **Yesterday** they telephoned me.

____

e. I visit them **rarely** anymore.

____

3. Create your own.

Describe the following pictures. Use at least two or three adjectives with every noun.

a.	**b.**	**c.**

What more complex forms of adjectives can I use?

STEP 20

'A man's character may be learned from the adjectives he uses in conversation.'

Mark Twain (1835–1910)
American writer

A Reflection

Look at the pair of sentences. Then complete the sentence which follows.

1. Tim finds Maths **confusing**.
2. Tim was very **confused** in the lecture yesterday.

The ~_______ form of the adjective is used to show a general truth, whereas the ~_______ form is used to show a feeling at a specific time.

B Contextualization

What is the grammatical construction of the following adjective phrases? Write your answers in the second column. Write other examples of each pattern in the third column.

Sentence with compound adjective	Grammatical structure of adjective phrase	Other examples
He's always forgetting things. He's so **absent-minded**.	*adjective + past participle*	*four-legged, middle-aged, old-fashioned*
Her children are very **good-looking**.		
Many religious people have **deeply rooted** beliefs.		
Plastic is a very **hard-wearing** material.		
He just bought a **five-door** car.		
The cakes were **home-made**. They were delicious!		
The politicians went on a **fact-finding** mission.		
This is a **smoke-free** restaurant.		

C Explanation

Which participle form of the adjective should I use?

The *~ing* form of an **ADJECTIVE** is used to show a general truth, whereas the *~ed* form is used to show a feeling at a specific time. Mixing up these two **PARTICIPLE** forms is a common mistake. So in the example presented in Part A, *Tim finds Maths confusing* refers to a general, ongoing truth: Tim *always* find Maths confusing. However, when the adjective is in the *~ed* form, the feelings expressed are only temporary: *Tim was very confused in the lecture yesterday*, but he will not be confused in *every* lecture.

Commonly confused participles

- amazing/amazed
- disappointing/disappointed
- embarrassing/embarrassed
- exciting/excited
- interesting/interested
- tiring/tired

What are adjective phrases?

An **ADJECTIVE PHRASE** is a combination of two or more words which together modify a noun. The constituent parts of an adjective phrase do not need to be adjectives, but can be a range of different word classes. There is often a **HYPHEN** joining these words. To identify whether a hyphen is needed, ask whether you can say the two parts separately.

- *An elephant is a large, grey animal.* (An elephant is large and grey. ✓)
  Here, it makes sense when the words are said separately, so no hyphen is needed.
- *That is a good-looking elephant.* (That elephant is good and looking. ✗)
  Here, it does not make sense when the words are said separately, so a hyphen is used.

The table below categorizes the most commonly used grammatical constructions of these adjective phrases, along with high-frequency examples.

Structure	Examples
adjective + past participle/*~ed* noun form	He's always forgetting things. He's so **absent-minded**. bad-tempered, big-headed, cold/warm-blooded, four-legged, left/right-handed, middle-aged, narrow-minded, old-fashioned
adjective + present participle	Her children are very **good-looking**. easy-going, free-standing, long-lasting, odd-sounding, rapidly increasing, slow-moving, smooth-talking
adverb + past participle/*~ed* noun form	Many religious people have **deeply rooted** beliefs. brightly lit, densely populated, hard-earned, highly strung, long-haired, short-sighted, well-known, well-prepared
adverb + present participle	Plastic is a very **hard-wearing** material. brightly shining, far-reaching, hard-drinking, never-ending
adjective + noun	He just bought a **five-door** car. full-length, high-volume, large-scale, last-minute, second-hand
noun + past participle	The cakes were **home-made**. They were delicious! sun-dried, wind-powered, market-driven
noun + present participle	The politicians went on a **fact-finding** mission. English-speaking, record-breaking, life-threatening, time-consuming
noun + adjective	This is a **smoke-free** restaurant. duty-free, tax-exempt, toll-free, trouble-free, world-famous

What is the difference between gradeable and ungradeable adjectives?

Certain adjectives cannot be **GRADED**, essentially meaning that they cannot be preceded by words like *very* or *quite*. For example, you could not say *This is a **very** smoke-free restaurant*. This is because *smoke-free* is a **CLASSIFYING ADJECTIVE. EXTREME ADJECTIVES**, where the word is already at the fullest extent of its possible meaning (e.g., *boiling*, *freezing*), are also **UNGRADEABLE.** (We can say *very hot* or *extremely cold*, but not *very boiling/freezing*.) **ABSOLUTE ADJECTIVES**, with which it is impossible to use a **COMPARATIVE** or **SUPERLATIVE** form, are also ungradeable (e.g., we cannot say something is *more dead* than something else).

Examples of ungradeable adjectives include the following.

- **Extreme adjectives:** see table to right
- **Absolute adjectives:** *correct*, *alive*, *dead*, *perfect*, *unique*, *certain*, *mortal*, *pregnant*
- **Classifying adjectives:** *nuclear*, *environmental*, *domestic*

Adjective	Extreme adjective
angry	furious
bad	awful
big	huge
crowded	packed
dirty	filthy
good	excellent
happy	overjoyed
hungry	starving
large	massive
scary	terrifying
small	tiny
tired	exhausted

What are nominal adjectives?

Certain adjectives can be used to talk about a whole class or group of people. To do this, the adjective is combined with a **DETERMINER** (usually *the*). Such adjectives are called **NOMINAL** because they function as nouns. High-frequency examples include *the poor*, *the elderly* and *the wealthy*. Some nationalities may also be referred to in this way, as in *the British* or *the Japanese*. Other common phrases used in this way include *the opposite* and *the contrary*.

Note: nominal adjectives can themselves also be modified by adjectives (*the unhappy poor*), are gradeable (*the very poor*), and can take comparative and superlative forms (*the poorest*).

What pairs of adjectives are commonly mistaken?

The following list gives commonly confused pairs of adjectives, with their meanings in brackets.

- **disinterested** (objective) vs **uninterested** (lacking interest)
- **economic** (relating to money) vs **economical** (good value)
- **extended** (lengthened) vs **extensive** (to a great degree)
- **fewer** (for countable and individual nouns) vs **less** (for uncountable and collective nouns)
- **high** (distance from ground) vs **tall** (height of vertical items)
- **historic** (famous) vs **historical** (in the past)
- **last** (opposite of *first*) vs **latter** (opposite of *former*)
- **many** (used with countable nouns) vs **much** (used with uncountable nouns)

Summary

1. There are two participle adjective forms: *~ing* and *~ed*.
2. Adjective phrases are adjectives composed of two or more words.
3. Adjectives can be gradeable or ungradeable.

D Activation

1. **Complete and comprehend.**

   Complete the following sentences in your own words.

   a. The difference between gradeable and ungradeable adjectives is

   ____

   b. A nominal adjective is

   ____

   c. Hyphens should be used in adjective phrases when

   ____

2. **Check your understanding.**

   Read through the following sentences and correct any adjective problems.

   a. He is a very unique singer. There is nobody else in the world who sounds like him.

   b. It was a very hot day yesterday. It was completely boiling!

   c. There are much reasons for this.

   d. Many famous historical people were born in London.

   e. That book was frightened – terrifying, in fact.

3. **Create your own.**

   a. **Rewrite each sentence using a nominal adjective.**

      1. Many people are afraid of new things.

         Many people are afraid of the new.

      2. I think rich members of society should pay more in taxes.

         ____

      3. People from Britain like to watch football.

         ____

      4. The government should provide more support to blind and deaf people.

         ____

   b. **Look up the meanings of five of the adjective phrases found in the table on page 84 and write sentences which show their meaning.**

      1. ______________________________
      2. ______________________________
      3. ______________________________
      4. ______________________________
      5. ______________________________

How can I use conjunctions and other linking words?

'I'm President of the United States, and I'm not going to eat any more broccoli!'

George H. W. Bush (1924–)
41st President of the United States

A Reflection

Read the two passages below. Which do you think is written in the better English?

1. The first job interview I ever had was a disaster. I left plenty of time to get to the train station. I was still nearly late. My bus broke down on the way. I had to walk the last kilometre. I finally arrived. I was very sweaty. Luckily, I had a spare shirt with me. If I had not had a spare shirt, I would have had to buy a new one. These were the problems. I got the job. They liked me so much, I got promoted!

2. The first job interview I ever had was a disaster. Although I left plenty of time to get to the train station, I was still nearly late because my bus broke down on the way. As a result, I had to walk the last kilometre. When I finally arrived, I was very sweaty. Luckily, I had a spare shirt with me; otherwise I would have had to buy a new one. In spite of these problems, I got the job. In fact, they liked me so much, I got promoted!

B Contextualization

Look back at the better passage in Part A. Underline the words/phrases which make it easier to read. You should find seven in total.

Complete the table below with the words/phrases you find. State what relationship each one shows, and what it links in the text.

Word/phrase	What relationship is it showing?	What is it linking?
although	concession/contrast	two clauses
as a result	cause and effect	two sentences

Think of other linking words for each relationship you have identified in the middle column.

Example: *cause and effect: as a result, therefore, since, thus, accordingly*

C Explanation

What are linking words?

LINKING WORDS are some of the most useful words in English. They help you show how your ideas are linked together. Commonly used linking words include **CONJUNCTIONS** (also sometimes called **CONNECTORS**) such as *although, because, when* and *while*, **ADVERBS** such as *however, otherwise, firstly* and *therefore*, and other phrases such as *in spite of* and *as a result*. Linking words help you to move from one idea to another and to show the relationships between different ideas.

Without these words, as in passage 1 in Part A, your speaking or writing sounds like a collection of bullet points: *Here's one fact. Here's another fact. Here's yet another fact.* Good use of linking words makes texts much easier to read because the relationships between the different statements are made explicit, as in passage 2.

What are the main relationships that linking words show?

There are many different ways in which linking words can be used in English. The table presents ten important functions which linking words can have, with examples.

Thinking point

When linking, ask two questions.

1. What am I linking? Are they clauses or sentences?
2. What is the relationship between these components?

Linking words	Example sentences
1. To show contrast or concession	
however, whereas, while, although, in contrast, on the other hand, despite, in spite of, nevertheless, yet	My father loves going to the cinema, **whereas** my mother prefers the theatre.
	Although it was raining, we still played football.
	Adverbs can be used as linking words; conjunctions, **however**, are far more common.
2. To emphasize or reinforce	
in fact, indeed, moreover	Linking words are very important. **In fact**, they are essential for good English.
	He loves playing football. **Indeed**, he barely does anything else!
3. To show a sequence or time relationship	
when, while, firstly/secondly/thirdly, after, until	Everybody was dancing **when** I arrived at the party.
	Until you understand how to use linking words, you will never be able to talk like a native speaker.
4. To show cause and effect	
since, because of, due to, as such, therefore, thus, for this reason, hence, accordingly	**Since** your library book is late, you must pay a small fine.
	His essay was so bad I couldn't mark it. I told him, **therefore**, that he had to do it again.
5. To add information	
besides, as well as, in addition, furthermore, moreover, also	To apply for this job, you should send your CV. **In addition**, you must write a covering letter.
	As well as comparisons, linking words are often used to signal transitions.

6. To compare	
similarly, in the same way, likewise, equally	You have to do four modules in the first year. **Likewise**, in the second year you do another four.
	Normally, only one linking word should be used in each sentence. **Similarly**, we should not use too many prepositions.
7. To present alternatives	
alternatively, on the other hand	You can get there via the high street. **Alternatively**, you can turn left onto George Street.
	I enjoyed *50 Steps to Improving Your Academic Writing*. It's a great book. **On the other hand**, *50 Steps to Improving Your Grammar* is fantastic, too.
8. To provide examples	
to illustrate this, for example, for instance, particularly, specifically, such as	She went on several holidays – **for example**, to New York, France and Morocco.
	I love racquet sports **such as** tennis and squash.
	Without linking words, text is difficult to read. **To illustrate this**, I will show you a bad piece of writing.
9. For transition	
regarding, with regards to, with respect to	**Regarding** our meeting – could we move it to Tuesday?
	Avoiding repetition is particularly important **with regards to** linking words.
10. To summarize	
in conclusion, in summary, to conclude, to sum up	**In summary**, we need 1,000 new customers in the next month.
	To sum up, linking words are crucial for good essays.

What do they link?

Linking devices can link either clauses with other clauses (C-C), or sentences with other sentences (S-S). The sentences below from Passage 2 in Part A show this.

1. **Although** I left plenty of time to get to the train station, I was still nearly late.
   dependent clause — independent clause

2. My bus broke down on the way. **As a result**, I had to walk the last kilometre.
   sentence — sentence

As sentence 1 shows, the linking device creates a **DEPENDENT CLAUSE**, which is followed by an **INDEPENDENT CLAUSE**. When a conjunction is used to create a dependent clause in this way, it is called a **SUBORDINATING CONJUNCTION**. It is possible to swap the two halves of the sentence around – *I was still nearly late, although I left plenty of time to get to the train station* – so long as the linking word still comes before the dependent clause. For more about dependent and independent clauses, see ▶Step 28. As in sentence 2, S-S linking words are always followed by a comma. Note that it is possible to place an S-S linking word after the subject, so long as it is surrounded by commas, as in sentence 4 below.

3. Adverbs are a word class used for linking. **However**, conjunctions are more common.
4. Adverbs are a word class used for linking. Conjunctions, **however**, are more common.

Summary

1. Linking words are an important part of English. They give shape and meaning to your language.
2. When linking, be sure whether clauses or sentences are being linked.
3. When linking, clearly identify the relationship between the two components.

D Activation

1. **Complete and comprehend.**
   Without looking at the previous pages, write as many linking words as you can in each category.

Contrast or concession	Emphasis or reinforcement	Showing a time relationship	Cause and effect	Adding information
Comparison	**Presenting alternatives**	**Providing examples**	**Transition**	**Summarizing**

2. **Check your understanding.**
   Complete each gap with an appropriate linking word or phrase.

The Chinese language has the most native speakers in the world, ______________________ English has the most total speakers (c. 1.5 billion). ______________________, English is the common international language of business. Several other languages, ______________________ French and Japanese, ______________________ have more than 100 million speakers. ______________________ the former is spoken by many people as a second language, the overwhelming majority (99 per cent) speak the latter as a first language.

3. **Create your own.**
   Read the following list of facts about Walt Disney. Then write a short paragraph about his life. Try to use at least four linking words.

- Walt Disney is famous for making cartoons, e.g., *Dumbo*, *Snow White*, *The Jungle Book*.
- He won 22 Oscars and four honorary Oscars.
- He created many famous characters: Donald Duck, Goofy, Mickey Mouse.
- He was the first voice of Mickey Mouse. He was not an actor.
- Non-TV/film interests: Disneyland theme park was opened in California in 1955. Disney World was opened in Florida in 1971.
- He died in 1966, aged 65. He had lung cancer.
- He had an enormous influence on media and leisure.

What are prepositions and how are they used in English?

STEP 22

'Prepositions are the most useful words in the language for compressing a clear meaning into few words.'

W. M. Baskervill (1850–1899) and **J. M. Sewell (1865–1955)**
American academics

A Reflection

A preposition is a word that is used before a noun, pronoun, or noun phrase, and which connects it to another word.

***At*, *in* and *on* are three common prepositions. List any others you know.**

The table shows some problems associated with using prepositions in English. Think about how often these things happen to you, and tick in the appropriate column.

Problem	Never	Sometimes	Frequently
I leave out prepositions when they are needed.			
I put the preposition in the wrong place.			
I use a preposition when it is not necessary.			
I guess which preposition I need to use.			

B Contextualization

Read the sentences below and underline all the prepositions you can find.

I love being in my garden in summer.
I've lived here for 11 years.
Who will the letter come from?
We met at a party.
It's under the chair.
We flew across the Atlantic.

Write each preposition in the correct gap below to show how it is used.

1. ___in___ refers to enclosed spaces and is also used for months or general periods of time.
2. ________ means lower than, or covered by, something else.
3. ________ describes movement from one side to another.
4. ________ indicates a specific place or position.
5. ________ refers to lengths of time.
6. ________ shows the origin, source or cause of something.

C Explanation

What are the most commonly used prepositions in English?

Of the 25 most commonly used words in English, eight are prepositions: *at*, *by*, *for*, *in*, *of*, *on*, *to* and *with*. This means that a good understanding of prepositions is important to speaking and writing good English. Other common prepositions are in the table below. Some of these words are also in other **WORD CLASSES** (in particular, **ADVERBS** and **CONJUNCTIONS**).

Most common prepositions in English						
about above across after against along	among around as before behind below	beneath beside between beyond but despite	down during except from inside into	like near off onto out outside	over past since through till towards	under until up upon within without

What are the major categories of prepositions in English?

The three main categories of prepositions generally used in English are **place and position**, **direction and movement**, and **time**. The table below gives definitions of commonly used prepositions in these categories, along with example sentences.

Place and position	Direction and movement	Time
At is used for a particular or exact position or place: *I'm at work. We met at a party.*	**To** and **towards** are used for a specific destination: *We went to Rio.*	**At** is used for specific times or ages: *Let's go at 10 o'clock. I work best at night.*
In is used for an enclosed or defined space: *I live in New York. She's in the garden.*	**Through** and **into** refer to movement in three-dimensional space: *I fell into the hole. The river flows through the city.*	**On** is used for specific days and dates: *It starts on Monday. My birthday is on 24th May.*
On is used to say that something is in physical contact with a surface: *The picture is on the wall.*	**Across** and **over** describe movement from one side to another: *We flew across the Atlantic.*	**In** is used for months, seasons or general periods of time: *The party is in May. We go on holiday in the summer.*
By, **near** and **beside** refer to objects which are close or touching: *The house is by the sea. The cinema is near my house.*	**Along** describes movement in the same direction or position on the same line: *We drove along the road.*	**Since** refers to a period of time between a moment or event in the past and now: *I've lived here since 2004. I've been ill since yesterday.*
Under, **below**, **underneath** and **beneath** mean lower than: *It's under the chair. The plane flew beneath the clouds.*	**On** and **onto** describe placing something somewhere, usually on a surface: *Put it on the table. Save it onto your desktop.*	**For** refers to lengths of time: *I've lived here for 11 years. I've been ill for 24 hours.*
Over and **above** mean higher than something: *Put the sign above the door. We are flying over the Atlantic ocean.*	**In** is used to describe movement towards the inside or middle: *Put the rubbish in the bin. Park in the garage.*	**Before** and **after** refer to earlier and later times: *She arrived before you. I'll do it after dinner.*

What other prepositions are commonly used in English?

Preposition	What it refers to	Examples
by	Cause of an action – a person, means or method	Who's that book **by**? It happened **by** mistake. We went **by** car.
for	Purpose or reason	What is this used **for**? **For** my birthday, I am going to a restaurant.
from	Origin, source or cause	It's made **from** glass. I received a letter **from** my friend.
of	Possession, origin, amount, relation of a part to a whole	Look at the first page **of** the book. Add a litre **of** water. The chair is made **of** wood.
with	Having, using or concerning	I want a room **with** a view.
without	Not having, using or concerning	She played football **without** skill.

How can I use prepositions well?

1. **Prepositions are difficult to learn**, so don't worry if you find them tricky.
2. **Prepositions generally have several different functions and uses.** For example, the *Oxford English Dictionary* lists 37 separate uses of *in*!
3. **Prepositions are a CLOSED CLASS of words**. This means that no new prepositions will be created. Once you know them, you know them all!
4. **If you are not sure which preposition to use, make an intelligent guess.** More often than not, you will be correct. You almost certainly know more than you think you do.
5. **Prepositions are often combined with NOUNS and VERBS to make commonly used PHRASES.** For example: *changes/differences in*, *evidence/reason for*, *suffer/benefit from*, *agree/adapt + to*. You should try to remember these as individual pieces of vocabulary.
6. **If you are unsure whether a preposition commonly goes with a noun or verb, check it online.** Look for particular phrases using a search engine to see if they really do exist, and how they can be used.
7. **Don't use too many prepositions in the same sentence.** Since the job of a preposition is to link words together, the more links you have, the more difficult it is to follow the sentence.
8. **Learn how to use combinations of prepositions.** Many useful phrases in English use two or more prepositions together, as in *according to, apart from, as for, because of, by means of, due to, except for, in order to, in place of, instead of, on account of, out of, up to, with regard to* and *with respect to.*
9. **In speaking, prepositions can have STRONG or WEAK FORMS.** Since prepositions are FUNCTIONAL WORDS, weak forms are commonly used. Note the difference: *Is this for* [/fə/] *me? What are you doing that for* [/fɔː/]*?*
10. **There is no grammatical reason why you cannot end a sentence with a preposition.** Some people think it is not good style, especially in formal situations. For the most part, though, ending a sentence with a preposition is acceptable and sounds more natural than the alternatives: compare *Who was the letter **from**?* with ***From** whom was the letter?*

Summary

1. Eight of the 25 most common words in English are prepositions, so you must know how they work.
2. Prepositions have many different uses.
3. Prepositions are often combined with nouns and verbs to make commonly used phrases.

D Activation

1. **Complete and comprehend.**
   Complete the statements about prepositions with appropriate words or phrases.

   a. The three main categories of prepositions are ______________________ and ______________________ (e.g., *at*, *under*), ______________________ and ____________ (e.g., *across*, *towards*) and __________________ (e.g., *since*, *after*).

   b. Prepositions are a closed class of words. This means that ______________________
   ____

   c. If you are unsure which preposition to use, you should ______________________
   ____

   d. To avoid confusion, don't use __________________ prepositions in a sentence.

2. **Check your understanding.**
   Complete each gap below with an appropriate preposition or prepositions. Sometimes more than one answer may be possible.

   My favourite object is a vase given __________________ me __________________ my mother __________________ 1998, __________________ my 18th birthday. She gave it __________________ me __________________ a beautiful card she made herself. I have had the vase __________________ 15 years. It is made mostly __________________ glass. I keep it __________________ a shelf __________________ my bedroom, __________________ a photograph __________________ my family. __________________ I die, I will leave it __________________ my daughter.

3. **Create your own.**
   Choose four of the prepositions from Part C and write a sentence using each one.

   a. ____

   b. ____

   c. ____

   d. ____

What are determiners and how are they used in English?

STEP 23

> *'Sometimes too much ... is barely enough.'*
>
> Mark Twain (1835–1910)
> *American writer*

A Reflection

In the sentences below, the determiners are highlighted. Read the sentences and then decide whether the statements which follow are true or false.

1. You can play **any** game you like. I know **other** games we could play.
2. **What** train shall we take? Is there **another** train leaving later?
3. **Their** favourite subject is English. **His** exam results were poor.
4. I don't like **this** house, but I do like **that** one. **Which** one do you like?
5. There's **not much** food left. You'd better hurry if you want **a** cake.
6. She has **little** experience of teaching. She needs to get **more** experience.
7. **Few** people passed **the** exam. **Fewer** people got **an** 'A' grade.
8. We'll have to meet in **either** London or Paris. I like **neither** London nor Paris.
9. Have you got **enough** money? I lost **both my** bank cards.

Statement	True	False
Determiners come before nouns/noun phrases.		
Determiners are content words, not function words.		
More than one determiner can be used in a phrase.		
Determiners are not used very often in English.		

B Contextualization

Write the determiners from Part A in the correct column in the table below.

	Article	Demonstrative	Possessive	Quantifier
Function	shows if something is known or unknown	shows if something is near or far	shows who owns something	shows how much or many of a thing there are
Examples		this	his	

Can you add any other determiners to the table?

C Explanation

What are determiners?

Determiners are a word class consisting of:

- **ARTICLES** (*a, an, the*)
- **POSSESSIVES** (*my, your, his, her, its, our, their*)
- **DEMONSTRATIVES** (*this/these, that/those*)
- **QUANTIFIERS** (e.g., *much, many, enough*)

Like other **FUNCTIONAL WORDS**, determiners do not change form, and do not have **SYNONYMS**. Although they are short and can easily be missed or forgotten, determiners have an important role in English. They tell us a lot about nouns – for example, whether the speaker is talking about something in general or thinking of specific examples, or how much or how many of something they are talking about. (**Note:** articles are dealt with separately in ▶Steps 24 and 25.)

What is the difference between general and specific determiners?

Determiners can be **general** or **specific**. General determiners are those used when talking about things in general, or when the listener/reader does not know exactly what we are talking about. They include *a*, *an*, *any*, *another*, *other* and *what*.

- *Any* is used with a singular or uncountable noun when talking about all of the items in a category: *You can play **any** game you like.*
- *Another* is used for an additional person/thing: *Is there **another** train leaving later?* *Other* is the **PLURAL** form: *I know **other** games we could play.*
- *What* is used for general questions: ***What** train shall we take?*

Specific determiners are those used when the listener/reader knows exactly what we are talking about. They include *the*, *which* and all demonstratives and possessives.

- Possessives are used to show ownership – what belongs to whom: ***His** exam results were poor. **Their** favourite subject is English.*
- Demonstratives are used to specify whether something is near in distance or time (*this/these*), or far in distance or time (*that/those*): *I don't like **this** house, but I do like **that** one.* See the table on the right.
- *Which* is used for questions about specified groups: ***Which** one do you like?*

	Near	Far
Singular	this	that
Plural	these	those

What are distributive determiners?

DISTRIBUTIVES are determiners which refer to individual components of a group, not the group as a whole. They refer to the specific parts of a general class.

- *Each* and *every* have very similar meanings. *Every* is used to emphasize that there are no exceptions: ***Every** student must attend. Each* places slightly more emphasis on the individuality of the people/things referred to: ***Each** student is responsible for their own work.*
- *Either* and *neither* refer to a choice between two possibilities. *Either* is positive, whereas *neither* is negative. *Either* combines with *or*, and *neither* with *nor*: *We'll have to meet in **either** London **or** Paris. I like **neither** London **nor** Paris.*

Distributives are usually used with singular nouns, although *each*, *either* and *neither* can be used with plural nouns if they are followed by *of*.

How do I use quantifiers?

Quantifiers provide information about the quantity of a noun. If the noun is **COUNTABLE** (*causes, problems*), the quantifier relates to how **many** there are; if the noun is **UNCOUNTABLE** (*evidence, interest*), it relates to how **much** there is. Some quantifiers can only be used with countable nouns, and some only with uncountable nouns. Others can be used with both.

Quantifier	Countable noun
many	causes
several	
a few	
few	
a couple of	

Quantifier	Uncountable noun
a great deal of	evidence
a good deal of	
a bit of	
a little	
little	
not much	
a lack of	

Quantifier	Countable or uncountable noun
all of the	causes evidence
a lot of	
lots of	
plenty of	
most of the	
some	
enough	
none of the	
no	

Notes

1. There is an important difference between *little/few* (= not enough) and *a little/a few* (= not much/many, but sufficient). For example, *She has little experience of teaching* implies that she does not have enough experience, whereas *She has a little experience of teaching* implies that the experience she has may be enough.
2. In academic and formal writing, it is best to use *many* and *much* rather than phrases such as *a lot of*, *lots of* or *plenty of*.
3. Although they may appear similar, there is an important difference between *no* and *a lack of*. *No* is an objective description, meaning that there is a zero quantity, whereas *a lack of* is more subjective, indicating that there is not enough of a particular object, and that more is needed.
   - **a.** In the last five years, there has been no interest in this subject.
   - **b.** In the last five years, there has been a lack of interest in this subject.

   Sentence a states an objective fact, but sentence b implies that the writer thinks that the situation described is bad, and should be rectified.

Can I use more than one determiner per noun?

As a general rule, no. It is not possible to say, for example, *the my phone* or *this your phone*. However, there is a group of words known as **PREDETERMINERS** which can be placed before determiners to make richer, more complex phrases. Predeterminers include multipliers (*double*, *twice*, *four/five times*), fractional expressions (*half*, *three-quarters*), **INTENSIFIERS** (*quite*, *rather*, *such*) and the words *both* and *either* (*I lost **both** my bank cards*).

Summary

1. Determiners come before nouns/noun phrases, and provide additional information about them.
2. Determiners can be general or specific.
3. When using quantifiers, consider whether or not the noun is countable.

D Activation

1. **Complete and comprehend.**
   Write brief descriptions of how the following determiners are used.

   any ______________________________

   this ______________________________

   that ______________________________

   its ______________________________

   several ______________________________

   some ______________________________

   each ______________________________

   neither ______________________________

   double ______________________________

2. **Check your understanding.**
   Select the determiners in each sentence which are possible.

   a. She doesn't drink *much / any / many* coffee – maybe two cups a week.

   b. To remain healthy, you should take *some / a lot of / an* exercise every day.

   c. I have lived in *both / either / neither* France and England.

   d. Please could you give me *this / that / your* coat.

3. **Create your own.**
   Identify and correct the mistake in each of the following sentences.

   a. There ~~are many~~ equipment in the laboratory.

   There is a lot of equipment in the laboratory.

   b. Did you buy big the house?

   ____

   c. She has few grey hairs. She's getting old!

   ____

   d. I'm really enjoying that ice cream.

   ____

How are articles used? (1)

'I'll give you a definite maybe.'

Sam Goldwyn (1882–1974)
American film producer

A Reflection

Follow this flow chart to think about how your own language is similar or different to English in how it uses articles. In particular, think about what you need to do to nouns if you want to identify them as being general or specific.

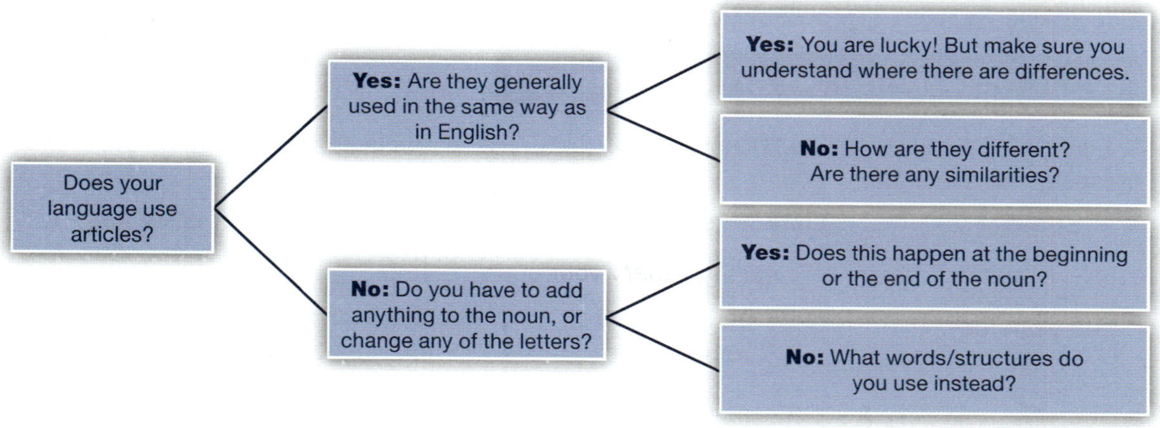

B Contextualization

Two possible answers are given to each question below. What is the difference in meaning between each answer?

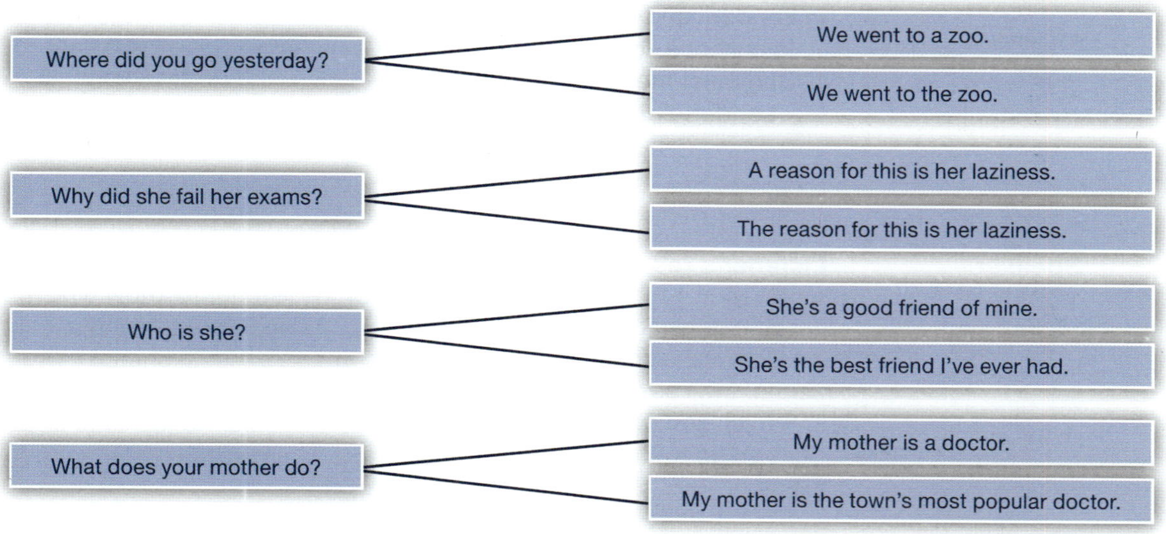

C Explanation

Why are articles important?

ARTICLES are difficult. They are also very important. As noted in ▶Step 23, they are a type of **DETERMINER**. This means that their grammatical job is to give more information about nouns, particularly by saying whether they are being used in a general or a specific way. There are three main reasons articles are important in English.

1. They are used extremely frequently. *The*, *a* and *an* constitute around 15 per cent of the words used in spoken and written English.
2. **NATIVE SPEAKERS** hardly ever make article mistakes. Therefore, if you want to sound more like a native speaker, a good understanding of articles is crucial.
3. Misusing articles can significantly change your meaning. If you use them incorrectly, you can easily confuse your listener/reader.

This step gives a general overview of articles. A deeper analysis is given in ▶Step 25.

What difference do articles make?

The following examples show how using *the* or *a/an* (or no article at all) can change the meaning of a sentence.

Speaker

We went to zoo yesterday.

Listener's response

Which zoo is she talking about?

In this example, the speaker has not used an article. Key information about the following noun (*zoo*) is therefore missing. This is confusing for the listener. It is also grammatically incorrect, and would sound very strange to a native speaker.

Speaker

We went to the zoo yesterday.

Listener's response

We both live in London, and there is only one zoo. She must mean London Zoo.

In this example, the speaker expects the listener to know which zoo is being talked about. Using *the* suggests that there is a shared understanding of what is being referred to. It is a sign to the listener that a particular zoo is meant.

Speaker

We went to a zoo yesterday.

Listener's response

She doesn't think I know the zoo she means. I will ask her, 'Which zoo did you go to?'

In this example, the speaker does not expect the listener to know which zoo is being talked about. Using *a* suggests that there is no shared understanding of what is being referred to. It is a sign to the listener to ask which zoo is meant.

What are the two articles in English?

The two articles in English are the **DEFINITE ARTICLE** and the **INDEFINITE ARTICLE**. Generally, the definite article (*the*) refers to things both the speaker and listener know the identity of. By contrast, the indefinite article (*a/an*) is used when there is no shared understanding of the thing being referred to.

Use of the definite article

Some of the specific situations in which *the* is used are as follows.

1. When we refer to something which has already been mentioned.
   - *Shall I retell* ***the*** *joke?* (The joke was told earlier.)
2. When it is clear which thing is meant because of a shared situation.
   - *Have you fed* ***the*** *cats?* (The cats belong to both of us.)
   - *Please can you shut* ***the*** *door?* (We are in the same room.)
3. For unique objects.
   - ***The*** *moon orbits* ***the*** *earth.* (There is only one moon and one earth.)
4. With superlatives.
   - *She's* ***the*** *best friend I've ever had.*
5. With ordinal numbers.
   - *Bolt was* ***the*** *first to finish, as usual.*
6. When we want to emphasize that only one thing is relevant.
   - ***The*** *reason for this is her laziness.* (There are no other reasons.)

Use of the indefinite article

Some of the specific situations in which *a/an* are used are as follows.

1. When introducing a situation or thing for the first time. (*The* can be used subsequently.)
   - *I bought* ***an*** *apple on the way to work.*
2. When there is no specific item intended, only something matching a description.
   - *Could I borrow* ***a*** *pen please?*
   - *Could you call* ***a*** *waiter?*
3. When classifying people or things, usually after a **COPULAR VERB**.
   - *A cat is* ***a*** *type of mammal.*
   - *My mother is* ***a*** *doctor.*

Summary

1. Articles are a type of determiner – a function word providing more information about nouns.
2. Articles are used very frequently: *the* makes up ten per cent of English usage, and *a/an* five per cent.
3. *The* is used for specific or known things, whereas *a/an* are used for general or unknown things.

D Activation

1. **Complete and comprehend.**
   a. **Write a brief summary of when you should use the definite article.**

   b. **Write a brief summary of when you should use the indefinite article.**

2. **Check your understanding.**
   Match the sentences (a–e) with the grammatical explanations (1–5).

a. Have you got a job?	**1.** Superlative form of the adjective, so definite article used.
b. That's the man I saw earlier.	**2.** Shared understanding, so definite article used.
c. He's the most amazing cook.	**3.** General classification/categorization, so indefinite article used.
d. Could I have a cup of tea, please?	**4.** General question to introduce a topic, so indefinite article used.
e. She is a very happy person.	**5.** General request, so indefinite article used.

3. **Create your own.**
   Complete the text below with definite and indefinite articles as appropriate.

New York is ________ very interesting city. In fact, it is probably ________ most interesting city I have ever visited. Although it's not ________ biggest city in ________ world, it does feel like it sometimes! ________ Empire State Building is ________ important symbol of ________ city, as is ________ Statue of Liberty. ________ interesting fact about ________ Statue of Liberty is that it was ________ present from France, back in 1886.

How are articles used? (2)

STEP 25

'It has long been an axiom of mine that the little things are infinitely the most important.'

Sherlock Holmes
character created by **Arthur Conan Doyle (1859–1930)**
Scottish writer

A Reflection

Why does an article come before *hospital* in some sentences, but not in others?

1. Is there a hospital near here?	**4.** The hospitals which I run are all clean.
2. The appointment is at the hospital.	**5.** My grandfather is in hospital.
3. Hospitals have to be clean places.	**6.** Admissions to hospitals have increased.

B Contextualization

Read the passage below and then answer the questions about the numbered phrases.

Last night[1], I went to a restaurant next to **the Thames**[2] in **London**[3]. I went to **the restaurant**[4] with my friend, **Charlotte**[3]. She had **pasta**[5], and I had **a pizza**[5]. Charlotte is originally from **France**[6], but now lives in **the United States**[6]. She is currently working as **an administrator**[7] at **a university**[8] in Los Angeles. She has been working there since **2012**[9] – **July**[9], I think. Ultimately, she would like to work for an international organization, such as **UNICEF**[10] or **the UNDP**[10].

[1] Why is no article used here?
[2] Why does *the Thames* need a definite article?
[3] Why do *London* and *Charlotte* not need articles?
[4] Why is *the* now used to refer to the restaurant instead of *a*?
[5] Why does *pizza* require an indefinite article here, but not *pasta*?
[6] Why does *the United States* need a definite article, but not *France*?
[7] Why does *administrator* need an article here?
[8] Why does *university* take *a* rather than *an*?
[9] Why are no articles needed before *2012* or *July*?
[10] Why does *UNDP* require a definite article here, but not *UNICEF*?

C Explanation

What difference does context make to article usage?

The context a word appears in is critically important when deciding whether the definite, indefinite or no article is required. For example, the six **SENTENCES** in Part A all use the noun *hospital*, but the article usage is different in each case. Sentences 1 and 2 demonstrate the use of the **DEFINITE** and **INDEFINITE ARTICLES** as outlined in ▶Step 24. The other sentences highlight other important aspects of article use.

- Sentences 3 and 6 show that when you are talking about things in general (i.e., making a wide-ranging point about something) using a **PLURAL**, an article is not needed. This is also the case for **UNCOUNTABLE NOUNS**: *Respect is important*. *Safety is critical*. Although sentence 4 also uses the plural *hospitals*, here a noun phrase is used to refer to a specific group of hospitals, so *the* is required.
- Sentence 5 uses the fixed expression *in hospital*. There are several common **PREPOSITIONAL PHRASES** in English related to place, time and movement which follow the same pattern, and do not require an article. Some such expressions are *at university/school, to university/school, at work, to work, at home, from home, by day, by phone/letter/email, by car/bus/plane/train, in bed, in prison, into town, on foot, on holiday, on time*.

What are some common article mistakes?

Sometimes people think that the rules for using articles are impossible to understand, and that there is no logic to them. This is not true. Although it can be difficult to know which article to use, it is not impossible. The passage in Part B highlights ten areas in which people frequently make article mistakes in English. Each is explained in detail below.

1. **last night** ✓ the last night ✗
   Last is already acting as a **DETERMINER** (▶Step 23): *last night* means 'the night immediately before this one'. As such, no additional determiner is required.
   Rule: Generally speaking, only one determiner is needed for each noun phrase.
2. **the Thames** ✓ Thames ✗
   It can be difficult to know which geographical features need an article and which do not. It is usual for the following to contain articles: rivers, oceans, seas (*the Atlantic Ocean*, *the Red Sea*), mountain ranges (*the Rockies*, *the Alps*), points on the globe (*the Equator*, *the South Pole*), geographical areas (*the Middle East*, *the Maghreb*), deserts (*the Sahara*) and forests (*the Amazonian rainforest*).
   Rule: Some geographical features use an article, but others do not.
3. **London** ✓ **Charlotte** ✓ the London ✗ the Charlotte ✗
   London and *Charlotte* are both **PROPER NOUNS**. Generally speaking, proper nouns do not require an article.
   Rule: Do not use articles with proper nouns.
4. **the restaurant** ✓ a restaurant ✗
   The restaurant being discussed is the same restaurant as in the previous sentence. Since there is a shared understanding of which restaurant is being referred to, the definite article is used.
   Rule: Once the indefinite article has been used to introduce something, the definite article should be used subsequently.

5. **pasta ✓ a pizza ✓** a pasta ✗ pizza ✗

   In this context, *pasta* is an uncountable noun, but *pizza* is countable. Uncountable nouns never require indefinite articles.

   Rule: Do not use indefinite articles with uncountable nouns.

6. **France ✓ the United States ✓** the France ✗ United States ✗

   In general, countries which have a **COUNTABLE NOUN** in their name (▶Step 8) require *the*; countries without such nouns do not. Since *State* is a countable noun, therefore, *United States* takes the definite article. On the other hand, if we referred to the United States simply as *America*, we would not need an article. Likewise, if we referred to *France* in its full form, i.e., *the Republic of France*, we would need to use the definite article, since *Republic* is a countable noun.

   Rule: Use *the* in country names when countable nouns are found in the names.

7. **an administrator ✓** administrator ✗

   In many languages, no article is used before a job title: *She is teacher. He is accountant*. In English, however, the indefinite article is required: *She is **a** teacher. He is **an** accountant*.

   Rule: Use an indefinite article when describing someone's job or role.

8. **a university ✓** an university ✗

   A common mistake when using the indefinite article is to use *an* before all words which begin with a **VOWEL LETTER**, rather than only before those which begin with a **VOWEL SOUND**. In this example, although *university* begins with the letter *u*, it begins with the sound /j/, a **CONSONANT SOUND**. We would also, for example, say *an MP* rather than *a MP,* because although the initial letter is *M*, a **CONSONANT LETTER**, the initial sound is /e/.

   Rule: Use *an* before vowel sounds rather than vowel letters, and *a* before consonant sounds rather than consonant letters.

9. **2012 ✓ July ✓** the 2012 ✗ the July ✗

   Many time words and phrases do not require an article. For days, months and years, articles are not required.

   Rule: Most time phrases do not need an article.

10. **UNICEF ✓ the UNDP ✓** the UNICEF ✗ UNDP ✗

    It is often difficult to know whether to use *the* before **ABBREVIATIONS**. To decide whether an article is required, it is necessary to distinguish **ACRONYMS** from **INITIALISMS**. Acronyms are abbreviations which can be said as a whole word, as in the example *UNICEF* (pronounced *you-knee-sef*). Initialisms, on the other hand, are abbreviations which must be spelt out – that is, when you read them, you have to say each letter separately, as in *UNDP* (*you-en-dee-pee*).

    Rule: Initialisms generally require *the*, but acronyms do not.

Summary

1. Although it may not always seem like it, article usage is governed by rules and logic. Learning a few key rules will make using articles much easier.
2. Articles are generally used with many geographical features and initialisms.
3. Articles are generally not used with other generalizations, determiners, proper nouns, countries, uncountable nouns, times and acronyms.

D Activation

1. **Complete and comprehend.**

   a. **The list below summarizes some of the key things to remember when using articles. Complete each gap with a relevant word or phrase.**

      1. Generally speaking, only one ______________ is needed for each noun phrase.
      2. Do not use articles with ______________ nouns.
      3. Use *the* with country names when ______________ nouns are found in the names.
      4. Only use *an* before vowel ______________.

   b. **Are the following statements about articles true or false? If they are false, correct them accordingly.**

      1. All geographical features require the definite article.
      2. Uncountable nouns usually take an indefinite article.
      3. Many time words and phrases do not require an article.
      4. Acronyms generally require *the*, but initialisms do not.
      5. Many fixed expressions do not need an article.

2. **Check your understanding.**
   Correct the article mistake(s) in each sentence.

   a. The trust is very important, particularly a trust between parents and the children.
   b. UNESCO and the UNICEF are part of the UN.
   c. The last time you were late, we missed film.
   d. The dogs are amazing animals.
   e. Is he still in the bed? We're going to be late if he doesn't get up.

3. **Create your own.**
   Complete each gap with the definite article (*the*), the indefinite article (*a*/*an*) or no article (Ø) depending on what you think is required.

   ______ BBC is ______ major international media organization based in ______ UK. It has ______ many thousands of employees who work in its ______ London headquarters. It was founded in ______ 1922. Critics of ______ organization say that it should not be given ______ money by ______ British government. Supporters say it provides ______ very good service.

What have I learnt so far about sentence structure?

'With sixty staring me in the face, I have developed inflammation of the sentence structure …'

attributed to **James Thurber (1894–1961)**
American writer and cartoonist

A Reflection

The following words and phrases have all been used in the first 25 steps of this book. Think about what they mean.

punctuation
subject-verb-object
countable noun
auxiliary verb
mother tongue
postmodification
premodification
function words
content words
passive voice

B Contextualization

All of the terms in the table below have been discussed in the first 25 steps. Try to identify at least one example of each in the text below.

China has the largest population of any country in the world, at around 1.4 billion. The capital city is Beijing, which in 2008 hosted the Olympic Games. Other large cities include Shanghai and Chongqing. They both have a population in excess of 10 million. One of the things which China is most famous for is its Great Wall. It is popularly supposed to be the only man-made object that can be seen from space.

1. proper noun	China	**5.** preposition of time	
2. verb in the present simple		**6.** regular past simple	
3. article		**7.** subject pronoun	
4. superlative adjective		**8.** relative pronoun	

See feedback on the above on page 109.

C Explanation

What has been taught in the first 25 steps about sentence structure?

If you have worked through the first 25 steps of this book, you already know quite a lot about **SENTENCE** structure (**SYNTAX**). Since this step comes halfway through the book, its purpose is to highlight some of the key points about sentence structure which have already been covered. If you do not understand some of these points, you might want to go back to the relevant steps and refresh your understanding, or look up the key words in the *Glossary* at the back of the book.

▶**Step 1** raises four key mistakes which have a negative impact on the overall quality of a sentence, namely: using the incorrect form of a word, using an incorrect sentence structure, using incorrect **PUNCTUATION** and using a poor **STYLE**.

▶**Step 2** gives an overview of the different word classes in English: **NOUN**, **VERB**, **ADJECTIVE**, **ADVERB**, **PRONOUN**, **DETERMINER**, **CONJUNCTION** and **PREPOSITION**. It also looks at the difference between **OPEN** and **CLOSED WORD CLASSES**. These groups of words have to be in balance within a sentence.

▶**Step 3** focuses on how small changes in grammar can have a significant impact on a sentence.

▶**Step 4** discusses how your **MOTHER TONGUE** (first language) can influence your English. This is true both at the word and the sentence level. Whilst there may be similarities to English in the way sentences are constructed in your own language, there are likely to be many differences as well.

▶**Step 5** looks at the difference between formal and informal grammar, and discusses how **GENRE** may affect the way in which English is written or spoken.

▶**Steps 6, 7 and 8** look at different categories of nouns and pronouns and how they are used. Nouns are the building blocks of a sentence.

▶**Steps 9 and 10** introduce **NOUN PHRASES**. Noun phrases can help make sentences more complex and detailed. Step 9 looks at **PREMODIFICATION** (where information in the form of adjectives, participles and other nouns are added before the noun), and Step 10 focuses on **POSTMODIFICATION** (where additional information appears after the main noun).

▶**Step 11** introduces verbs. Since every sentence must contain at least one verb, understanding how they work is critical.

▶**Step 12** looks at different ways of categorizing verbs. For example, they can be **TRANSITIVE** or **INTRANSITIVE**, **MAIN VERBS** or **AUXILIARY VERBS**, **STATIVE** or **DYNAMIC**, and **REGULAR** or **IRREGULAR**.

▶**Steps 13 and 14** examine the 12 verb forms of English, looking in particular at **TENSE** (when something happens) and **ASPECT** (how something happens). These steps also discuss the verb forms which are most commonly used in sentences.

▶**Step 15** shows that there is more than one possible **WORD ORDER** in English. Verbs can sometimes be put into the **PASSIVE VOICE** (object-verb-subject) rather than the **ACTIVE VOICE (SUBJECT-VERB-OBJECT)**.

▶**Steps 16 and 17** introduce adjectives and adverbs, two major word classes which have an important role to play in sentences. The former adds information to nouns, while the latter provides more information about other words, usually verbs.

▶**Step 18** focuses on **COMPARATIVE** and **SUPERLATIVE** forms of adjectives and adverbs.

▶**Step 19** discusses where adjectives and adverbs should be positioned in a sentence. Word order is critically important in sentence construction.

▶**Step 20** looks at more complex forms of adjectives, including **ADJECTIVE PHRASES**.

▶**Step 21** focuses on conjunctions and other **LINKING WORDS**, looking at the ways in which **CLAUSES** and sentences can be linked.

▶**Step 22** gives an overview of how prepositions are used. Prepositions have a very important function in the sentence: they show the relationship between content words such as nouns and verbs. Using prepositions incorrectly can make it very difficult to understand sentences.

▶**Step 23** focuses on determiners, a word class which provides key information about nouns.

▶**Steps 24 and 25** look in more detail at **ARTICLES**, a very commonly used type of determiner.

Feedback on Part B

The relevant words for each category are marked in the passage with the numbers from the table (i.e., 1 = proper noun, 2 = verb in the present simple, etc.).

China^{1} has^{2} the^{3} largest^{4} population of any country in the^{3} world, at around 1.4 billion. The^{3} capital city is^{2} Beijing^{1}, which^{8} in^{5} 2008 hosted^{6} the^{3} Olympic Games^{1}. Other large cities include^{2} Shanghai^{1} and Chongqing^{1}. They^{7} both have^{2} a^{3} population in excess of 10 million. One of the^{3} things which^{8} China^{1} is^{2} most famous^{4} for is^{2} its Great Wall^{1}. It^{7} is popularly supposed to be the^{3} only man-made object that^{8} can be seen from space.

Summary

1. You already know more about English sentences than you probably think you do.
2. To be able to write a good sentence, you need to have a good understanding of the different word classes, and how they work together.
3. The normal order of words in English is subject-verb-object.

D Activation

1. **Complete and comprehend.**

   Answer the following questions. If you are unsure, check the relevant step to find the answer.

   a. Is the normal word order of English the same as in your mother tongue? If not, what problems might this create?

   b. What is the usual position for adjectives?

   c. Where in a sentence do adverbs normally go?

   d. What do relative pronouns do?

2. **Check your understanding.**

   Fill in the table about the word classes of English with the correct information.

Word class	Examples	Function
Noun		*Refers to people, places or things*
Verb		
Adjective		
Adverb		
Pronoun		
Preposition		
Conjunction		
Determiner		

3. **Create your own.**

   Reorder the jumbled words to make sentences. Sometimes it may be possible to reorder the words in more than one correct way.

a. brown jumped dog a over quick the fox lazy	*The quick brown fox jumped over a lazy dog.*
b. I to the yesterday shops went	
c. met the they at museum the café next to	
d. was Terry flatmate returned working his when	
e. black ball got its off ran the dog and	

What are phrases?

> *'I summed up all systems in a phrase, and all existence in an epigram.'*
>
> **Oscar Wilde (1854–1900)**
> ***Irish playwright and poet***

A Reflection

Place the words in the box in the correct place in the diagram on the right.

~~letters~~ whole texts words phrases clauses paragraphs ~~sentences~~

letters
make
make
make
make
sentences
make
make

Look up the following words in a dictionary, and explain in your own words what they mean.

phrase ______________________________

____

____

clause ______________________________

____

____

B Contextualization

There are different types of phrases in English. A noun phrase, for example, is a phrase in which the main word is a noun, e.g., *my friend Sam*.

Read the passage. Write each highlighted phrase in the appropriate column.

My friend Sam went to the café because he was hungry. As he was waiting for his food, he saw a well-known celebrity in the corner. The food arrived quite quickly, but Sam kept looking at the woman. Eventually, the celebrity's friend arrived. He had arrived really late and she was very clearly annoyed.

Noun phrase	Verb phrase	Prepositional phrase	Adjective phrase	Adverb phrase
My friend Sam				

C Explanation

What is a phrase?

The diagram on the right shows the hierarchy of written English – the different components and the relationships they have with each other. To make your written English clear, it is important to know how these components fit together. This step focuses on **PHRASES**, while ▶Step 28 looks at **CLAUSES** and ▶Steps 29 and 30 look at whole **SENTENCES**.

letters
make
words
make
phrases
make
clauses
make
sentences
make
paragraphs
make
whole texts

Four key facts about phrases are as follows.

1. **A phrase is a group of words which works as a single unit.** Phrases can be thought of as the 'building blocks' of a sentence.
2. **Unlike a clause, you cannot have a phrase by itself in a piece of writing.** A phrase must be combined with another phrase to make sense. Phrases are only ever used by themselves in informal speaking or very informal pieces of writing, where different conventions may apply.
3. **A phrase consists of two parts: the HEAD WORD(S) and the dependent words.** The head word is the main idea, whereas the job of the dependent words is to add more information.
4. **The number of words in a phrase can vary hugely.** For example, a noun phrase can be just one word (e.g., *I, Angela*), or it can be many words (e.g., *the large green tree which is in the corner of the field*).

> **Top tip**
> Thinking about written English as a series of phrases (rather than isolated words) can help your reading become quicker and more successful, and your writing clearer and more accurate.

What is a noun phrase?

NOUN PHRASES were looked at in detail in ▶Steps 9 and 10. Refer back to these steps if necessary.

What is a verb phrase?

The head word in a **VERB PHRASE** is a **MAIN VERB**. As in a noun phrase, information may come before or after the main verb in order to create the whole verb phrase. Consider the main verb *eat,* for example. Additional words which may precede it include:

- **AUXILIARY VERBS** (including **MODAL VERBS**)**:** *I **did** eat it. I **have** eaten some. I **am** eating it. I **may** eat some. I **will** eat some.*
- **NEGATIVE WORDS:** *I **never** eat it.*
- **ADVERBS:** *I **already** ate dinner. I **willingly** ate it.*

The two most common structures which follow the main verb are as follows.

- **OBJECTS:** When the main verb is **TRANSITIVE**, a **DIRECT OBJECT** is required: *I never eat **bread**.* Depending on the verb used, and the context, an **INDIRECT OBJECT** may also be needed: *I gave **her** my **bread*** – here, *bread* is the direct object and *her* is the indirect object.

- **COMPLEMENTS:** Some verbs, such as *seem*, *be*, *feel* and *appear* cannot take a direct object, but do require other information. There are many different types of **COMPLEMENT** which can follow these verbs, the simplest of which is an adjective such as *happy*.

What is a prepositional phrase?

Phrases in which a **PREPOSITION** (▶Step 22) is the main word are very useful. They can provide more information about the nouns and verbs in a sentence. Three key facts about **PREPOSITIONAL PHRASES** (PPs) are as follows.

1. When it adds information to nouns, the PP acts like an adjective. For example, in *Who is that person **in the car**?* the PP gives information about the person.
2. When it adds information to verbs, the PP acts like an adverb. For example, in *Could you tell me **in the morning**?* the PP says how and when the telling should take place.
3. PPs never contain the subject of the sentence.

PPs can turn **SIMPLE** or **COMPOUND SENTENCES** into **COMPLEX SENTENCES**. The best way to add PPs is to write the basic sentence, and then ask a question about each part. For example:

Sam bought a drink, sat down, and waited.

Where did Sam buy a drink? Where did Sam sit down? Who was Sam waiting for?

*Sam bought a drink **at the bar**, sat down **in the corner**, and waited **for them**.*

What is an adjective phrase?

ADJECTIVE PHRASES have already been looked at in detail in ▶Step 20, where the various grammatical constructions which can be used to make adjective phrases are outlined in detail. These include adverb + adjective (*very good*), adjective + **PRESENT PARTICIPLE** (*good-looking*), adverb + **PAST PARTICIPLE** (*well-known*) and adjective + noun (*last-minute*).

What is an adverb phrase?

An **ADVERB PHRASE** is an adverb composed of two or more words. Like an adverb (▶Step 17), the grammatical job of an adverb phrase is to modify a verb, adjective or another adverb. Very often a **QUALIFIER** (a word, often an adverb, which increases or decreases the meaning of the main adverb) is combined with an adverb to make an adverb phrase.

- Qualifiers which 'decrease': *He comes to visit **only** occasionally. The food arrived **quite** quickly. She was **somewhat** happier.*
- Qualifiers which 'increase': *She was **very** clearly annoyed. He had arrived **really** late.*

An adverb phrase can appear at the beginning, middle or end of a sentence.

Summary

1. There are five main types of phrase: noun, verb, prepositional, adjective and adverb.
2. Phrases cannot exist by themselves in writing, although they may in informal contexts.
3. Phrases are composed of a head word and dependent words.

D Activation

1. **Complete and comprehend.**
   Write out in detail the grammatical construction of each of these phrases from Part B.

Phrase	Phrase type	Construction
a. my friend Sam	noun phrase	possessive adjective + countable noun + proper noun
b. he was waiting	verb phrase	
c. for his food	prepositional phrase	
d. well-known	adjective phrase	
e. quite quickly	adverb phrase	

2. **Check your understanding.**
   Divide the following sentences into their constituent phrases.
   a. The old dog was asleep in front of the fire.
   [The old dog] [was asleep] [in front of the fire]. ____
   b. My parents have always supported me and my brother.
   ____
   c. Your birthday present is going to be a holiday in Los Angeles.
   ____
   d. I used to work in a factory next to a river.
   ____

3. **Create your own.**
   Write phrases with the same structure as in Exercise 1.
   a. my friend Sam: your dad Dave, her boss Misha, his girlfriend Nigella ____
   b. he was waiting: ____
   c. for his food: ____
   d. well-known: ____
   e. quite quickly: ____

What are clauses?

STEP 28

'In bourgeois society capital is independent and has individuality, while the living person is dependent and has no individuality.'

Karl Marx (1818–1883)
German political philosopher

A Reflection

Look at the 12 phrases in the box below. Combine them to make five sentences.

my front door	and I played football	while you were watching television	before leaving home
at the weekend	those are the socks	which I was looking for	~~even though it was raining~~
~~we went to the park~~	I went to the cinema	I finished writing my essay	I locked

1. We went to the park even though it was raining.
2. __________
3. __________
4. __________
5. __________

B Contextualization

Look at the following pairs of clauses. In each case, one represents a complete idea and the other an incomplete idea. Decide which is which.

1. a. it was raining	complete	**b.** because it was raining	incomplete
2. a. although I was late		**b.** I was late	
3. a. after our meeting		**b.** I went back to work	
4. a. let's go to New York		**b.** rather than Paris	
5. a. which goes very fast		**b.** the car is expensive	

What is the difference between the following sentences? Focus in particular on the use of *which* in the relative clauses.

- Let's meet at the café which is next to the river.
- Yesterday I went to an amazing café, which is next to the river.

What other words can be used in relative clauses? How, specifically, are they used?

C Explanation

What is a clause?

In the grammatical hierarchy given on page 112, a **CLAUSE** comes between a **PHRASE** and a **SENTENCE.** A useful general definition of a clause is 'a group of words containing at least a subject and a verb'. There are two main types of clause in English: **INDEPENDENT CLAUSES** (ICs) and **DEPENDENT CLAUSES** (DCs). The table below compares the key features of these clauses.

	Independent clauses	**Dependent clauses**
What do they include?	subject + verb	**DEPENDENT MARKER WORD** + subject + verb
What do they represent?	A complete thought	An incomplete thought
Can they appear on their own?	Yes: an IC can be a sentence.	No: a DC must be combined with an IC.
Examples	*it was raining, I was late*	*as it was raining, although I was late*

What are dependent marker words?

Dependent clauses always begin with a **DEPENDENT MARKER WORD** (DMW). Below are four key facts about DMWs and a table showing how some common DMWs are used.

1. A DMW indicates that a clause is dependent.
2. A DMW is almost always the first word of the clause.
3. There are two types of DMWs: **SUBORDINATING CONJUNCTIONS** and **RELATIVE PRONOUNS.**
4. DMWs express many different types of relationship.

time (*after, as, as soon as, before, once, since, until, when, while*)
manner (*as, as if, as though, like*)
cause and effect (*although, though, whereas, while, except, that*)
reason (*because, in that, now that, since, so that*)
condition (*if, in case, provided [that], unless, as/so long as*)
purpose (*so that, in order that*)
comparison (*as … as, more than, less than, than*)

DMW + clause content	**Examples**
after/before + event which comes after/before the event in the IC	I went back to work **after** our meeting. **Before** leaving home, I locked my front door.
as/so long as + event which is a condition of the event in the IC	**So long as** you sign the contract today, you'll get the 50% discount.
because + reason/explanation for event in IC	She was late **because** her train was delayed.
in order that / so that + purpose/goal to be achieved by action in IC	I am going to study hard in the next month **so that** I pass my English exam.
now that + recent event which is a condition of event in IC	**Now that** you've arrived, we can eat.
rather than + worse option than action in IC	**Rather than** Paris, let's go to New York.
until/till + event which must happen for the situation described in IC to change	I am not leaving **until** I've finished my essay.
when/while + event happening at same time as event in IC	**While** you were watching television, I finished writing my essay.

How can clauses be combined?

There are many different ways in which clauses can be combined to form sentences. The main ways in which this happens in English are outlined in ▶Step 29. Generally speaking, there are two ways of combining an independent and a dependent clause. They provide different emphases.

1. independent clause + dependent clause: *We went to the park even though it was raining.*
2. dependent clause + independent clause: *Even though it was raining, we went to the park.*

Dependent clauses represent incomplete ideas, and so cannot be sentences in their own right. They must appear in connection with an independent clause.

What is a relative clause?

A **RELATIVE CLAUSE** is a common type of dependent clause. Relative clauses have already been introduced in ▶Step 10. They are very useful, especially in writing, since they provide an easy way to **POSTMODIFY** nouns. The purpose of a relative clause is to provide information about something or someone who has already been specified.

Three key facts about relative clauses are as follows.

1. They come after the nouns they are qualifying.
2. They are often introduced by a **RELATIVE PRONOUN**.
3. They can be **DEFINING** or **NON-DEFINING**.

> **Relative pronouns**
> The relative pronouns are:
> *that, which, who, whose, whom, what, where, when, why.*

Defining relative clauses

Here, the information which describes the noun is essential to the meaning of the sentence. For example, in *Let's meet at the café* ***which is next to the river***, the information *which is next to the river* is a defining relative clause because it defines what is meant by *the café*. If that information was not there, the sentence would have, or might have, a different meaning altogether.

Non-defining relative clauses

Here, the information which describes the noun is considered 'additional'. It is not essential to understanding the sentence. For example, in *Yesterday, I went to an amazing café,* ***which is next to the river***, the information *which is next to the river* does not, in this case, actually define the noun phrase *an amazing café* – it just describes one of its qualities.

> **Top tip**
> One difference between a defining and a non-defining relative clause is that the latter always has a **COMMA** before it. In addition, *that* cannot appear in a non-defining relative clause.

Summary

1. A clause comes between a phrase and a sentence in the grammatical hierarchy.
2. An independent clause can exist by itself, and consists of at least a subject and a verb; a dependent clause cannot exist by itself, and contains a dependent marker word.
3. Relative clauses are very useful for adding more detail to your writing.

D Activation

1. **Complete and comprehend.**

   Complete the two paragraphs below with the appropriate phrases from the box.

subject + verb	incomplete	do not make sense
complete	make sense	dependent marker word + subject + verb

Independent clauses consist of at least a ______________________.
They represent a thought or idea which is ______________________.
As such, they ______________________ independently of other clauses.

Dependent clauses consist of at least a ______________________.
They represent a thought or idea which is ______________________.
As such, they ______________________ without an independent clause.

2. **Check your understanding.**

   Are the following clauses independent or dependent? Write *IC* or *DC* next to each of them.

a. which is next to the post office	DC	**f.** whose author is very well known	
b. that's got my name on it		**g.** who was born in 1930	
c. that's the man		**h.** whom I worked with last year	
d. let's meet in the bookshop	IC	**i.** this is a book	
e. Buzz Aldrin was the second person on the moon		**j.** could you pass me the towel	

3. **Create your own.**

   Combine the clauses a–j above in pairs to make good sentences. Ensure you use a comma where it is needed. Sometimes you may need to separate some of the phrases in a clause.

   a. Let's meet in the bookshop which is next to the post office. (d, 1)
   b. ______________________
   c. ______________________
   d. ______________________
   e. ______________________

What are the main types of sentence in English?

'A sentence is enough for a sensible man.'

Plautus (c.250–184 BCE)
Roman playwright

A Reflection

What is the purpose of each sentence in Groups A–C? In each group, there is an example of each function 1, 2, 3 and 4.

1. Making a statement	2. Asking a question	3. Giving orders or instructions	4. Talking about something surprising

Group A	I went there yesterday.	1	Do you know Sue?	____
	Open the window.	____	That's wonderful!	____
Group B	I'll help you later.	____	Please be quiet.	____
	I'm shocked!	____	Where does she live?	____
Group C	You must be joking!	____	He likes chocolate.	____
	It's her birthday, isn't it?	____	Don't go outside!	____

Does the punctuation give you any clues about how to categorize the sentences?

B Contextualization

Match sentences 1–4 to the structures in the boxes below. Two will not be needed.

IC	DC	IC + DC	IC + CC + DC	IC + CC + IC	IC + CC + IC + DC

IC = independent clause, DC = dependent clause, CC = coordinating conjunction

1. She was drinking coffee.

   ____

2. She was drinking coffee and he was eating a cake.

   ____

3. She was drinking coffee because she was tired.

   ____

4. She was drinking coffee and he was eating a cake because they were tired and hungry.

   ____

C Explanation

What is a sentence?

A **SENTENCE** is not an easy idea to define. It can be as short as two words (*I do*) and as long as many thousands of words – although this is not advisable! It may contain just one **CLAUSE** (▶Step 28) or many clauses joined together.

A sentence is often unique. When you create a sentence, it is likely that it will be the first time that anybody has written or spoken that particular group of words in that particular way.

A key question to ask before you create any sentence is: *Why am I making this sentence? What is its purpose?*

There are four main functions a sentence can have. These are given in the table below. The overwhelming majority of sentences in English are declarative.

Function	Purpose	Examples	Punctuation required
DECLARATIVE	To share information; to make statements.	I went there yesterday. I'll help you later. He likes chocolate.	A **FULL STOP**
INTERROGATIVE (▶Step 35)	To ask questions; to request or check information.	Do you know Sue? Where does she live? It's her birthday, isn't it?	A **QUESTION MARK**
IMPERATIVE	To give orders; to tell somebody what to do, politely or impolitely.	Open the window. Please be quiet. Don't go outside!	A full stop or **EXCLAMATION MARK**
EXCLAMATIVE	To talk about interesting, surprising or amazing things.	That's wonderful! I'm shocked! You must be joking!	An exclamation mark

How are sentences constructed?

There are four main types of sentence, according to their grammatical construction: **SIMPLE**, **COMPOUND**, **COMPLEX** and **COMPLEX–COMPOUND**. Details of these four types are presented below.

What is a simple sentence?

[She was drinking coffee][1].

[1]IC

The most basic sentence type is the simple sentence. Although it is called simple, this does not mean that it is a bad sentence. Some of the most effective sentences in English are simple.

A simple sentence consists of a single **INDEPENDENT CLAUSE** (▶Step 28). (Since a **DEPENDENT CLAUSE** does not form a complete idea, it cannot be a sentence by itself (▶Steps 28, 30).) This means that a simple sentence may consist of just a **SUBJECT** and a **VERB**. Although most simple sentences have more than just two words, they do tend to be relatively short. This type of sentence is quite easy to write, and you are unlikely to make mistakes.

What is a compound sentence?

[She was drinking coffee][1] [and][2] [he was eating a cake][3].
[1]IC [2]CC [3]IC

A compound sentence contains two or more independent clauses. The word *compound* means *together*. Compound sentences are a good way of joining together clauses which talk about similar ideas. There are three ways of joining these clauses.

1. Using a **COORDINATING CONJUNCTION** (*for*, *and*, *nor*, *but*, *or*, *yet*, *so*)
2. Using a **SEMICOLON** (▶Step 43)
3. Using a **COLON** (▶Step 43)

What is a complex sentence?

[She was drinking coffee][1] [because she was tired][2].
[1]IC [2]DC

A complex sentence contains an independent clause and one or more dependent clauses. As noted in ▶Step 28, a dependent clause must contain a **DEPENDENT MARKER WORD** (either a **SUBORDINATING CONJUNCTION** or a **RELATIVE PRONOUN**), which can be used to signify various different kinds of relationship with the independent clause. By contrast, in a compound sentence, the two clauses are of equal importance, and the relationship between them, if there is one, can only be implied, not stated. For example, compare the following sentences.

1. She was drinking coffee because she was tired.
2. She was drinking coffee; she was tired.

The complex sentence (1) **tells** the reader why she was drinking coffee; the compound sentence (2) only **implies** it, but does not state it.

What is a complex–compound sentence?

[She was drinking coffee][1] [and][2] [he was eating a cake][3] [because they were tired and hungry][4].
[1]IC [2]CC [3]IC [4]DC

A complex–compound sentence is a mixture of the two previous sentence types. It consists of at least two independent clauses and at least one dependent clause.

Summary of the clauses used in the four sentence types

Type of sentence	Independent clauses	Dependent clauses
Simple	1	None
Compound	2+	None
Complex	1	1+
Complex–compound	2+	1+

Summary

1. There are four main sentence functions: declarative, interrogative, imperative and exclamative.
2. There are four sentence types: simple, compound, complex and complex–compound.
3. When writing a sentence, think about why you are writing it and what types of clause are required.

D Activation

1. **Complete and comprehend.**

   Complete the table with the information in the box below.

1+	1	None	2+	None	1	2+	1+

Type of sentence	Independent clauses	Dependent clauses
Simple		
Compound		
Complex		
Complex–compound		

2. **Check your understanding.**

   Read the passage. Write the sentence letters (a–f) in the table according to their type.

Esperanto is an artificial language, which is a term meaning 'a language created by humans'.[a] It was invented by L. L. Zamenhof in 1887.[b] His primary aim was to create an easy-to-learn language which was politically neutral, so as to lead ultimately to world peace.[c] The word 'Esperanto' means 'one who hopes'.[d]

Over time, many other artificial languages have been invented, but none have had as much influence as Esperanto.[e] Although it has no native speakers, more than 100,000 people speak Esperanto around the world, and there are nearly 200,000 Esperanto articles on Wikipedia.[f]

Simple	
Compound	
Complex	*a*
Complex–compound	

3. **Create your own.**

   Using the clauses given, create four sentences with appropriate punctuation.

since I love watching films	the students are working hard	but my friends didn't want to	I suggested we go to the cinema
my train was delayed	because they have an exam	I went to the park with my dog	so I was late for my meeting

Simple	
Compound	
Complex	
Complex–compound	

How can I write better sentences and avoid mistakes?

'Sentence first – verdict afterwards.'

Lewis Carroll (1832–1898)
English writer and mathematician

A Reflection

Which of the following statements are true, and which are false?

1.	It is important to think about why you are writing a sentence.	**True / False**
2.	Sentences should be as long as possible.	**True / False**
3.	Mixing the types and lengths of your sentences is a good strategy.	**True / False**
4.	Grammatical accuracy is the most important thing when writing a sentence.	**True / False**

B Contextualization

What is the problem with each text a–h? Match the texts with comments 1–8.

a. She has two children the girl is 15 and the boy is 12.

b. I went to Barcelona in 2013. Madrid is far less pretty than Barcelona, which is a beautiful city.

c. I live in Doha. I have one sister. She is 11 years old.

d. Many of my classmates are worried about their English exam and their Maths exam, because they found the courses difficult, and as such they are staying up late to revise, but I don't think this is a good idea.

e. Michael told Nigel that he was going to be late.

f. When he arrived home.

g. Having finished her essay, the computer was turned off.

h. There are three things you need to remember: set your alarm, bring the tickets and don't be arriving late.

1. The sentence is too long.	d	**5.** The information is in the wrong order.	
2. Too many short sentences are used.		**6.** It is unclear who the pronoun refers to.	
3. The sentence is incomplete.		**7.** Phrases in the sentence do not all use the same type of construction.	
4. One sentence runs into another.		**8.** The use of modifiers is unclear.	

C Explanation

What kinds of sentence should I use?

You should use whatever kind of **SENTENCE** is appropriate in the circumstances. Some people think that a good sentence is a long sentence. This is not true! Your sentences should be as long or short as they need to be. Remember that a short and accurate sentence is better than a long and inaccurate sentence.

Four general points to bear in mind about writing sentences in English are as follows. Compare them with your responses to the statements in Part A.

1. Before you write a sentence, it is important to think about **why** you are writing it. What is its purpose? What are you trying to achieve? Asking these questions will help you to decide which grammatical constructions you need to use. See ▶Step 29.
2. If you think a sentence is too long, then everybody else will too.
3. Using a mixture of different types and lengths of sentence will make your text more readable.
4. Even if your sentence is grammatically correct, it may still not make sense. The American linguist Noam Chomsky used the sentence *Colourless green ideas sleep furiously* to emphasize this point. It is grammatically correct, but it makes no sense at all!

What common mistakes are made with sentences?

This section discusses the eight common mistakes identified in Part B. Do you make any of these mistakes?

1. **The sentence is too long (text d).**

   Rewrite: *Many of my classmates are worried about their English and Maths exams because they found the courses difficult. As such, they are staying up late to revise, but I don't think this is a good idea.*

   As noted above, a long sentence is not necessarily a good sentence. In the example, too many **CLAUSES** are used. When this occurs, it can become difficult to know how the clauses relate to each other.

2. **Too many short sentences are used (text c).**

   Rewrite: *I live in Doha and have one sister, who is 11 years old.*

   Whilst short sentences can help your writing to sound clear and focused, you should not only use short sentences. If you do, your writing will sound incoherent and 'out of breath', like a list of statements which are not related to each other. Where two sentences next to each other are of equal importance, you might be able to join them using a **COORDINATING CONJUNCTION**; where one sentence is more important than the other, you can use a **SUBORDINATING CONJUNCTION**.

3. **The sentence is incomplete (text f).**

   Rewrite: *We ate dinner when he arrived home.*

   Every sentence must have at least a **SUBJECT** and a **VERB**. If either one of these is missing, the sentence is not complete. In addition, if your sentence includes a **DEPENDENT MARKER WORD** (▶Step 28), there must be at least two clauses in the sentence, one of which must be an **INDEPENDENT CLAUSE**. A **DEPENDENT CLAUSE**, such as *when he arrived home*, cannot be a sentence on its own.

4. **One sentence runs into another (text a).**

   Rewrite: *She has two children. The girl is 15, and the boy is 12.*

   You must ensure that sentences are clearly separated by placing a **FULL STOP**, or other **PUNCTUATION** (▶Steps 41, 43), between them. An alternative solution is to join sentences using coordinating or subordinating conjunctions.

5. **The information comes in the wrong order (text b).**

   Rewrite: *I went to Barcelona in 2013. It is a beautiful city, far prettier than Madrid.*

   In English, the usual order in which information is introduced is 'familiar' or 'known', followed by 'new' or 'unknown'. Information doesn't always have to be stated in this order, but most of the time it does. In the example, Barcelona is introduced in the first sentence, so it is logical to reverse the order of information in the second sentence so that Madrid is introduced at the end.

6. **It is unclear who the pronoun refers to (text e).**

   Rewrite 1: *Michael was going to be late. He told Nigel.*
   Rewrite 2: *Michael knew Nigel was going to be late, so he told him.*

   PRONOUNS help you to avoid repetition, improving the quality of your writing (▶Step 7). However, you need to make sure that it is clear who or what each pronoun refers to. In the example sentence, it is not clear who *he* refers to: it could be either Michael or Nigel who is going to be late. The rewritten versions show the two possible interpretations. This can be a particular problem in long sentences where there are many words between the pronoun and the word it replaces.

7. **Phrases in the sentence do not all use the same type of construction (text h).**

   Rewrite: *There are three things you need to remember: set your alarm, bring the tickets and ensure you are not late.*

   Sentences sound better when they use parallel structures. The example in Part B, for example, has a list with two verb forms in the present simple (*set* and *bring*) and one in the negative present continuous (*don't be arriving*). Whilst the grammar here is accurate, the **STYLE** is poor. The rewritten version puts the final point into the present simple to match the others, and moves the negative so that it is not before the verb. This improves the flow of the sentence.

8. **The use of modifiers is unclear (text g).**

   Rewrite: *Having finished her essay, she turned the computer off.*

   In the example, the introductory **MODIFIER** (*having finished her essay*) uses a pronoun (*her*) which does not correspond to the subject of the sentence (*computer*). In the rewritten version, the main sentence is put into the **ACTIVE VOICE** so that the subject (*she*) matches the pronoun.

Summary

1. A long sentence is not necessarily a good sentence. A short and accurate sentence is better than a long and inaccurate sentence.
2. Be aware of common sentence problems in English, and identify strategies for avoiding them.
3. Even if your sentence is grammatically correct, it may still not make sense.

D Activation

1. **Complete and comprehend.**

   In your own words, write the solution(s) to each of the problems identified in Part C.

	Problem	Solution
a.	1	Ask how many clauses there are. Break up the sentence into shorter ones.
b.	2	
c.	3	
d.	4	
e.	5	
f.	6	
g.	7	
h.	8	

2. **Check your understanding.**

   The following sentences are incorrect. Write the number of the problem from Part C.

Sentence	Problem
a. Whereas my mother likes playing tennis.	3
b. Bill Clinton was one of the most powerful people in the world. He used to be President of the USA.	
c. I went to the beach, the hotel and the gym we then went to the restaurant for dinner.	
d. Helen told Rachel that she had to leave.	

3. **Create your own.**

   Rewrite the sentences from above so that they are correct.

   a. ______________________________

   b. ______________________________

   c. ______________________________

   d. ______________________________

How can I show possibility and probability?

> *'If nature has taught us anything it is that the impossible is probable.'*
>
> Ilyas Kassam (1986–)
> *British writer, philosopher and chef*

A Reflection

Look at the words in the box and write them in the correct categories below.

~~can~~ certain possibly potential likely could perhaps might couldn't probably may can't

Modal verbs	*can*
Adjectives	
Adverbs	

B Contextualization

Match the condition and result clauses in these conditional sentences.

Condition clause

1. If you heat water,
2. If you want any more advice,
3. If I won the lottery,
4. If she'd been there,
5. If she'd caught her train,
6. If you worked harder,

Result clause

a. I would go on holiday.
b. it would never have happened.
c. I'll give you some.
d. you would have got a better job by now.
e. it boils.
f. she would be here now.

What is the grammatical structure of each sentence?

Sentence parts	Condition clause structure	Result clause structure
1. *e*	*if + present simple*	*present simple*
2.		
3.		
4.		
5.		
6.		

C Explanation

How can conditionals be used to talk about possibility and probability?

CONDITIONAL SENTENCES are one of the main ways to talk about the possibility or probability of something happening. Conditional sentences have two halves: a condition clause (CC) and a result clause (RC). The RC is an **INDEPENDENT CLAUSE** (▶Step 28), usually containing a **MAIN VERB** with *will* or *would*, while the CC is a **DEPENDENT CLAUSE** starting with *if*, which is a **DEPENDENT MARKER WORD.** Some of the most commonly used conditional structures in English are given in the table below.

Name	Description	Form	Example	Uses
Zero	If the condition exists, the result will always follow.	CC: *if* + present simple RC: present simple	If you heat water, it boils.	Stating general truths and facts
1st	If the condition exists, the result is very likely.	CC: *if* + present simple RC: future simple	If you want any more advice, I'll give you some.	Talking about possible future events
2nd	The condition is not real; it is imagined. It may be quite a remote possibility.	CC: *if* + past simple RC: *would* + infinitive	If I won the lottery, I would go on holiday.	Giving advice; talking about hypothetical situations
3rd	The condition did not happen, so neither did the result.	CC: *if* + past perfect RC: *would have* + past participle	If she'd been there, it would never have happened.	Regret; talking about how a situation might have been different
Mixed type A	The condition did not happen, so the present situation is different to the result. 3rd conditional CC + 2nd conditional RC.	CC: *if* + past perfect RC: *would* + infinitive	If she'd caught her train, she would be here now.	Regret; inferring what happened in the past
Mixed type B	The condition is an imagined ongoing situation which would have caused the result at some point in the past. 2nd conditional CC + 3rd conditional RC.	CC: *if* + past simple RC: *would have* + past participle	If you worked harder, you would have got a better job by now.	Regret; encouraging or criticizing

Three key facts about conditional sentences

1. The order of the clauses can normally be reversed. For example, for the 2nd conditional sentence above, you could say instead *I would go on holiday if I won the lottery.* In some circumstances, **PUNCTUATION** (especially **COMMAS**) may have to change.
2. Other **CONJUNCTIONS** which may introduce condition clauses are *unless* (meaning 'if not') and *provided/providing that*, *so/as long as* and *on condition that* (all meaning 'only if').
3. In the 2nd conditional, where the condition clause uses the verb *be*, *were* rather than *was* is often used for the 1st and 3rd person. For example: *If I were you, I'd go to school.*

How can adjectives and adverbs be used to talk about possibility and probability?

Using **ADJECTIVES** with **NOUNS**, or **ADVERBS** with **VERBS**, is a relatively easy way of indicating possibility or probability. Common adjectives which can be used in this way include *likely*, *possible*, *potential* and *probable*; adverbs include *probably*, *possibly*, *maybe* and *perhaps*. *Certain* (adjective) or *certainly* (adverb) can be used if you are sure (▶Step 39).

How can modal verbs be used to talk about possibility and probability?

As outlined in ▶Step 12, **MODAL VERBS** are a type of **AUXILIARY VERB**. Many modal verbs can be used to talk about possibility or probability.

- **Can** is used to make general statements about what is possible: *You **can** smoke in the next room. She **can** speak French*. It is often followed by the **PASSIVE VOICE**: *Many items **can** now be bought online.*
- **Can't** (= **cannot**) is used to say something is impossible: *That **can't** be true!*
- **Could** is often used to talk about a general ability in the past: *When I was a child, I **could** do what I wanted*. It is used to suggest plans for the future: *We **could** go to the cinema.* It can also be used to form the present perfect to talk about a past possibility: *We **could** have gone to France.*

> *be able to*
>
> This has a similar meaning to *can*, but is less commonly used. However, it can be extremely useful in situations where it is not possible to use *can*, for example, with the present perfect: *I haven't been able to sleep recently.*

- **Couldn't** performs the same roles in the negative: *I **couldn't** swim until I was 15. They **couldn't** have done any more.*
- **Must** is used when we have evidence which makes us certain something is true: *You've been running. You **must** be thirsty. Must have* can be used to form the present perfect in order to talk in a similar way about the past: *He **must have** known about that.*
- **Should** is used to talk about things which we assume, or have good reason to think, are true. *Should* is not quite as strong as *must*, and is often used in implied questions: *They **shouldn't** be back soon, **should** they?*
- **May** and **might** are used to say that something is a possibility in the future, but that there is no certainty. They have a very similar meaning: *It **may** rain tomorrow*. *She **might** be late*. They can be used with the present perfect to talk about past or present possibilities: *She **might** have had a headache. They **may** have arrived already.* They are also sometimes used in the present perfect continuous to talk about past possibilities: *He **might** have been worrying about his exams*.

Summary

1. There are four major types of conditional sentences in English, plus two mixed types. These sentences are composed of a condition clause (using *if*) and a result clause.
2. Adjectives (e.g., *likely*, *potential*) and adverbs (e.g., *maybe*, *perhaps*) can also be used to show possibility and probability.
3. Modal verbs can be combined with main verbs to show probability and possibility.

D Activation

1. **Complete and comprehend.**
   Match each sentence to its purpose.

fact	possibility	regret	advice

   a. If I were you, I wouldn't tell him until tomorrow. ______________
   b. If she'd told us, we could have helped sooner. ______________
   c. If the weather's nice, we'll go to the park later. ______________
   d. If I complain, he ignores me. ______________

2. **Check your understanding.**
   Complete the following sentences with an appropriate modal verb.
   a. His favourite actor ______________ be Tom Cruise. He's got all his DVDs.
   b. I've finished! I ______________ finally submit my essay.
   c. Before she arrived in London, she ______________ speak a word of English.
   d. Our boss ______________ agree with you, but I doubt it.
   e. Emma and Nigel went to the zoo yesterday. They ______________ seen some lions.

3. **Create your own.**
   a. **Complete the sentences about yourself, using an appropriate form of the conditional.**
      1. If I exercised more, ______________
      2. If I didn't go to work tomorrow, ______________
      3. If I'd been born in the UK, ______________
      4. If I go to bed late tonight, ______________

   b. **Now write three more sentences using some of the phrases in the box below.**

unless	on condition that	provided that	providing that	as long as	so long as

      1. ______________
      ____
      2. ______________
      ____
      3. ______________
      ____

How can I use phrasal verbs correctly?

STEP 32

'The whole is more than the sum of its parts.'

Aristotle (384–322 BCE)
Greek philosopher and scientist

A Reflection

Some examples of phrasal verbs are *carry out*, *drop in*, *get by*, *give out* and *find out*. Decide whether the following statements about phrasal verbs are true or false.

Statement	True	False
Phrasal verbs are composed of more than one part.	✓	
It is usually possible to guess the meaning of a phrasal verb.		
Phrasal verbs are not very common in formal, written English.		
Phrasal verbs are always transitive.		
Phrasal verbs can only have one meaning.		

What other phrasal verbs do you know? Take a minute to write as many as you can.

B Contextualization

Match each verb from the box to its phrasal equivalent below.

admire survive ~~complete~~ discover visit succeed distribute examine

carry out	complete	*get by*	________
drop in	________	*give out*	________
look up to	________	*find out*	________
get ahead	________	*check up on*	________

C Explanation

What are ten facts about phrasal verbs?

1. A phrasal verb is composed of two different kinds of word: a **VERB** and a **PARTICLE**. A particle is either a **PREPOSITION** (▶Step 22) or an **ADVERB** (▶Step 17).
2. Phrasal verbs are very common in spoken English and informal writing. However, they are not commonly used in **FORMAL** speaking and writing. In formal situations, it is better to use a one-word equivalent. For example, *admire* can replace *look up to.*
3. The verbs used in phrasal verbs are generally common verbs, such as *break*, *come*, *look*, *make* and *take*. These verbs can be combined with many different prepositions and adverbs. For example, *look* can be combined with *at*, *in*, *into* and *over.*
4. The meaning of a phrasal verb can sometimes be guessed from its parts. On other occasions this may not be possible, and the phrasal verb has to be learnt separately.
5. Some phrasal verbs have more than one meaning. For example, *blow up* means *inflate* (*blow up a balloon*) but also *destroy* (*blow up a building*). Phrasal verbs may have both a literal and a figurative meaning.
6. The majority of phrasal verbs consist of two words, but some have three (*look up to*, *get along with*).
7. Phrasal verbs can be **TRANSITIVE** or **INTRANSITIVE** (▶Step 12). An example of a transitive phrasal verb is *fill out* (*I filled out the form*); an example of an intransitive verb is *break down* (*My car broke down*). Remember: intransitive verbs may take an **INDIRECT OBJECT.**
8. Some phrasal verbs are separable. This means that the object may come between the verb and its particle, as in *She **wrote** his address **down***. The object may also come after the phrasal verb, as in *She **wrote down** his address*. Where the object is a pronoun, however, the verb **must** be separated, with the pronoun placed between the verb and the particle. Whenever a phrasal verb is separated, the sentence structure is: subject + verb + object + particle. Note that all separable phrasal verbs are also transitive.
9. Other phrasal verbs are inseparable, meaning that the verb component cannot be separated from the particle. *Look after*, for example, is an inseparable phrasal verb: we can say *She **looked after** her niece*, but not *She **looked** her niece **after***. Inseparable phrasal verbs can be transitive or intransitive.

> **Top tip**
> A dictionary will tell you whether or not a phrasal verb is separable, and whether or not it is transitive.

10. Some phrasal verbs can be turned into nouns. For example: *The television is on **standby**. Technical **backup** can be provided if necessary.* The particle may go before or after the main verb. Other common phrasal nouns include *breakaway, changeover*, *input*, *onset*, *payback*, *payoff*, *playback*, *put-down*, *setback* and *take-off.*

What are some of the most commonly used phrasal verbs in English?

Separable phrasal verbs

- What **brought** this situation **about**?
  bring about = cause to happen
- You need to **calm** him **down** before he leaves.
  calm down = become/make calm, feel less stressed
- Has the government **carried** this policy **out** yet?
  carry out = complete, perform, accomplish
- **Give** these notes **out** to everyone in the lecture.
  give out = distribute

Inseparable phrasal verbs

Transitive

- Can you **check up on** her when you get home?
  check up on = examine, verify
- I'd like to **do without** coffee, but I couldn't.
  do without = manage without something
- Did they find him or did he **get away with** it?
  get away with = be bad without getting caught
- Who do you **look up to**?
  look up to = admire
- If you borrow my car, you'll have to **take care of** it.
  take care of = protect

Intransitive

- What does *e.g.* **stand for**?
  stand for = mean, represent (often for an abbreviation)
- She has really **fallen behind** in her classes.
  fall behind = fail to do something quickly enough
- **Drop in** any time. It would be great to see you.
  drop in = visit someone without notice
- He wants to **get ahead** in the company.
  get ahead = be successful in the work you do
- My daughter **ran away** from that scary dog.
  run away = go quickly in the opposite direction

Other separable phrasal verbs

blow up, bring up, call off, fill out, fill up, find out, give away, give back, hand in, hang up, hold up, leave out, look over, look up, make out, make up, pick out, pick up, point out, put away, put off, put on, put out, set up, take down, take off, take over, talk over, throw away, try out, turn down, turn up, turn off

Other transitive inseparable phrasal verbs

back out of, call for, call on, care for, come by for, fall back on, get around, get over, go over, go through, hear of, live up to, look after, look down on, look into, make up for, put up with, run across, run into, see about, see to, stick to, take after, talk over, turn into, wait on, wait up for

Other intransitive inseparable phrasal verbs

back down, catch on, clear out, come back, come in, come to, eat out, get by, get off, get up, go back, go on, grow up, keep away, lie down, look on, pass out, show off, show up, slow up, stand by, stay over, take off, wake up, walk back, watch out, wear out

Summary

1. Phrasal verbs are made up of two kinds of word: verb and particle.
2. Phrasal verbs are a very common feature of spoken English and informal writing. In formal writing, a one-word equivalent should be used.
3. Two key considerations when using phrasal verbs are whether they are transitive or intransitive, and whether they are separable or inseparable.

D Activation

1. **Complete and comprehend.**
   Fill in the gaps with appropriate words. Try not to refer back to the text.
   - **a.** A phrasal verb is composed of a verb followed by either a ______________ or an ______________.
   - **b.** Phrasal verbs are ______________ in spoken English and informal writing, but ______________ common in academic speaking and writing.
   - **c.** Phrasal verbs can have ______________ one meaning.
   - **d.** Phrasal verbs may be transitive, meaning that they must be followed by an ______________, or intransitive, meaning that they must not. If the verb is ______________, the object can come after the whole verb, or else between the components.
   - **e.** When the phrasal verb is inseparable, the object must ______________ the particle.

2. **Check your understanding.**
   Rewrite each sentence using an appropriate phrasal verb.
   - **a.** If you ever come to London, please visit.
     If you ever come to London, please drop in.
   - **b.** The case caused a change in the law.
     ____
   - **c.** She managed without any help from her parents.
     ____
   - **d.** The doctors performed the operation last night.
     ____
   - **e.** He really admires his elder sister.
     ____

3. **Create your own.**
   Choose three phrasal verbs from the boxes on page 133. Look them up in a dictionary and then write three sentences to show their meaning.
   - **a.** ____
   - **b.** ____
   - **c.** ____

What grammar should I use to show relationships in time?

STEP 33

'Lost time is never found again.'

Benjamin Franklin (1706–1790)
American politician, writer and scientist

A Reflection

Categorize the adverbs.

~~today~~	later	seldom	always	not long	tomorrow
all day	never	yesterday	~~for a while~~	now	~~monthly~~
yearly	sometimes	often	since last week	regularly	

When	How long	How often
today	for a while	monthly

B Contextualization

Complete each gap with an appropriate time word from the box.

before after since on at for ~~in~~ when as soon as

1. She's going to university ____in____ September.
2. Did you arrive ______________ or ______________ Emily?
3. You can open your presents ______________ 9 o'clock ______________ your birthday.
4. She's been teaching ______________ 10 o'clock – ______________ nearly six hours!
5. I was writing my essay ______________ my computer crashed.
6. We'll leave ______________ your father gets home.

Match the verb forms in the word box to the sentence functions (▶Step 14).

present simple present continuous present perfect past simple

Sentence function	Verb form
To make generalizations	
To talk about changes over a period of time	
To show an action is unfinished at the present moment	
To show an action began and finished at a specific past moment	

C Explanation

What are the four main ways to talk about time in English?

There are many different ways to talk about time in English. This step identifies four of the simplest and most effective ways of doing so. Combining several of these strategies together can help you to write about time in an even more interesting and intelligent way.

> *used to*
>
> This **AUXILIARY VERB** is used in order to say that something regularly happened in the past, but no longer happens.
>
> - *I **used to play** football when I was younger. Now I'm too old.*
> - *He **used to smoke** 20 cigarettes a day, but he quit last year.*
>
> *Used to* is followed by the verb in the bare infinitive.

1. **Using verbs**

   VERBS are the main **WORD CLASS** used to refer to relationship in time. ▶Steps 13 and 14 explain in detail which verb forms should be used in each situation. Two key areas to remember are **TENSE** (when something happens) and **ASPECT** (how something happens). Four of the main verb forms used in English, and their common uses, are outlined below.

   - **Present simple**
     I go to school every day. *English is difficult*.
     Used to state general truths or facts, to make generalizations, to describe repeated actions or to indicate a future action or event which is planned or timetabled.
   - **Present continuous**
     She's reading a book. *We're leaving tonight*.
     Used to show action is unfinished at the present moment, to say you are in the middle of doing something, to discuss things that are generally true at the moment or to indicate an event which will occur in the near future.
   - **Past simple**
     They returned home late last night. As a child, she lived in Berlin.
     Used to show that an action started and finished at a specific point in the past, to show something happened in the past for a period of time or to show past habits, truths or facts.
   - **Present perfect**
     We've been talking for ages. They've been here before.
     Used to show an event or events took place in the past, but not at a specific time, to talk about changes over a period of time or to show that actions/events which began in the past have continued until the present.

2. **Using adverbs**

   ADVERBS of time can provide more information about time relationships in three areas.

   - **When** something happens: *today*, *yesterday*, *tomorrow*, *later*, *now*, *last week/month/year*.
   - **How long** something happens for: *all day/week/month/year*, *not long*, *for a while*, *since last week*.
   - **How often** something happens: *never*, *seldom*, *sometimes*, *often*, *always*, *monthly*, *yearly*. This group can be divided into adverbs of definite frequency (e.g., *annually*, *daily*, *fortnightly*, *hourly*, *nightly*, *quarterly*, *weekly*) and adverbs of indefinite frequency (e.g., *constantly*, *ever*, *frequently*, *generally*, *infrequently*, *normally*, *occasionally*, *rarely*, *regularly*, *usually*).

3. **Using subordinating conjunctions**
   Many **SUBORDINATING CONJUNCTIONS** can be used to talk about time. They can be used in three different ways.
   - To show that events occurred at different times: *after*, *before*
     Did you arrive before or after Emily?
   - To show two things occurred at the same time: *while, when*
     I was writing my essay when my computer crashed.
   - To show that for one event to occur, another event has to happen first: *as soon as, once, until*
     We'll leave as soon as your father gets home.

4. **Using prepositions**
   As noted in ▶Step 22, there are a number of **PREPOSITIONS** used in English which are related to time. *In*, *on* and *at* are three of the most common. *In* refers to general periods of time, whilst *on* and *at* are more specific.

in

Seasons	Months	Parts of the day	Years, centuries
in spring, in summer, in autumn, in winter	*in May, in June, in July*	*in the morning/ afternoon/evening*	*in 2013, in the 20th Century*

on

Days	Special days	Dates	Part of a specific day
on Sunday, on Monday, on Tuesday	*on Christmas Day, on my birthday*	*on 29th December, on 24th January*	*on the morning of 4th July*

at

Clock times	Mealtimes	Specific phrases	Festivals
at ten o'clock, at half past nine	*at breakfast, at lunchtime, at dinner*	*at night, at the weekend*	*at Christmas, at Eid, at Diwali*

Since and *for* are two more commonly used – and commonly confused – prepositions. They are generally used with the present perfect and present perfect continuous verb forms. *Since* refers to the point in time when something began, whereas *for* refers to a duration of time. Therefore, *since* must be followed by times (*12 o'clock, this morning*), dates (*1989, 24th May, last Tuesday*) or events (*the end of the Second World War, the General Election*), whereas *for* must be followed by lengths of time (*three seconds, seven hours, 41 days, millions of years*). For example, we could say either *She's been teaching* ***since*** *10 o'clock* or *She's been teaching* ***for*** *nearly two hours*.

Summary

1. Verbs are the most common way to talk about relationships in time. Focus on being able to correctly use the four main verb forms: present simple, present continuous, present perfect and past simple.
2. Adverbs of time can help you say when something happens, how long it happens for and how often it happens.
3. Five common time prepositions are *in, on, at, since* and *for*.

D Activation

1. **Complete and comprehend.**

   a. **Write as many of the uses of these four verb forms as you can remember.**

Present simple	Present continuous
Past simple	**Present perfect**

   b. **Which of the verb forms above are the following adverbs most likely to go with? Sometimes two forms may be equally likely.**

   1. yesterday *past simple*
   2. since yesterday ______
   3. never ______
   4. later ______
   5. daily ______

2. **Check your understanding.**
   Use an appropriate subordinating conjunction to complete each sentence.

   a. I saw my friend *while* I was waiting for a bus.
   b. I'll call you back ______ my lesson.
   c. We'll let you know if you got the job ______ we have interviewed everyone.
   d. ______ I know my final marks, I don't know where I'm going to college.
   e. ______ she was a fashion designer, Victoria Beckham was a pop star.

3. **Create your own.**
   Complete each sentence with an appropriate time phrase.

   a. I last went to the cinema on *Monday / my birthday / 13th June*.
   b. She's been working on that computer since ______.
   c. They finally arrived at ______.
   d. At ______, we'll be staying with my friends Tim and Tom.
   e. My parents have lived in their house for ______. They moved there in ______, I think.
   f. We ______ go on holiday there all the time, but it became too expensive.

What grammar should I use to talk about negatives?

STEP 34

'If two negatives make an affirmative ... does it follow that two nobodies shall be somebody?'

Samuel Laman Blanchard (1804–1845)
English poet and journalist

A Reflection

Underline the 13 negative words in the passage.

I have been teaching for 25 years, and I have never seen such a difficult exam. There was no way this was reasonable. In fact, I would say it was unfair. Nothing – or hardly anything – from the curriculum was in the exam. In terms of the results, neither the weakest nor the strongest students did well. Barely any students got more than 50%. None got more than 60%. They just could not understand the questions! In my opinion, nobody benefits from such a difficult exam. I disagree with what the examiners did. The questions came from nowhere.

B Contextualization

Write each negative word from the passage next to the correct description.

An adverb meaning 'not at any time'	*never*	A two-word combination meaning 'not either of two things/people'	
A pronoun meaning 'not any' or 'not one'		A pronoun meaning 'not anything'	
A determiner meaning 'not any'		A verb with a negative prefix	
An adverb used in a verb phrase to form the negative		Two adverbs meaning 'almost not'	
A pronoun meaning 'no person at all'		A pronoun or adverb meaning 'no place'	
An adjective with a negative prefix			

Write down any negative words you know beginning with the following prefixes.

dis~	*disagree*	in~	
il~		ir~	
im~		un~	*unfair*

C Explanation

What is the purpose of negative words in English?

There are many reasons to use **NEGATIVE** words in English, primarily:

- to say something is not true, did not happen or does not exist
- to give a negative response to a question
- to present a negative attitude towards something

What are the main negative words in English?

In general, negative words are either **DETERMINERS** (Step ▶23), **PRONOUNS** (Step ▶7) or **ADVERBS** (Step ▶17). The table below gives definitions of the most common words; an example sentence which shows how the word is used is also given in each case. Notes relating to specific words appear beneath the table.

Words	Definition	Example
no	A determiner meaning 'not any'	There was **no** way this was reasonable.
not[1, 2]	An adverb used in a verb phrase to form the negative	They just could **not** understand the questions!
none	A pronoun meaning 'not any' or 'not one'	**None** got more than 60%.
never	An adverb meaning 'not at any time'	… I have **never** seen such a difficult exam.
nobody, no one[3]	Pronouns meaning 'no person at all'	… **nobody** benefits from such a difficult exam.
nothing	A pronoun meaning 'not anything'	**Nothing** … from the curriculum was in the exam.
neither … nor	A two-word combination meaning 'not either of two things/people'.	… **neither** the weakest **nor** the strongest students did well.
nowhere	A pronoun or adverb meaning 'no place'	The questions came from **nowhere**.

Notes

1 *Not* can be used in conjunction with an **AUXILIARY VERB**. It appears after the first auxiliary verb in the **VERB PHRASE**. For example: *She is not coming later. They may not arrive on time. You have not been listening properly. My brother might not be going.* In spoken English and informal written English, *not* is often combined with the auxiliary verb in a contracted form. This results in forms such as:

- *be* as an auxiliary: *isn't, aren't, wasn't, weren't, won't* (**Note:** *isn't* not *amn't*.)
- *have* as an auxiliary: *hasn't, haven't, hadn't*
- *do* as an auxiliary: *don't, doesn't, didn't*
- modal auxiliaries: *can't, couldn't, mustn't, shouldn't, wouldn't*

2 When there is no auxiliary verb (e.g., in the present simple or past simple), use the appropriate form of *do* (*do/does/did*) plus the **BARE INFINITIVE**. For example: *They do not like cricket. She does not eat fish. We didn't go to the cinema.*

3 *No one* does not usually have a **HYPHEN**, but some people use one (*no-one*).

Top tip

NATIVE SPEAKERS of some English dialects sometimes use two negatives in the same clause for negative emphasis, without the intention that one should cancel the other out. For example, *I don't want nothing* can be used to mean *I don't want anything*, even though in many contexts, such as in academic writing, it could only mean the opposite (*I want something*). You should always avoid using double negatives for emphasis in academic and formal speaking and writing, since in this context they are incorrect.

What negative adverbs can I use?

There are several negative adverbs meaning 'almost not', such as *hardly*, *scarcely* and *barely*. When using these adverbs, you should **not** use an additional negative form. Because the negative meaning is already contained in the adverb, the other words in the clause must appear in their positive forms. For example, the negative determiner *no* is replaced by *a/an* for singular nouns, and *any* for plural or uncountable nouns.

- *There is **barely a** single piece of evidence for this theory.*
- *He had **hardly any** sleep last night.*

The negative adverb/pronoun *nowhere* is replaced by *anywhere*.

- *Since her accident, she **hardly** goes **anywhere**.*

The negative adverb *never* is replaced by *ever*.

- *I **scarcely ever** go.*

What negative prefixes are there?

Knowing how to use negative **PREFIXES** can make your writing easier to follow and less complicated. In each of the following pairs of sentences, both sentences are acceptable, but sentence b is easier to read and more concise.

1. **a.** I do not agree with what the examiners did.
b. I disagree with what the examiners did.

2. **a.** In fact, I would say it was not fair.
b. In fact, I would say it was unfair.

Some of the most commonly used negative prefixes are *dis~*, *il~*, *im~*, *in~*, *ir~* and *un~*. Three common words for each are given below.

dis~	il~	im~	in~	ir~	un~
disadvantage	illegal	immoral	inaccurate	irregular	unclear
disappear	illegible	imperfect	inadequate	irrelevant	undo
dishonest	illogical	impossible	inappropriate	irresponsible	unhappy

Other prefixes which may indicate a negative meaning include *a/an~* (*amoral*), *anti~* (*antisocial*), *contra~* (*contradiction*), *counter~* (*counterargument*), *de~* (*decentralize*), *mis~* (*misuse*), *non~* (*nonsense*). The **SUFFIX** *~less* also has a negative meaning, as in *faultless*, *hopeless*, *useless*.

Summary

1. The main negative words are *no, not, none, no one, nobody, nothing, neither … nor, nowhere* and *never.*
2. These words are generally used as pronouns, determiners or adverbs.
3. Using negative prefixes such as *dis~*, *in~* and *un~* can make your writing more concise.

D Activation

1. **Complete and comprehend.**
   a. **Answer the following questions in your own words.**
      1. What are the main reasons for using negatives in English?
      2. How do you use the word *not* with a verb phrase?
      3. What are double negatives? Should you use them?
      4. Name three negative adverbs.

   b. **How many negative prefixes/suffixes commonly used in English can you remember (14 were mentioned)? Try to think of at least one example word for each.**

2. **Check your understanding.**
   Complete each sentence with an appropriate negative word.
   a. I have ___________ reason to help you.
   b. She has ___________ been to America.
   c. I tried everything, but ___________ made him happy.
   d. I knew ___________ at the party.
   e. I have been to London and Paris, but I like ___________.
   f. She is ___________ going to believe you.
   g. ___________ of you arrived on time.

3. **Create your own.**
   Rewrite the following sentences using different negative forms.
   a. At no point in my life have I played basketball.
      I have never played basketball.
   b. It is not possible to leave after 11 o'clock.
      ____
   c. There aren't any places left to visit in this town.
      ____
   d. He was so nervous, only a few words came out of his mouth.
      ____
   e. They don't know anything.
      ____

What grammar should I use to ask questions?

STEP 35

'Who questions much, shall learn much, and retain much.'

Francis Bacon (1561–1626)
English philosopher and statesman

A Reflection

Make notes about what you can remember about interrogative sentences (▶Step 29).

B Contextualization

Which answer type from the box below would you expect for the following questions?

a. *yes*	**b.** a person	**c.** a place	**d.** *no*
e. a reason	**f.** either *yes* or *no*	**g.** a time	

The weather's not getting any better, is it? d

Has she left? ___

Did he live in London? ___

When did he go to school this morning? ___

She goes to university, doesn't she? ___

Where did she live in London? ___

Can his brother swim? ___

Why is it raining? ___

Do you speak German? ___

Who did you meet in town? ___

Does he live in Berlin? ___

Did he go to school this morning? ___

You're arriving at nine o'clock, aren't you? ___

Which of them is the youngest? ___

What is the difference in tone between the questions in each pair below? In each case, decide which is formal and which informal, and why.

1. a. I wonder whether she liked it. ______

b. She liked it? ______

2. a. They're leaving when? ______

b. When are they leaving? ______

C Explanation

What is the main way of asking questions in English?

As discussed in ▶Step 29, **INTERROGATIVES** are one of the four sentence types in English. This type of sentence can be used (i) to ask questions, (ii) to request information or (iii) to check information. The easiest and most common way to ask questions is to invert (reverse the order of) the **SUBJECT** and the first **AUXILIARY VERB** in a **DECLARATIVE SENTENCE**. You should also replace the **FULL STOP** with a **QUESTION MARK**. Take the following example in the present continuous.

It is raining.
(subject + auxiliary verb + main verb)
→
Is it raining?
(auxiliary verb + subject + main verb)

Examples of declarative and interrogative sentences using other verb forms can be seen in the table below.

Verb form	Declarative sentence	Interrogative sentence
Present perfect	She has left.	Has she left?
Present perfect continuous	Your friend has been working.	Has your friend been working?
Past continuous	They were waiting in the queue.	Were they waiting in the queue?
Modal + present simple	His brother can swim.	Can his brother swim?

Some declarative sentences, such as those in the present simple and past simple, do not contain auxiliary verbs. When there is no auxiliary verb in the declarative sentence, the auxiliary verb *do* is used to make the question. The main verb changes to the **BARE INFINITIVE** form.

Verb form	Declarative sentence	Interrogative sentence
Present simple	He lives in Berlin.	Does he live in Berlin?
Past simple	He lived in London.	Did he live in London?

Using prepositional verbs in questions

When a **PREPOSITIONAL VERB** is used in a question, the preposition normally comes at the end: *Which book are you looking for?*

What are *Wh~* questions?

Wh~ questions begin with a **QUESTION WORD**. The question words are *what*, *where*, *when*, *which*, *who*, *whom*, *whose* and *why*. *How* is also included, although it does not begin with *wh~*.

- *Why is it raining?*
- *Which of them is youngest?*
- *When did he go to school this morning?*
- *Where did she live in London?*
- *Who did you meet in town?*

Wh~ questions are useful when you require more than a *yes* or *no* answer – when you require specific information. Each of the question words refers to a specific type of information desired. *Where*, for example, asks for a location, *when* a time and *why* a reason.

What are question tags and how can they be used?

In the question types discussed on the previous page, the person asking the question does not know the answer. However, there may be occasions when you think you know the answer, but want to check that you are correct. To do this, you can use a **QUESTION TAG** – a phrase at the end of a declarative sentence which indicates that you want the listener to confirm what you have said. For example: *You're arriving at nine o'clock,* ***aren't you****?*

To form a question using a question tag, follow either of these formulas.

1. positive declarative sentence + negative question tag
2. negative declarative sentence + positive question tag

When there is an auxiliary verb in the declarative sentence, the question tag uses the same auxiliary verb and inverts it with the subject. Thus, *you're* in the declarative sentence corresponds to the question tag *aren't you*: *You're arriving at nine o'clock, aren't you?* Similarly, *it was* in the declarative sentence corresponds to the question tag *wasn't it*: *It was raining when we arrived, wasn't it?*

When there is no auxiliary verb in the declarative sentence, the auxiliary verb *do* is used in the question tag: *She goes to university, doesn't she?*

Question tags are more common in spoken English. The way you say the question tag can affect its meaning. If your voice goes down, this suggests that you are almost certain that the information is correct. If your voice goes up, this suggests that you are uncertain.

What are the formal and informal ways of asking questions?

Depending on the context, questions may be asked in a more formal or informal way.

Formal questions

A question can be made more formal by rephrasing it to ask explicitly about the listener's knowledge or ability. Doing this can make a question sound less like a demand. If you need to be polite or deferential, it is often a good idea to ask a question in this way.

Do you know *if it is raining?*	***Do you know*** *why it is raining?*
Are you able to tell me *where she lived in London?*	***Could you tell me*** *where she lived in London?*

Informal questions

In spoken English, native speakers may not form questions in a grammatically accurate way. Instead, they may use a declarative sentence with a **RISING TONE**.

She liked it? You're coming later? You want to go to the cinema? They're leaving at 12?

Summary

1. The basic way of forming questions in English is to invert the auxiliary verb and the subject. If there is no auxiliary verb, use *do/does/did*.
2. If you want to find out specific information, use a question word (*what, where, when, which, who, whom, whose, why, how*).
3. Question tags can be used after declarative sentences to create informal questions.

D Activation

1. Complete and comprehend.

Complete the table.

Verb form	Declarative sentence	Interrogative sentence
Present simple	He's often very impatient.	Is he often very impatient?
Past continuous	______ Thursday's lecture.	Were you discussing Thursday's lecture?
______	His brother's decided to study English.	______ to study English?
Present continuous	She's suggesting his argument is flawed.	______ his argument is flawed?
Past simple	You ______ some new ideas.	______ develop some new ideas?
______	She has been working very hard this year.	______ very hard this year?

2. Check your understanding.

Rearrange the jumbled words to make questions.

a. going to are be you late — Are you going to be late?

b. is China the capital of what ______

c. said you do why that think he ______

d. do answer you the understand ______

e. she computer fix her did ______

f. not answer the is that's it ______

3. Create your own.

Write sample questions which could have the following answers. In each case, many different answers are possible.

Sample question	Answers
a. Does he like watching films?	Yes, he does.
b.	Last year.
c.	No, it isn't.
d.	New York.
e.	Because it was so hot.
f.	Yes, I think it's going to be late.

What is agreement?

'All colours will agree in the dark.'

Francis Bacon (1561–1626)
English philosopher and statesman

A Reflection

Read the sentences below. In each case, there is one problem relating to agreement. Identify the problem and correct it.

1. My friends is coming to see me tonight.
2. She haves a very large house.
3. Both is available.
4. She wishes she could go on holiday soon.
5. Three months are a long time to be away.
6. Paper catchs fire more quickly than wood.
7. My aunt are visiting tomorrow.
8. Anything are possible.
9. Half of the cakes has been sold.
10. Twenty pounds are expensive for a ticket.
11. The train arrived at his destination.
12. There were no light.
13. My friend Tom, as well as his parents, are going on holiday.
14. The man arrived at her office.
15. She, along with her sister, have been coming here for years.
16. You be late.

B Contextualization

Look at the list of rules about agreement. Match the rules to the sentences in Part A.

Rule	Sentences
Subjects and verbs must agree with each other in number.	1, 7
Some verbs in the present simple are irregular.	
Some verbs in the 3rd person present simple take ~*es*, not ~*s*.	
Some indefinite pronouns require a singular verb, while others require a plural verb.	
Be careful when the subject and verb are separated from each other.	
When using *of* to talk about parts of a whole, identify whether the noun is singular or plural.	
Sums of money and periods of time take a singular verb.	
Nouns and pronouns must agree in gender.	

Which of the following sentences are correct?

Note: sometimes both sentences in the pair may be correct.

1. **a.** The company is expanding. **b.** The company are expanding.
2. **a.** The government was voted out. **b.** The government were voted out.
3. **a.** Who made the decision? **b.** Whom made the decision?
4. **a.** Who did you see? **b.** Whom did you see?

C Explanation

What is grammatical agreement?

Grammatical **AGREEMENT** means that in a sentence or text, words belonging to the same grammatical category (e.g., number, person or **GENDER**) must bear the correct relationship to one another. For example, in *The boys walked their dog*, the subject (*boys*) is **PLURAL**, so the plural possessive adjective (*their*) must be used. If the sentence was rewritten as *The boys walked his dog*, the subject and the adjective would no longer agree.

Unlike in some languages, where agreement is a critical issue (for example, in languages where nouns are gendered), in English there are relatively few areas in which words can agree. The areas in which agreement is important are outlined below.

What are the top ten rules to follow regarding agreement?

1. **Subjects and verbs must agree with each other in number.**

   If a **SUBJECT** is singular, the **VERB** must also be singular; if a subject is plural, the verb must also be plural.

   - *My friends are coming to see me tonight.*
   - *My aunt is visiting tomorrow.*
   - *There was no light.*

2. **Some verbs in the present simple are irregular.**

   Whilst there are many verbs in English which are **IRREGULAR** in the past simple, there are a small group of common verbs which are irregular in the present simple as well. The verbs *be*, *have*, *do* and *go* are all irregular in the third person (*is, has, does, goes*). The verb *be* is also irregular in the 1st person (*I am*, *we are*) and the 2nd person (*you are*).

   - *She has a very large house.*
   - *You are late.*

3. **Some verbs in the 3rd person present simple take *~es*, not *~s*.**

   Verbs which end in **SIBILANT** sounds (*sh*, *ch*, *ss*, *zz*) take *~es* rather than *~s* in the 3rd person singular.

   - *She wishes she could go on holiday soon.*
   - *Paper catches fire more quickly than wood.*

4. **Some indefinite pronouns require a singular verb, while others require a plural verb.**

   Singular **INDEFINITE PRONOUNS** (▶Step 7) take singular verbs. These include *each*, *either*, *neither*, *one*, *no one*, *nobody*, *nothing*, *anyone*, *anybody*, *anything*, *someone*, *somebody*, *something*, *everyone*, *everybody* and *everything*.

   - *Anything is possible.*

   Plural indefinite pronouns take plural verbs. These include *several*, *few*, *both* and *many*.

   - *Both are available.*

> **Singular or plural indefinite pronouns**
>
> Five indefinite pronouns (*some*, *any*, *none*, *all*, *most*) may be used with a singular or a plural verb, depending on the noun which follows. In the examples below, since *water* is **UNCOUNTABLE**, the verb is singular; since *cups* are **COUNTABLE** and in the plural, the verb is plural.
>
> - *Some of the water was spilt.*
> - *Some of the cups were broken.*

5. **Be careful when the subject and verb are separated from each other.**

Sometimes a subject and its verb may be separated in a sentence, for example by a **DEPENDENT CLAUSE** (▶Step 28). When deciding whether the verb should be singular or plural, identify the subject of the **SENTENCE**: the verb should always agree with the subject. Sentences may be particularly confusing when phrases such as *along with*, *as well as*, *in addition to* are used. For example, in the sentence *My friend Tom, along with his parents,* ***is*** *going on holiday*, the subject is *my friend Tom*, which is singular. The plural form of the verb can only be used if the sentence is rewritten so that the subject is pluralized: *My friend Tom and his parents* ***are*** *going on holiday.*

6. **Collective nouns may be singular or plural, depending on how they are used.**

A **COLLECTIVE NOUN** is a noun which refers to a group of people, animals or things. Collective nouns can be thought of either as singular or plural ideas. For example: *The company is/are expanding. The government was/were voted out. My family has/have been living there.* Other collective nouns include *army*, *audience*, *committee*, *enemy*, *gang*, *group*, *herd*, *media*, *public*, *staff* and *team*. **Note:** in American English, collective nouns are generally treated as singular.

7. **When using *of* with parts of a whole, the noun can be singular or plural.**

As noted in ▶Step 8, some nouns can be both countable and uncountable. Many can be used with phrases such as *per cent of*, *part of*, *half of*, *fraction of*, *some of*, *all of*, *none of*, *majority of*, *minority of*. When they are used with these phrases, the verb should be either singular or plural in correspondence with the noun.

- *Half of the cakes have been sold.*
- *Half of the cake has been eaten.*

8. **Sums of money and periods of time take a singular verb.**

Even though the noun may be pluralized, the verb should always be singular.

- *Twenty pounds is expensive for a ticket.*
- *Three months is a long time to be away.*

9. ***Whom* is correct in some circumstances, but it can sound strange.**

In formal English, *who* should be used as a subject and *whom* as an object.

- *Who made the decision?*
- *Whom did you see?*

In many contexts, however, *whom* is becoming less common, as it is often considered to be too formal. Very often, *who* is used as both a subject and an object.

10. **Nouns and pronouns must agree in gender.**

Although it is not very common in English, there are occasions when nouns which are gendered must be followed by the correct gendered pronoun.

- *The* ***man*** *arrived at* ***his*** *office.*

This is also the case with words which are neutral, i.e., neither male nor female.

- *The* ***train*** *arrived at* ***its*** *destination.*

Summary

1. Compared to many languages, agreement is a minor issue in English, but it still requires consideration.
2. Verbs are the main area where there are issues related to agreement.
3. Nouns and pronouns should agree in gender.

D Activation

1. Complete and comprehend.

In each pair, one sentence is correct and one incorrect. Tick the correct sentences.

	1.		2.	
a.	There were no light.	☐	There was no light.	☐
b.	Ali, unlike his teammates, trains three times a week.	☐	Ali, unlike his teammates, train three times a week.	☐
c.	Five per cent of the profits is donated to charity.	☐	Five per cent of the profits are donated to charity.	☐
d.	The government was unpopular, but they still gained a majority.	☐	The government was unpopular, but it still gained a majority.	☐

2. Check your understanding.

Complete each sentence with an appropriate form of the verb in brackets.

a. If she ____________________ (*pass*) the ball, we'll score a goal.

b. Nothing ____________________ (*achieve*) yesterday. It was a disaster.

c. Ten years ____________________ (*be*) a long time to work in one company.

3. Create your own.

Write an example sentence to show your understanding of each of the ten rules regarding agreement in English.

a.	
b.	
c.	
d.	
e.	
f.	
g.	
h.	
i.	
j.	

What grammar can I use to increase my cohesion?

STEP 37

'The only completely consistent people are the dead.'

Aldous Huxley (1894–1963)
English novelist

A Reflection

Complete the sentences below with the phrases from the box.

demonstrative pronouns	linking words	pronoun	proper nouns
common nouns	punctuation	adverbs	word family

1. The grammatical job of a ____________________ is to replace a noun. Examples include *we*, *us*, *our* and *ours*.
2. *London* and *Chris* are examples of ____________________, while *television* and *milk* are examples of ____________________.
3. *This*, *that*, *these* and *those* are ____________________. Their grammatical job is to refer specifically to people, places or things.
4. *Clear*, *clearly*, *clarity* and *clarify* are all in the same ____________________.
5. *However* and *although* are examples of ____________________, respectively joining together sentences and clauses.
6. ____________________, like *similarly* or *accordingly*, can be used at the beginning of a sentence to link ideas.

B Contextualization

How do the following pairs of sentences differ? Which is better in each case?

1. a. Mr Smith went to Washington with his wife. They went by car because she lost her train ticket!	**b.** Mr Smith went to Washington with his wife. Mr and Mrs Smith went by car because Mrs Smith lost her train ticket.
2. a. I live in London. London is very large.	**b.** I live in London. The city is very large.
3. a. Nicolaus Copernicus discovered that the earth moved around the sun. This idea was revolutionary.	**b.** Nicolaus Copernicus discovered that the earth moved around the sun. The idea that the earth moved around the sun was revolutionary.
4. a. Everyone wants to succeed in life. To succeed requires a lot of hard work. When a job you do succeeds, remember what you did, so that you can repeat it. By doing this, you can succeed even more often.	**b.** Everyone wants to succeed in life. To be successful requires a lot of hard work. When you do a job successfully, remember what you did, so that you can repeat it. By doing this, you can attain even more successes!

C Explanation

What is cohesion?

COHESION is a difficult idea to define. In general, it means the way that the different parts of a text link together. If your language is not cohesive, then it will be very difficult for your listener or reader to follow what you are saying. If they cannot follow what you are saying, then you will not be able to communicate properly.

What follows is a list of ten ways in which you can make your speaking and writing more cohesive. You should try to use these strategies in connection with each other.

1. **Using pronouns**

   As outlined in ▶Step 7, the grammatical job of a **PRONOUN** is to replace a noun. Using pronouns will make your English both easier to follow and less repetitive. Repeating the same nouns in a text again and again will make it boring and difficult to read. Whenever you use pronouns, the listener or reader must link them to previous statements, which means the cohesion of the text is increased. In the following text, the four pronouns are highlighted. What does each one refer to?

   *Mr Smith went to Washington with **his** wife. **They** went by car because **she** lost **her** train ticket!*

2. **Switching between proper and common nouns**

   Texts can become very repetitive if the same words are used all the time. In addition to using pronouns, you can also switch between **PROPER** and **COMMON NOUNS** (▶Step 6). In the following example, *London* is the proper noun and *city* is the common noun, used with the definite article to make clear that London is being referred to.

   I live in London. The city is very large.

3. **Using demonstrative pronouns**

   The **DEMONSTRATIVE PRONOUNS** *this*, *that*, *these* and *those* can create cohesion by referring both backwards and forwards within a text.

   - Backwards cohesion: *Nicolaus Copernicus discovered that the earth moved around the sun. This idea was revolutionary.*
   - Forwards cohesion: *This is what the letter said: firstly, that …*

4. **Using words from the same word family**

   Using words in different **WORD CLASSES** from the same **ROOT** can be a way to create more cohesion within a text. The two texts below demonstrate that using words from different classes not only improves the style of a text, but also makes it easier to follow.

Text using the same word	Text using words from different classes
Everyone wants to succeed in life. To succeed requires a lot of hard work. When a job you do succeeds, remember what you did, so that you can repeat it. By doing this, you can succeed even more often.	Everyone wants to succeed in life. To be successful requires a lot of hard work. When you do a job successfully, remember what you did, so that you can repeat it. By doing this, you can attain even more successes!

5. **Putting old information before new information**

   The expectation in English is that old information (i.e., information which the reader or listener already knows) should come at the beginning of the sentence, with new information coming afterwards.

6. **Using linking words**

LINKING WORDS (CONJUNCTIONS and ADVERBS) can show the relationships between ideas either within a SENTENCE (between CLAUSES) or between different sentences. See ▶Step 21.

7. **Using parallel structures**

✗ *In my spare time, I like to play football, going to the cinema and to read books.*
✓ *In my spare time, I like playing football, going to the cinema and reading books.*

Using the same verb forms in the second sentence creates a kind of 'echo effect'. This emphasizes that the three items are in a list, and that they all relate to the first part of the sentence. Jumping between different forms unnecessarily can be confusing for a reader/listener, making it difficult to follow what has been said. A further example can be seen in the ten numbered headings in this step. In order to show that the sections are all related to the same idea, each heading has the same structure: *~ing* form + NOUN PHRASE.

8. **Using introductory adverbs**

When an adverb is placed at the beginning of a sentence, it can have two functions.

a. **It can show the listener/reader how the sentence links to the previous one.**
For example, *similarly* shows that the sentence has the same focus as the previous sentence. *Consequently* shows that the sentence which follows is the result or outcome of the sentences coming before. Other adverbs which can be used at the start of a sentence include *accordingly*, *alternatively* and *specifically*.

b. **It can tell the listener/reader something about the whole of the sentence.**
If a sentence were to begin *Interestingly*, ... this would be the speaker or writer's way of saying, 'I think this sentence is particularly interesting.' Similar adverbs include *critically*, *crucially* and *importantly*. Sometimes these adverbs tell us something about the feelings of the speaker or writer, e.g., *annoyingly*, *disappointingly*, *happily*, *sadly*.

9. **Using synonyms**

Using SYNONYMS can help you avoid some of the problems discussed in point 4. The rewritten passage below shows a text containing not only a range of word classes, but words from different roots as well.

*Everyone wants to **do well** in life. To be successful requires a lot of hard work. When you do a job **effectively**, remember what you did, so that you can repeat it. By doing this, you can attain even more **accomplishments**!*

10. **Using punctuation correctly**

Punctuation marks, such as FULL STOPS, SEMICOLONS, COLONS and COMMAS, show the relationships between clauses and sentences. For example, a comma may indicate a list, and a semicolon can show that two sentences have a close relationship. See ▶Steps 41–45.

Summary

1. If what you say or write is not cohesive, then you will not be able to communicate properly.
2. Key strategies for increasing cohesion include the use of pronouns, proper/common nouns, demonstrative pronouns, words in the same family, the definite article, linking words, parallel structures, introductory adverbs, synonyms and punctuation.
3. Cohesion is best achieved by combining several of these strategies.

D Activation

1. Complete and comprehend.

Look at the word cloud below. Some of the key points from this step are presented here. Reflect on how they can make your writing and speaking more cohesive.

word families definite article
parallel structures
pronouns proper/common nouns
synonyms demonstrative pronouns
introductory adverbs
punctuation linking words

2. Check your understanding.

Complete the sentences below to make them cohesive using phrases from the box.

accordingly	the building	similarly	it	were eating
ate	them	they	went	were going

a. When we were at the park yesterday, we ________________ to the museum, played football and ________________ ice cream.

b. No rules were broken; ________________, there will be no punishment.

c. Are the instructions clear? Do you understand ________________?

d. Buckingham Palace is where the Queen lives. ________________ is large and quite ugly.

3. Create your own.

Rewrite the following passage to make it more cohesive.

Last year, I went on holiday with my parents and brother to New York. Me, my parents and brother had not been on holiday together for many years. New York is an interesting city. New York has hundreds of great places to visit. The great places in New York include museums, zoos and galleries. On our first day, we went to the Metropolitan Museum of Art before going to Central Park Zoo.

Why should I be precise in my choice of grammar?

STEP 38

'Precision is next to godliness.'

attributed to **Samuel Beckett (1906–1989)**
Irish playwright, novelist and poet

A Reflection

The content words in the following sets of sentences are the same. The functional words, however, are different. Read each set of sentences and decide how the meaning changes.

1. **a.** Amy saw the film last week.
   b. Amy saw the film last Thursday.
   c. Amy saw the film five days ago.
   d. Amy has seen the film before.
2. **a.** Angela would phone her mother …
   b. Angela should phone her mother …
   c. Angela could phone her mother …
3. **a.** The cup was made in China.
   b. The cup was made of china.
4. **a.** Olivia likes the dog …
   b. Olivia likes dogs …

Some nouns can have both a countable and an uncountable form. Complete the table which follows. Sometimes more than one option may be possible.

Countable	Uncountable	Countable	Uncountable
an adaptation	adaptability	an immigrant	
a cooperative			liberalism
	coordination	a participant	
an identity			symbolism

B Contextualization

Write (a), (b) or (c) for sentences 2 and 4 in the spaces below to complete them.

2. ______________ if her phone was working.
   ______________, but she doesn't want to.
   ______________ because she has been unwell.

4. ______________ because they are usually friendly.
   ______________ next to that tree.

C Explanation

Why is it important to be precise?

As the sentences in Part A show, just one or two words can make a huge difference to a sentence. In some cases, the meaning of the sentence changes, whereas in other cases, the emphasis of the sentence changes. The purpose of this step is to remind you to be precise in your grammatical choices so that the **BUTTERFLY EFFECT** does not cause you any problems.

This step outlines five specific areas where you need to be careful about the form of the word you use.

Note: these points refer to the groups of sentences in Part A.

1. **Main verbs**

   In example 1 in Part A, sentences (a), (b) and (c) all refer to an event which happened at a specific point in the past. Therefore, these sentences all use the past simple. Sentence (d), however, refers to the event as having happened at an unspecified time before the present. This sentence, therefore, uses the past perfect.

2. **Modal verbs**

   MODAL VERBS are an area where it is easy to make mistakes. The reason for this is that many of them sound the same – for example, *would*, *should* and *could* – and so are easily confused.

   - *Would* refers to something that will happen in a hypothetical situation.
     Angela would phone her mother if her phone was working.
   - *Should* refers to things which it is correct or appropriate to do.
     Angela should phone her mother because she has been unwell.
   - *Could* refers to things which it is possible to do.
     Angela could phone her mother, but she doesn't want to.

3. **Prepositions**

   Using the wrong preposition can change the meaning of a sentence and, potentially, confuse your audience. For example, the two sentences in example 3 in Part A, *The cup was made in China* and *The cup was made of china*, are both correct, but the meaning is different, as the pictures below demonstrate.

in refers to where the cup was made

of refers to the material the cup is made from

4. Determiners

DETERMINERS (▶Step 23) can alter the meaning of a sentence quite considerably. Sentence (a) in example 4 in Part A, *Olivia likes the dog*, refers to a specific dog which is known to the speaker and listener. Sentence (b), however, which contains no determiner, refers to dogs in general: *Olivia likes dogs.*

5. Nouns

Some words have more than one form in a particular word class. This is particularly common with **NOUNS**. Often, nouns which have the same **ROOT** may appear in either a **COUNTABLE** or an **UNCOUNTABLE** form. Sometimes the same noun can be used in either a countable or an uncountable way. See the table for a list of common nouns which have more than one form – and which you should therefore be particularly careful about.

Countable noun	Uncountable noun
adaptation	adaptation, adaptability
assistant	assistance
clarification	clarification, clarity
consultation, consultant	consultation
cooperator, cooperative	cooperation
coordinator, coordinate	coordination
creation	creation, creativity
document	documentation
expert	expertise
facilitator, facility	facilitation, facility
function	functionality
identity, identification	identification
immigrant	immigration
individual	individuality, individualism
liberal	liberalism, liberalization
participant	participation
prediction	predictability
priority	prioritization
professional	professionalism
researcher	research
supervisor	supervision
symbol	symbolism
uniform	uniformity

Summary

1. It is important to be as precise as possible in your use of English so as to avoid any misinterpretation. A small mistake may change the meaning or emphasis of a sentence dramatically.
2. Verbs are a word class where you should be especially careful to be precise, both with main verbs and modal verbs.
3. Prepositions, determiners and nouns are three other word classes where care is needed.

D Activation

1. **Complete and comprehend.**

   Explain the mistake which has been made in each sentence.

Sentence	Mistake
a. Pass me this cup over there, would you?	Wrong determiner is being used – replace *this* with *that*.
b. The department really needs more coordinator.	
c. I should go later – it depends whether it's raining or not.	
d. She'll be there in 10 o'clock.	

2. **Check your understanding.**

   Complete each sentence with an appropriate word of the type given in brackets.

   a. He's been living in London ________________ (preposition) 2008.

   b. Come and look at ________________ (determiner) moon through my telescope.

   c. She ________________ (verb) me the day before yesterday.

   d. Immigration is a concern in some countries, but other countries actively encourage ________________ (noun) to come.

3. **Create your own.**

   Write three sentences which show the different meanings of *would*, *should* and *could*, as in Part B.

Modal verb	Example sentence
would	
should	
could	

How can I use grammar for emphasis?

'No iron can stab the heart with such force as a full stop put just at the right place.'

Isaac Babel (1894–1940)
Russian short story writer

A Reflection

Read the pairs of sentences. In each case, one sentence (a or b) is more emphatic than the other. Decide which one it is, and explain or underline the key language which shows this.

1. **a.** Make sure the rules are clear, simple and direct.
   b. The rules need to be clear. They also need to be simple and direct.
2. **a.** The largest city in Japan is Tokyo.
   b. Tokyo is the largest city in Japan.
3. **a.** The email was sent on time.
   b. Importantly, the email was sent on time.
4. **a.** I do like your cooking – honestly!
   b. I like your cooking – honestly!
5. **a.** She left yesterday.
   b. She left and went back to her own house yesterday afternoon.
6. **a.** The President made a mistake.
   b. Mistakes were made.
7. **a.** I think it's amazing.
   b. I think it's amazing!
8. **a.** It is Alan who works hardest at school.
   b. Alan works hardest at school.
9. **a.** What we want is less homework.
   b. We want less homework.
10. **a.** Never have I seen such a brilliant film.
    b. I have never seen such a brilliant film.

B Contextualization

Match the descriptions below to the sentence numbers above. In each case, the description refers to the more emphatic sentence in the pair. If you do not know the meaning of some of the words, look them up in the *Glossary* at the back of the book.

Present information in groups of three.	1	Use a short sentence.	
Reverse the normal word order.		Use a dummy auxiliary.	
Use different punctuation.		Start with an emphatic adverb.	
Use the active voice.		Use a *what* cleft sentence.	
Start with a negative adverb.		Use an *it* cleft sentence.	

C Explanation

What grammatical strategies can I use to make my English more emphatic?

The ten strategies given here should not be used all the time in your speaking or writing. If you were to use them all the time, their impact would be lost! Instead, it is better to use them occasionally, in order to maximize the effect which they can have.

You may be familiar with some of the strategies presented here, since they have been introduced earlier in the book.

1. **Present information in groups of three.**

   Make sure the rules are clear, simple and direct.

   When listing information or giving examples, presenting your points in groups of three can be an effective strategy for emphasis. 'Tripling' can give a phrase a distinct pattern, shape and form, and therefore make it more memorable. Some of the most famous speeches in history use triple structures: 'life, liberty, and the pursuit of happiness', 'government of the people, by the people, for the people', 'friends, Romans, countrymen'.

   If you are using a triple structure, you should use the same grammatical structure in each part. For example, the phrase *government of the people, by the people, for the people* uses exactly the same grammatical structure for each of the three parts (*government* + **PREPOSITION** + *the people*).

2. **Reverse the normal word order.**

   The largest city in Japan is Tokyo.

   In most English **SENTENCES**, general or already-known information comes before specific or new information. In short, this means that you have to introduce a topic before you comment on it. For emphasis, however, it can be effective to introduce new information before making clear what is being referred to, as in *The largest city in Japan is Tokyo.*

3. **Start with an emphatic adverb.**

   Importantly, the email was sent on time.

   Emphatic adverbs, often placed at the beginning of a sentence, can say something about the whole sentence. Such adverbs often show your opinion of the information which follows (*interestingly, controversially*) or show its relationship with the previous sentence (*particularly, specifically*). See ▶Step 17 for more information about adverbs.

4. **Use a dummy auxiliary.**

   I do like your cooking – honestly!

   Historically – for example, when William Shakespeare was writing – the verb *do* was commonly used for emphasis as an **AUXILIARY VERB** in positive statements. Although this use, sometimes called the 'dummy auxiliary', is less common nowadays, it can still be very effective. It can also be used in the past: *She did arrive on time.*

5. **Use a short sentence.**

   She left yesterday.

   Short, simple sentences can often be very effective for communicating your idea emphatically. In writing, short sentences can be particularly effective at the beginning of a paragraph (to present a concise overview of the paragraph) or at the end of a paragraph (to provide a focused summary). A short sentence can also work well as the first or last sentence of a whole essay. However, be careful not to overuse short sentences; otherwise your writing may lack **COHERENCE**.

6. **Use the active voice.**

   The President made a mistake.

   Although the **PASSIVE VOICE** has an important function in English (▶Step 15), the **ACTIVE VOICE** is more commonly used. The active voice tends to be more emphatic because it says who is doing something, and so increases the strength of the sentence.

7. **Use different punctuation.**

   I think it's amazing!

   Using an **EXCLAMATION MARK** (▶Step 41) is a very effective way of adding emphasis to a **DECLARATIVE SENTENCE**. You should only do this very occasionally, however. Rewriting a sentence so that it is **INTERROGATIVE** and, if appropriate, adding a **QUESTION MARK** (▶Step 41), can also occasionally be a useful strategy.

8. **Use an *it* cleft sentence.**

   It is Alan who works hardest at school.

   A **CLEFT SENTENCE** uses a special construction to focus the reader or listener on specific information. One common cleft sentence construction is: *it* clause + **RELATIVE CLAUSE**. The structure of the *it* clause is: *it* + *be* form + phrase. Here, the *it* clause *It is Alan* is followed by the relative clause *who works hardest at school*.

9. **Use a *what* cleft sentence.**

   What we want is less homework.

   Another common cleft sentence construction is: *what* clause + *be* form + phrase. In the example here, the *what* clause is *What we want*, which is followed by the *be* form (*is*) and the phrase *less homework*. Often, an emotive verb is used in the construction, such as *dislike*, *enjoy*, *hate*, *like*, *love*, *need*, *prefer* or *want*. Remember that a **FULL STOP**, not a question mark, is needed when using this construction – even though the sentence begins with *what*.

10. **Start with a negative adverb.**

    Never have I seen such a brilliant film.

    Using a **NEGATIVE** adverb at the beginning of a sentence is a way of emphasizing a point very strongly. Use the construction: negative adverb + auxiliary/modal verb + subject + main verb + object.

Summary

1. Carefully choose the times when you use the techniques in this unit. If you overuse them, their effect and impact will be lost.
2. One key strategy for creating emphasis is to focus on the kind of information placed at the beginning of a sentence.
3. Other important strategies include choosing the correct verb form and using rhetorical techniques such as short sentences and triple structures.

D Activation

1. **Complete and comprehend.**
   Explain why using the following strategies can make your writing more emphatic.

Groups of three	
Dummy auxiliaries	
Short sentences	
Question marks and exclamation marks	

2. **Check your understanding.**
   Rewrite the following sentences using the indicated strategies from Part C.

   a. I admire Robert the most. (strategy 8)

   ____

   b. I enjoy going out to dinner with my friends most of all. (strategy 9)

   ____

   c. That's the best cake I've ever eaten. (strategy 7)

   ____

   d. My parents enjoyed going to London. (strategy 4)

   ____

3. **Create your own.**
   Choose four of the strategies listed in Part C and write your own sentences.

Which strategy?	Example sentence

How can I avoid making grammatical mistakes?

STEP 40

'Experience is the name everyone gives to their mistakes.'

Oscar Wilde (1854–1900)
Irish playwright and poet

A Reflection

The table below contains answers to questions about English. These topics have been covered earlier in the book. Write an appropriate question for each, using the information in ▶Step 35 to help you form the question, if needed.

Question	Answer
1. What is the normal word order of English?	subject-verb-object
2.	A subject and a verb
3.	The former is used when there is a shared understanding of what is being referred to, while the latter is used when this does not exist.
4.	The former make their past simple and past participle forms by adding ~*ed*; the latter must be learnt separately.

B Contextualization

What is wrong with each sentence? Correct any mistakes which you see.

1. The boy the ball kicked.
2. She's playing football every week.
3. Arrived home late last night.
4. She's coming at Saturday.
5. That's a same dog we saw in the park.
6. Let's meet at the café, which is nearest to the station.
7. I writed a letter to my nephew.
8. Three equipments in the gym were broken.
9. Take the desk out of my office and paint it.
10. Correctly she answered the question.

C Explanation

What are some of the most common grammatical mistakes in English?

Although it is difficult to generalize about the mistakes people make, there are particular areas that English learners often find hard. Ten common problems are discussed below.

1. **Placing words in the wrong order (▶Steps 4, 15)**

   The boy the ball kicked.

   In English, unlike some languages, **WORD ORDER** is important. The usual word order of English is **SUBJECT-VERB-OBJECT (SVO)**. The order can be reversed if the verb is in the **PASSIVE VOICE**.

   To avoid mistakes: know the word order differences between English and your language.

2. **Using the wrong verb form (▶Steps 13, 14)**

   She~~'s playing~~ (plays) football every week.

   When using verbs, remember that you must decide on their **TENSE** and **ASPECT**. There are a number of verb forms which are commonly confused; this is often the result of **MOTHER TONGUE INFLUENCE**. Two of the most commonly confused pairs of verb forms are the present simple and present continuous (*I play* and *I am playing*), and the past simple and present perfect (*I went* and *I have gone*).

   To avoid mistakes: for the present simple/present continuous, ask if what you are talking about happens regularly (= present simple) or if it is a temporary current event (= present continuous). For the past simple/present perfect, ask if what you are talking about has already finished (= past simple) or if it is still ongoing or might happen again (= present perfect).

3. **Writing incomplete sentences (▶Steps 28, 29)**

   I arrived home late last night.

   Every **SENTENCE** must contain a **SUBJECT** and a **VERB**.

   To avoid mistakes: when checking your writing, tick the subject and verb in each sentence to make sure you have not forgotten one or the other.

4. **Using the wrong preposition (▶Step 22)**

   She's coming ~~at~~ (on) Saturday.

   PREPOSITIONS are quite difficult to use. They are often forgotten or used incorrectly.

   To avoid mistakes: try searching online for verb-preposition and noun-preposition combinations. For example, *on Saturday* gets millions of hits if you type this combination into a search engine, whereas *at Saturday* and *in Saturday* both get very few.

5. **Using articles incorrectly (▶Steps 24, 25)**

   That's ~~a~~ (the) same dog we saw in the park.

   Since **ARTICLES** are not used in many languages, many learners of English find them difficult.

   To avoid mistakes: make sure you understand the uses of the **DEFINITE** and **INDEFINITE ARTICLES**. See ▶Step 25 for tips on avoiding the most common article mistakes.

6. **Mixing up defining and non-defining relative clauses (▶Step 28)**

no comma needed

Let's meet at the café, which is nearest to the station.

A **RELATIVE CLAUSE** uses a **RELATIVE PRONOUN** such as *who*, *whose*, *which* or *that* to provide more information about the noun phrase which comes before. There are two types of relative clause, namely **DEFINING** and **NON-DEFINING**.

To avoid mistakes: defining relative clauses contain essential information about the noun. Both *that* and *which* can be used, and no **COMMA** is required. Non-defining relative clauses contain additional information. They cannot use *that*, and require a comma.

7. **Confusing irregular and regular verbs (▶Step 12)**

wrote

I ~~writed~~ a letter to my nephew.

Although the majority of verbs in English are **REGULAR**, many of the most commonly used verbs are **IRREGULAR**.

To avoid mistakes: learn the irregular forms of commonly used verbs. Whilst you may know very common ones (*go-went-gone*), you may not be familiar with others (*grow-grew-grown*, *write-wrote-written*).

8. **Confusing countable and uncountable nouns (▶Step 8)**

Some equipment in the gym was broken.

~~Three equipments in the gym were broken.~~

English distinguishes between **COUNTABLE NOUNS**, which can have a number placed before them (*table*, *dog*), and **UNCOUNTABLE NOUNS**, which cannot (*air*, *water*). This distinction does not exist in many languages.

To avoid mistakes: learn which **COMMON NOUNS** in English are generally considered to be uncountable, which countable and which can be both.

9. **Being unclear about what a pronoun is referring to (▶Step 7)**

the desk

Take the desk out of my office and paint ~~it~~.

When there are many words between a noun and the **PRONOUN** which replaces it, the sentence may be ambiguous.

To avoid mistakes: check each pronoun, and make sure it is clear which word it refers to. If not, change the structure of the sentence, or use the original noun.

10. **Putting adverbs in the wrong place in a sentence (▶Step 19)**

correctly She answered the question.

ADVERBS should come either in initial, mid or end position according to their type and function in the sentence.

To avoid mistakes: study the table on page 80 to help you decide where to place an adverb.

Summary

1. It is useful to recognize common problem areas in English, and to identify strategies for dealing with them.
2. Some of these problems concern structure (word order, incomplete sentences).
3. Other problems concern specific word classes, such as verbs (confusing verb forms, regular/irregular verbs) and function words (prepositions, articles).

D Activation

1. Complete and comprehend.

Without looking at Part A, answer the following questions.

a. What is the normal word order of English?	
b. What are the two things that every sentence must contain?	
c. When are definite and indefinite articles used?	
d. What is the difference between regular and irregular verbs?	

2. Check your understanding.

Read the following passage. Correct any mistakes you find.

Sally lived in London since three years. His house is small flat above a train station. It is having five rooms. Two bedrooms, a lounge, a kitchen and a bathroom. There are a lot of furnitures in the rooms. Best thing about the house is the view at the window of London.

3. Create your own.

Write sentences which contain the following features.

Features to include	Example sentence
a. Contrast of the present simple with the present continuous	I usually play basketball on Fridays, but at the moment I am playing on Tuesdays.
b. The past form of *meet* and a non-defining relative clause	
c. A defining relative clause	
d. Correct placement of *yesterday* in a sentence using the past simple	

What is punctuation for?

'I have been immensely busy. I took out a comma … Then I put back the comma.'

Oscar Wilde (1854–1900)
Irish playwright and poet

A Reflection

The passage below has no punctuation or capitals. What effect does this have?

what is the united nations
the united nations un is an international organization which was founded in San Francisco in 1945 originally there were 51 member states now there are an incredible 193 theyre led by a secretary general and their main areas of responsibility are as follows law security economics human rights and political freedom in recent years they have also had to deal with the terrible spread of hivaids equality is at the centre of the uns constitution which says that it believes in the dignity of the human person and in the equal rights of men and women

B Contextualization

Now read the corrected passage. Highlight the capitals and the 12 types of punctuation mark. When are they used? Write the marks and their names in the table below.

What is the United Nations?
The United Nations (UN) is an international organization which was founded in San Francisco in 1945. Originally there were 51 member states; now there are an incredible 193! They're led by a Secretary-General, and their main areas of responsibility are as follows: law, security, economics, human rights and political freedom. In recent years, they have also had to deal with the terrible spread of HIV/AIDS. Equality is at the centre of the UN's constitution, which says that it believes 'in the dignity … of the human person, and in the equal rights of men and women'.

Marks the end of a sentence	full stop .	Provides a definition or extra information	
Shows the exact words that have been said or written		Shows that a sentence is a question	
Denotes missing information		Says something is surprising or interesting	
Indicates possession or missing letters		Presents a choice or alternative	
Divides a sentence into smaller units		Shows two clauses are closely related	
Joins two words/syllables together		Shows two sentence parts are connected	

C Explanation

What is the purpose of punctuation?

When we speak, we can add pauses or change the tone or volume of our voices to show that we are asking a question, to add emphasis or to indicate that we have finished making a point. To do the same in writing, **PUNCTUATION** is needed. Punctuation helps your reader understand you.

Marks the end of a **SENTENCE**	**FULL STOP** .	Provides a definition or extra information	**BRACKETS** ( )
Shows the exact words that have been said or written	**QUOTATION MARKS** ' ' and " "	Shows that a sentence is a question	**QUESTION MARK** ?
Denotes missing information	**ELLIPSIS** ...	Says something is surprising or interesting	**EXCLAMATION MARK** !
Indicates possession or missing letters	**APOSTROPHE** '	Presents a choice or alternative	**OBLIQUE** /
Divides a sentence into smaller units	**COMMA** ,	Shows two clauses are closely related	**SEMICOLON** ;
Joins two words or **SYLLABLES** together	**HYPHEN** -	Shows two sentence parts are connected	**COLON** :

Three key facts about each of these 12 punctuation marks are presented below.

1. **Quotation marks (' ' and " ") – show the exact words that have been said or written**
   - Choosing single (' ') or double (" ") quotation marks is generally a matter of style.
   - Quotation marks can be used around the title or name of something.
   - They can indicate that a particular word is controversial or debatable.
2. **Question mark (?) – shows that a sentence is a question**
   - Question marks should not be used for indirect questions.
   - They are sometimes (but not always) used for **RHETORICAL QUESTIONS**.
   - There should never be more than one at the end of a sentence.
3. **Apostrophe (') – indicates possession or missing letters**
   - Adding ~*'s* is the usual way of indicating possession in English.
   - **CONTRACTIONS** such as *isn't* are used in informal English. In formal English, use full forms.
   - Remember that ~*s* is used without an apostrophe to pluralize nouns.
4. **Comma (,) (▶Step 42) – divides a sentence into smaller units**
   - A comma in writing is similar to a pause in speaking.
   - Commas are commonly used to separate items in a list.
   - A comma cannot separate two **INDEPENDENT CLAUSES**. Use a full stop or semicolon instead.
5. **Exclamation mark (!) – says something is surprising or interesting**
   - Exclamation marks are not common in formal English.
   - Use them very sparingly unless the text is very informal, e.g., an email to a friend.
   - Never use more than one at the end of a sentence.
6. **Oblique (/) – presents a choice or alternative**

- Generally, there is no space before or after the oblique: *Dear Sir/Madam*.
- They are sometimes used in **ABBREVIATIONS**: *n/a* means *not applicable*.
- The oblique is also known as a **SLASH**.

7. **Full stop (.) – marks the end of a sentence**
   - When typing, one space should be left after a full stop.
   - They can be used after people's initials (*T.S. Eliot*) and in abbreviations (*Mon.*, *Tues.*).
   - They are also used in web addresses: *www.garneteducation.com*.
8. **Hyphen (-) (▶Step 44) – joins two words or syllables together**
   - The purpose of hyphens is to clarify meaning and avoid confusion.
   - They are sometimes used in noun and adjective phrases: *Secretary-General*.
   - They are used in written numbers between 21 (*twenty-one*) and 99 (*ninety-nine*).
9. **Ellipsis (…) – denotes missing information**
   - The ellipsis is used to show that some material has been left out of a quotation.
   - It can be used at the end of a sentence to imply that more could be said.
   - A space should be used before and after an ellipsis.
10. **Brackets (( )) – provide a definition or extra information**
    - Brackets are often used for definitions, particularly to give abbreviations.
    - They are used to give information or comments which are not essential to the meaning of the sentence: *Khalid (Ahmed's brother) was very angry.*
    - If there is a bracket at the end of the sentence, the final punctuation mark appears outside it, unless the whole sentence is in brackets.
11. **Semicolon (;) (▶Step 43) – shows two clauses are closely related**
    - Semicolons can be followed by a **LINKING WORD** showing the relationship between the clauses.
    - They can be used to separate items in a list when using commas would be confusing.
    - Semicolons are followed by lower-case (not capital) letters.
12. **Colon (:) (▶Step 43) – shows two sentence parts are connected**
    - Colons show relationships such as explanations, reasons and definitions.
    - Colons are also commonly used to indicate the start of a list or series.
    - Colons are followed by lower-case (not capital) letters.

When are capital letters used?

Capital letters (*ABC* …) are used in the following situations.

- When beginning sentences (***T**hey're led …*)
- For **PROPER NOUNS** (***U**nited **N**ations*)
- For most **ACRONYMS** and **INITIALISMS** (***HIV/AIDS***)
- In titles of authored works (***O**liver **T**wist*)

Summary
1. Punctuation is important because it gives shape and meaning to writing.
2. Full stops, question marks and exclamation marks show the end of a sentence.
3. Most punctuation marks can be used in a variety of ways.

D Activation

1. **Complete and comprehend.**

Read the passage below and complete the statements by saying why each piece of punctuation is used.

The history of Western[(a)] feminism can be divided into three well-known[(b)] 'waves'.[(c)] The first wave focused on *de jure* (official)[(d)] inequalities. The second wave, sometimes known as the women's[(e)] liberation movement, focused on legal and social equality for women. The third wave,[(f)] which began in the 1990s, challenges the dominance of middle-class/white[(g)] women in debate about feminism.

a. A capital letter is used *because Western is a proper noun.*

b. A hyphen is used ______

c. Quotation marks are used ______

d. Brackets are used ______

e. An apostrophe is used ______

f. A comma is used ______

g. An oblique is used ______

2. **Check your understanding.**

Each of the sentences below contains punctuation or capital letter mistakes. Write out the sentences correctly.

a. My mother, is a teacher

______

b. do you still speak to your ex-husband.

______

c. the british broadcasting corporation bbc is a large tv company in the uk.

______

d. She asked 'have you seen my fathers glasses'

______

3. **Create your own.**

The following passage has no punctuation or capitals. Correct it.

in 1893 new zealand became the first county to grant universal suffrage a vote for every citizen nine years later the same occurred in australia in the uk things took slightly longer a movement called the suffragettes led by emmeline pankhurst was founded in 1903 the suffragettes main demand was simple equal political rights this was finally achieved in 1928

When should I use commas?

STEP 42

'Another sport which wastes unlimited time is comma-hunting.'

Francis Cornford (1874–1943)
English classical scholar and humorist

A Reflection

What are the differences in meaning between the following pairs of sentences?

1. **a.** Let's eat Grandad. **b.** Let's eat, Grandad.
2. **a.** I like cooking my family and my dog. **b.** I like cooking, my family and my dog.

Now complete the following sentence in your own words.

Commas are important because ____

____

B Contextualization

Read this passage and match each comma use to its description in the table below.

Margaret Thatcher,[1] the first female Prime Minister of the United Kingdom, entered Parliament in 1959. She defeated Ted Heath,[2] who was her leader, in a party election in 1975. After defeating Heath,[3] she led her party to victory in the 1979 general election by 2,165,000[4] votes. Overall,[5] she won three general elections: in 1979,[6] 1983 and 1987. Therefore,[7] it can be said that she was one of the most successful British Prime Ministers,[8] but she still remains a controversial,[9] divisive figure today. As one famous historian argued,[10] 'You either loved her or hated her. There was no middle ground.'

When commas are used	Number
After a noun/noun phrase when using a non-defining relative clause	
When defining a noun/noun phrase	1
To separate elements in a series or list	
To separate adjectives when they come before a noun	
Before a coordinating conjunction which links two independent clauses	
After a dependent clause when it begins the sentence	
Between a reporting expression and direct speech	
To divide large numbers into thousands and millions	
After introductory phrases	
After linking words which connect two sentences	

C Explanation

What are commas for?

COMMAS are important because they can change or clarify meaning, as in the differences in meaning in the pairs of sentences in Part A. Let's look at example 2 in detail.

a. *I like cooking my family and my dog* is a combination of these two ideas: (i) I like cooking my family and (ii) I like cooking my dog.

b. *I like cooking, my family and my dog* is a combination of these three ideas: (i) I like cooking, (ii) I like my family and (iii) I like my dog.

Language learners often find commas difficult. This is because commas are either not used in their own language, or else are used in a different way. The rules for using commas in English can seem complicated. Indeed, **NATIVE SPEAKERS** of English often use commas incorrectly. The issue is complicated by the fact that usage of the comma in **BRITISH ENGLISH** (**BrE**) and **AMERICAN ENGLISH** (**AmE**) is different. However, by following a few key rules, your ability to use commas correctly will increase considerably. These rules, which apply to BrE, are presented below.

What are the most common uses of the comma in English?

1. **When defining a noun/noun phrase**

   Margaret Thatcher, the first female Prime Minister of the United Kingdom, entered Parliament in 1959.

   The normal structure of a **SENTENCE** in which you give a definition is as follows: **NOUN/NOUN PHRASE** + comma + definition + comma + **VERB PHRASE**.

2. **After a noun/noun phrase when using a non-defining relative clause**

   She defeated Ted Heath, who was her leader, in a party election in 1975.

   RELATIVE CLAUSES (▶Step 28) provide information about the noun or noun phrase which comes before. When this information is considered additional or non-essential, a comma is used before and after the relative clause. In the example, the information *who was her leader* is not essential to understanding the sentence – we would still understand the sentence without it. Therefore, commas are used.

3. **After a dependent clause when it begins the sentence**

   After defeating Heath, she led her party to victory …

   In many English sentences with an **INDEPENDENT** and a **DEPENDENT CLAUSE** (▶Step 28), the independent clause comes first. However, this order may be reversed. The writer could have said *She led her party to victory after defeating Heath*, but chose to invert the order to change the emphasis. When this happens, a comma must follow the dependent clause. Dependent clauses often begin with **CONJUNCTIONS**.

4. **To divide large numbers into thousands and millions**

   … by 2,165,000 votes.

   Generally, in numbers larger than 999, a comma is added after the number of thousands and, if applicable, after the number of millions. However, note that commas are **not** used in dates (*July 2013*, not *July 2,013*) or for a decimal point (£*1.45*, not £*1,45*; *3.14*, not *3,14*).

5. **After introductory phrases**

   Overall, she won three general elections: …

   Introductory phrases provide information which the reader needs to know before understanding the rest of the sentence. Sometimes an introductory phrase may be a one-word **ADVERB**; at other times it may be an **ADVERB PHRASE** or **PREPOSITIONAL PHRASE**.

6. **To separate elements in a series or list**
   ... in 1979, 1983 and 1987.
   When two elements are in a list, only *and* or *or* is needed to join them. For example: *Margaret Thatcher was re-elected in 1983* ***and*** *1987.* However, when there are three or more elements, the items in the list are separated by commas. Sometimes a comma may be used before the *and* or *or* (see Grammar box).

> **The Oxford comma**
>
> Some people prefer to put a comma before the *and* or *or* in all such lists. This is known as the 'Oxford' or 'serial' comma. It is commonly used in American English, but less so in British English. However, inserting this additional comma can help to clarify meaning where there is a change of idea or form in a list. For example: *Margaret Thatcher was controversial, divisive, and someone who provoked either love or hate in others.*

7. **After linking words which connect two sentences**
   She won three general elections: in 1979, 1983 and 1987. Therefore, it can be said that ...
   When two sentences are logically connected by a **LINKING WORD** such as an adverb or conjunction (▶Steps 17 and 21), a comma is used after the linking word.
8. **Before a coordinating conjunction which links two independent clauses**
   ... it can be said that she was one of the most successful British Prime Ministers, but she still remains a controversial, divisive figure today.
   When independent clauses are linked by a **COORDINATING CONJUNCTION** such as *and*, *but* or *yet*, a comma is used before the conjunction.
9. **To separate adjectives when they come before a noun**
   ... a controversial, divisive figure today.
   When more than one adjective is used, commas must be used to separate them.
10. **Between a reporting expression and direct speech**
   As one famous historian argued, 'You either ... no middle ground.'
   When a reporting verb such as *state* or *argue* precedes a quotation, a comma comes after the verb (before the **QUOTATION MARKS**). When the quotation comes first, the comma comes after the final quotation mark: '*... no middle ground*', *argued one famous historian.*

How can I avoid comma mistakes in English?

1. **Don't use a comma when a full stop or semicolon is needed.** Commas cannot be used between independent clauses unless a coordinating conjunction is used. If it is not appropriate to link the clauses using a conjunction, use a **FULL STOP** or a **SEMICOLON**.
2. **Don't use commas with all relative clauses.** Only use them with non-defining relative clauses; they are not needed with defining relative clauses (▶Step 28).
3. **Don't place a comma between a subject and a verb.** This is a common mistake when the subject is long: *The food I like most in the world, is chocolate* should read *The food I like most in the world is chocolate.*
4. **Don't use too many commas in one sentence.** Every time a comma is used, it makes the sentence more complicated. If too many commas are used in a sentence (three is usually enough), it is possible that the reader will not be able to understand what you are saying.

Summary
1. A comma's main job is to divide text into smaller units so that it can be understood more clearly.
2. If there is a pause in speaking, there is likely to be a comma in writing.
3. If there are more than three commas in a sentence, it may be difficult to understand.

D Activation

1. **Complete and comprehend.**

   The following passage has no commas. Insert them where you think they should be.

> Margaret Thatcher's first ministry which took place between 1979 and 1983 was very controversial. Three key events of this ministry were economic reforms the restriction of trade unions' power and going to war against Argentina. Interestingly many people think that Thatcher only won the 1983 general election because she won this war. However others argue that her economic reforms were necessary and this is what won her the election. Since she won the election so convincingly her decisions in her second ministry were even more radical.

2. **Check your understanding.**

   Next to each comma above, write a number 1–10 according to the rules presented in Part C.
   Note: you will not need all the numbers.

3. **Create your own.**

   a. **Using the following notes, taken from a lecture entitled 'Margaret Thatcher's economic policies', write a paragraph summarizing the topic.**

> Margaret Thatcher's economic policies
>
> In general – MT's economic policy was about freedom
>
> Believed in monetarism = an economic system where the government has little influence
>
> 3 benefits of monetarism: low inflation and greater efficiency and less borrowing
>
> BUT – caused unemployment to rise above 3 million. MT believed she was still right – even though lots of people lost their jobs

   b. **Check your use of commas in your paragraph. As in Exercise 2, write a number 1–10 according to the use of each comma.**

When should I use colons and semicolons?

STEP 43

'Here is a lesson in creative writing. First rule: do not use semicolons ... All they do is show you've been to college.'

Kurt Vonnegut (1922–2007)
American novelist

A Reflection

Decide whether the following apply to colons (:), semicolons (;), both or neither.

Statement	Colon	Semicolon	Neither
Can be followed by an independent clause			
Can be followed by a dependent clause			
Should appear at least once in every paragraph			
Can be useful for dividing up long sentences			
Are followed by a lower-case letter			

B Contextualization

These sentences show the different uses of the semicolon. Match them in the table.

1. At the shop, I bought a red, juicy apple; a long, green cucumber; and a soft, blue towel.
2. I spoke to my Mum on the phone yesterday; she likes me to call once a week.
3. We wanted to go to the cinema; however, we didn't have enough money.

When semicolons are used	Sentence
To show a close relationship between independent clauses which are not linked by a coordinating conjunction	
To show a close relationship between independent clauses which are linked by a linking word	
To separate items in a list which already contains punctuation	

These sentences show the different uses of the colon. Match them in the table.

1. At the cinema, I saw the 20:00 showing of *Legally Blonde 2: Red, White and Blonde*.
2. There are three things you mustn't forget: your tickets, passport and money.
3. I love books: I particularly like the Harry Potter novels.

When colons are used	Sentence
To introduce a list or series	
Between figures in times and between titles and subtitles	
To explain, summarize or define	

C Explanation

Why are colons and semicolons important?

FULL STOPS and **COMMAS** are the most commonly used pieces of **PUNCTUATION** in English. However, **COLONS** and **SEMICOLONS** are also relatively common, especially in **FORMAL ENGLISH**. Knowing how to use them properly can improve the quality and accuracy of your writing. **NATIVE** and non-native speakers of English frequently make mistakes in using them; however, by following a few key rules, you can quickly gain a good understanding of how they should be used.

> **Note**
> It is sometimes thought that a semicolon is more like a comma than a full stop, when actually it is the other way around.

What are the most common uses of the semicolon in English?

1. **To separate items in a list which already contains punctuation**
   At the shop, I bought a red, juicy apple; a long, green cucumber; and a soft, blue towel.
   Semicolons can be used in lists where commas are also used, in order to show which items are being separated. In the example sentence, imagine that the semicolons were replaced by commas. It would be much harder to understand.

2. **To show a close relationship between independent clauses which are not linked by a coordinating conjunction**
   I spoke to my Mum on the phone yesterday; she likes me to call once a week.
   If you link two **INDEPENDENT CLAUSES** with a semicolon, you are showing that they are of equal weight and importance. Using a semicolon instead of a full stop shows that the sentences have a close relationship.

> **Note**
> Do not use a semicolon if you are joining the **CLAUSES** with a **COORDINATING CONJUNCTION** such as *for*, *and*, *nor*, *but*, *or*, *yet* or *so*.

3. **To show a close relationship between independent clauses which are linked by a linking word**
   We wanted to go to the cinema; however, we didn't have enough money.
   Where sentences have a close relationship and are linked by a **LINKING WORD** such as *otherwise*, *therefore*, *however*, *consequently* or *similarly*, a semicolon can be used to separate them rather than a full stop.

> **Am I using the semicolon correctly?**
> Ask yourself, 'Could I use a full stop instead?' or 'Could I join the sentences with *and*?' If the answer is yes, then you are using it correctly.

What are the most common uses of the colon in English?

1. **Between figures in times and between titles and subtitles**

   At the cinema, I saw the 20:00 showing of Legally Blonde 2: Red, White and Blonde.

   When referring to times of day, the colon divides hours and minutes; in titles, it separates the main title from the subtitle.

2. **To introduce a list or series**

   There are three things you mustn't forget: your tickets, passport and money.

   The information before a colon should always form an independent clause. In less formal writing, this rule can be relaxed. When writing lists, the information which follows can sometimes use bullet points.

3. **To explain, summarize or define**

   I love books: I particularly like the Harry Potter novels.

   A colon can be used where the second clause explains, summarizes or defines the first clause, and where there is no coordinating conjunction.

Use of colons in academic English

In addition, colons have two specific uses in academic English.

1. For in-text references: *According to Smith (2010: 208) ...*
2. To introduce long quotations: *Smith (2010) argues that: ' ... '.* On these occasions, the quotation should begin on the next line if it is particularly long.

What are the similarities between colons and semicolons?

1. **Both colons and semicolons must be followed by a lower-case letter.**

   This rule applies unless the word which follows is *I*, a **PROPER NOUN** (*Sam*, *London*, etc.) or where the colon signifies that the following text is a subheading or topic (as in the title of the film above).

2. **Both colons and semicolons can be useful for dividing up longer sentences.**

   Don't overuse them, however. There is no specific number of times that you should use a colon or semicolon per paragraph. Sometimes, using shorter sentences is better. Instead of using a colon, it is sometimes better to use a comma followed by a phrase like *such as, namely, that is* or *for example.*

   *There are three things you mustn't forget, **namely** your tickets, passport and money.*

   However, you should remember that only an independent clause can follow a semicolon; either an independent or a dependent clause can follow a colon.

Summary

1. Although colons and semicolons are not as common as full stops or commas, they can help to make your writing clearer and more accurate.
2. Semicolons show close relationships between sentences, and can be useful in separating items in lists.
3. Colons are useful for explaining, summarizing, defining and putting items in a series or list.

D Activation

1. **Complete and comprehend.**

   A student has taken notes about how colons and semicolons are used. Complete the gaps in their notes with appropriate words.

Usage

They are both followed by ___________-case letters.

Function

Semicolons show ___________ relationships between sentences.

Colons can be used to introduce many different types of statement or text, e.g.,

____

Grammar

Semicolons must be followed by an ______________________ clause.

Colons can be followed by a _______________________________________.

In essays

The colon has two specific uses in academic writing: for ___________ references and when introducing ___________ quotations.

2. **Check your understanding.**

   Is the colon or semicolon used correctly? Make any changes necessary.

   a. I'll meet you at 12;30.

   b. A wolf can be defined as follows: the largest member of the dog family, which lives in the wild.

   c. New York is the largest city in the USA; but it is not the capital city.

   d. I have lots of pets; two dogs, three cats and a snake!

3. **Create your own.**

   Rewrite the following sentences using a colon or semicolon as appropriate.

   a. I have four exams tomorrow. The exams are Maths, English, History and Geography.

   ____

   b. I have to leave now. Otherwise, I will miss my train.

   ____

   c. My diet isn't going very well. For breakfast, I ate eggs, bacon and chips. For lunch, I had a hamburger and chips. For dinner, I ate another hamburger, more chips and some ice cream.

   ____

   ____

   ____

When should I use hyphens?

'There is no room in this country for hyphenated Americanism.'

Theodore Roosevelt (1858–1919)
26th President of the United States

A Reflection

How does the hyphen change the meaning in each pair of sentences?

1. **a.** I'm afraid you'll have to resign. **b.** I'm afraid you'll have to re-sign.
2. **a.** There are 250 year-old trees. **b.** There are 250-year-old trees.
3. **a.** I resent the suggested revisions to Chapter 2. **b.** I re-sent the suggested revisions to Chapter 2.

B Contextualization

Which of the following are correct? Tick those you think are acceptable in English, and put a cross next to those which are not. In some cases, both options might be possible.

a. Richard Nixon is an <u>ex-president ✓ / expresident ✗</u> of the USA.

b. During his time as president, Bill Clinton sent only two <u>e-mails / emails</u>.

c. George W. Bush is a former president who is very <u>well-known / well known</u>.

d. <u>Three-quarters / Three quarters</u> of the 44 US presidents have been millionaires.

e. Abraham Lincoln has been voted America's <u>best-ever / best ever</u> president.

C Explanation

Why are hyphens used in English?

The main use of **HYPHENS** in English is to join words together. Unfortunately, there is not always universal agreement on when hyphens should be used. Many dictionaries and style manuals disagree on certain points. Some words occur in both hyphenated and non-hyphenated forms, for example, *email/e-mail*, *postmortem/post-mortem* and *voiceover/voice-over*.

In general, the use of the hyphen in written English is decreasing. Words which have a hyphen tend to lose it over time. However, there are still many occasions when hyphens should be used. The general rules are outlined below.

When should hyphens be used?

The main circumstances in which hyphens should be used in English are as follows.

1. **To form adjective phrases**
   ADJECTIVE PHRASE structures take many forms, including **NOUN + ADJECTIVE** (*world-famous*), **NOUN + PARTICIPLE** (*custom-built*) and **ADJECTIVE + PARTICIPLE** (*good-looking*). See ▶Step 20 for more examples of adjective phrases.

> **Note**
> Many adjective phrases become unhyphenated if they come after the noun.
> - *Brian is a very* ***well-known*** *bank robber.*
> - *Brian is a bank robber who is very* ***well known****.*

2. **To form compound nouns**
   Hyphenating **COMPOUND NOUNS** used to be common, but is increasingly regarded as unnecessary. Many are commonly written as one word (*website*) or two unhyphenated words (*car park*). Many compound nouns can be written in more than one form (*counterargument/counter-argument, chatroom/chat room/chat-room*). Not all forms are always possible, however, so check a dictionary if you are unsure. When more than one form is possible, make sure you are consistent in your usage. There are a few compound nouns which should always be hyphenated; these include *mother-in-law* and *father-in-law*, and phrases involving single-letter components like *X-ray* and *T-shirt*.

3. **To form numbers between 21 and 99** (*forty-three*, *two hundred and eighty-six*) and **fractions** (*one-third*, *three-quarters*)

4. **With prefixes in particular situations**
   - A hyphen is used when a **PREFIX** comes before a proper noun (*pre-Socratic*, *un-American*). Note that the proper noun should be capitalized, but the prefix should not (unless it is at the beginning of a sentence).
   - A hyphen is often used when a prefix ends with the same vowel which starts the following word (*re-enter*, *semi-industrialized*). In cases involving the prefix *co~*, often both hyphenated and unhyphenated versions are possible (*co-operative/cooperative*, *co-ordinate/coordinate*).
   - A hyphen is used with the following prefixes: *ex~*, *self~*, *all~* (*ex-president*, *self-control*, *all-powerful*).
   - A hyphen is used where the prefix comes before a date (*post-1945*).

5. **To clarify the structure of the sentence**
For example, the sentence *There are 250 year old trees* is ambiguous without hyphens: it is unclear whether there are (i) 250 trees which are one year old or (ii) an unspecified number of trees which are 250 years old. Using hyphens makes clear which meaning is intended: (i) *There are 250 year-old trees* or (ii) *There are 250-year-old trees*.

6. **To distinguish two different words which have the same spelling**
For example, *resign* means to leave a job, but *re-sign* means to sign again. There are many examples of this use of the hyphen with the prefix *re~*: *resent/re-sent*, *reform/re-form*, *recover/re-cover*, *represent/re-present*.

Hyphens vs dashes

Although they look similar, the hyphen (-) and the DASH (–) are different pieces of punctuation with completely distinct uses. However, they are often confused, and many people use them interchangeably. The main uses of the dash are:

- to show a break in thought: *This is what I – and many others – think.*
- to indicate a range of values: *ages 20–40, 1939–1945, 10:00–11:30*
- to show a binary relationship: *Paris–Dakar rally, father–daughter relationship*

Also beware the underscore (_), which is most commonly found in web and email addresses, where spaces are not allowed.

When should hyphens not be used?

Although you may think it necessary, do **not** use hyphens in the following situations.

- For the majority of prefixes: *proactive*, *disinterested*, *prefix*, *postmodern*, *microchip*, *reassess*, *biannual*, *megabyte*
- After ADVERBS ending in *~ly*: *totally brilliant idea*, *recently discovered coin*
- After a letter or numeral which is the second part of a description or name: *number one priority*, *class A drug*, *Type 2 diabetes*
- For VERB and PREPOSITION combinations: *look into*, *break down*, *go in*
- Where the adjective in a compound is in its COMPARATIVE or SUPERLATIVE form: *the less popular president*, *the most likely reason*
- In chemical formulas: *carbon monoxide*, *potassium permanganate*

Summary

1. The main purpose of hyphens is to clarify meaning. When they can do this, use them; if they do not, don't.
2. Hyphens are most commonly used to form compound words.
3. Hyphens are used with prefixes in a few special situations, but otherwise are not.

D Activation

1. **Complete and comprehend.**

   In which of the following situations would you use a hyphen?

   ✓ = always needed ✗ = never needed ? = depends on the situation

Situation	✓	✗	?
a. To distinguish between homonyms			
b. To form compound nouns			
c. After prefixes			
d. For verb and preposition combinations			
a. To form adjective phrases where the adjective is a superlative			

2. **Check your understanding.**

   Read through the following sentences, and in each case decide whether the hyphenated or non-hyphenated version of the word or phrase is correct.

   a. We were late because our car broke-down / broke down.

   b. The basic rate of income-tax / income tax in the UK is 20 per cent.

   c. Do you have any pre-existing / preexisting medical conditions?

   d. The chair needs to be re-covered / recovered.

   e. She is the best-known / best known singer in my country.

   f. The nearest town is about ten kilo-metres / kilometres away.

3. **Create your own.**

   Rewrite the following sentences using hyphenated phrases.

   a. When I was in India, I went to a wedding which lasted for three days.

   When I was in India, I went to a three-day wedding.

   b. George W. Bush, who used to be president, was at the event.

   ____

   c. Seventy-five per cent of the class passed the exam.

   ____

   d. She is the sister of my wife.

   ____

   e. I don't know much about history before 1900.

   ____

How can I improve my spelling?

STEP 45

'It is a poor mind which can't think of at least two ways to spell any word.'

Andrew Jackson (1767–1845)
7th President of the United States

A Reflection

For each word below, identify the correct plural form. Sometimes more than one form is correct.

1.	**activity**	**a.** activitys	**b.** activities	**c.** activityes
2.	**bus**	**a.** buses	**b.** busses	**c.** buss
3.	**child**	**a.** childs	**b.** children	**c.** childes
4.	**formula**	**a.** formula	**b.** formulae	**c.** formulas
5.	**half**	**a.** halfs	**b.** halfes	**c.** halves
6.	**hero**	**a.** heroes	**b.** heros	**c.** heroies

B Contextualization

The passage below contains some of the most frequent spelling mistakes made in English. There are 16 in total. Underline all those you can find.

In resent years, Brittish goverments have becum more interested in the enviroment. Untill the mid-1990s, there atitude was that it wasn't realy impotent – that it wasn't neccessary too do much about it. Therefor, many governments just ignored the issue. Buisnesses tended to have the same attitude, wich meant that basicly only charities and pressure groups were doing anything.

Write the correct spellings of the words you underlined above.

Misspelt word	Correct spelling	Misspelt word	Correct spelling
resent	recent		

UNIT I Punctuation and spelling

Step 45

C Explanation

Why is spelling important?

Spelling is important not only because incorrect spelling can result in misunderstanding, but also because correct spelling gives a positive impression to the person you are writing to. Since most writing is now done electronically, and spellcheckers are extremely common, there is no excuse for many of the spelling mistakes which are made.

What words are commonly misspelt?

The following list includes some of the most frequently misspelt words in English. Words spelt incorrectly in the passage from Part B appear in green.

accommodate, achieve, acknowledge, across, actually, analyze, apparently, appearance, appreciate, argument, attitude, basically, become, beginning, belief, business, coming, completely, criticism, definitely, dependent, difference, discipline, discussed, eighth, eliminate, embarrass, environment, especially, excellent, existence, experience, extremely, familiar, finally, foreign, forty, forward, further, government, guarantee, immediately, important, independent, intelligence, knowledge, laboratory, library, meant, millennium, necessary, neither, nuclear, occasionally, occurrence, parallel, persuade, physically, possession, possible, practical, psychology, really, receipt, recent, recommend, reference, remember, repetition, rhythm, ridiculous, scene, schedule, separate, surprise, their, therefore, thoroughly, truly, until, usually, which

What are some of the common mistakes?

Learners often find spelling difficult because English contains words from many different languages. Below is a list of some of the main problems, along with useful rules and examples.

1. **Not writing silent letters**
   Some words have 'silent' letters which appear in writing, but are not spoken. They can be found at the start of a word (*knight* is pronounced in the same way as *night*), in the middle (in *government*, the first *n* is often silent), or at the end (in *engine*, the final *e* is not pronounced).
2. **Writing long vowel sounds incorrectly**
   You may know how to say a word, but not how to write it. The long /ee/ and /oo/ sounds are particularly difficult as they can be written in many different ways.
   /**ee**/ sound: *l**ea**p, p**eo**ple, br**ie**f, m**e**, s**ei**ze, k**ey**, sk**i***
   /**oo**/ sound: *tr**u**th, gr**ou**p, fr**ui**t, sh**oe**, bl**ew**, bl**ue**, thr**ough***
3. **Using the wrong version of a heterograph**
   HETEROGRAPHS are words which have the same sound, but which are spelt differently, such as *there*, *their* and *they're*. Knowing which version to use can be difficult. A list of commonly used heterographs appears below.

accept/except	*buy/by/bye*	*meat/meet*	*their/there/they're*
allowed/aloud	*flour/flower*	*one/won*	*to/too*
ante~/anti~	*for/four*	*peace/piece*	*wait/weight*
are/our	*hear/here*	*right/write*	*way/weigh*
ate/eight	*hole/whole*	*sea/see*	*weak/week*
band/banned	*hour/our*	*some/sum*	*wear/where*
bean/been	*know/no*	*son/sun*	
brake/break	*mail/male*	*stationary/stationery*	

4. **Mixing up double and single consonants**
One of the most difficult aspects of English spelling is knowing when, and when not, to double a **CONSONANT LETTER** in a word. *Attitude,* for example, has a double *t*, while *British* only has one. Unfortunately, there is no reliable rule to predict when a consonant should or should not be doubled. Common problem letters include *bb* (*hobby/liberal*), *dd* (*hidden/medical*), *ll* (*follow/politics*), *mm* (*summary/limit*) and *rr* (*carry/very*).

5. **Using the wrong plural form of a word**
Notwithstanding irregular **PLURALS** (see Grammar box), the vast majority of English nouns are pluralized by adding ~*s* to the end of the word. Some exceptions are as follows.
   - For nouns ending in an ~*o* which is preceded by a consonant (*hero*, *potato*), the plural is made by adding ~*es* (*heroes*, *potatoes*).
   - For **NOUNS** ending in an /f/ sound (*half*, *life*), the plural is made by changing *f* to *v* and adding ~*es* (*halves*, *lives*).
   - For nouns ending in ~*y* (*sky*, *lady*), the plural is made by changing it to ~*ies* (*skies*, *ladies*).
   - For nouns ending in a **SIBILANT** sound (/s/, /z/, /ʃ/, /ʒ/, /tʃ/ or /dʒ/) such as *kiss* or *wash*, add ~*es* (*kisses*, *washes*).

Irregular plurals

Singular	Plural
aircraft	aircraft
analysis	analyses
child	children
crisis	crises
datum	data
foot	feet
man	men
phenomenon	phenomena
species	species
thesis	theses
tooth	teeth
woman	women

6. **Mixing different types of English together**
There are many different versions of English. The two most commonly used are **BRITISH ENGLISH** (**BrE**) and **AMERICAN ENGLISH** (**AmE**). This book uses British English. Whichever type of English you are using, you should be sure not to mix up features from different types. As well as sometimes using completely different words for the same thing, BrE and AmE often use different spellings of the same word. The four main ways in which spellings may differ are outlined in the table below. The common examples are given in BrE.

~our **(BrE) vs** ***~or*** **(AmE)** **BrE:** Red is my favourite colour. **AmE:** Red is my favorite color. **Common examples:** *armour, behaviour, endeavour, flavour, harbour, honour, humour, labour, neighbour, odour, rumour, splendour*	***~ise*** **(BrE) vs** ***~ize*** **(AmE)** **BrE:** I work for a small organisation. **AmE:** I work for a small organization. **Common examples:** *authorise, characterise, civilise, colonise, criticise, emphasise, equalise, mobilise, realise, recognise, symbolise*
~re **(BrE) vs** ***~er*** **(AmE)** **BrE:** I live in the city centre. **AmE:** I live in the city center. **Common examples:** *calibre, centimetre, kilometre, litre, metre, theatre*	***~ogue*** **(BrE) vs** ***~og*** **(AmE)** **BrE:** Did you see their new catalogue? **AmE:** Did you see their new catalog? **Common examples:** *analogue, dialogue, epilogue, monologue, prologue*

Note: this book uses ~*ize* word endings. This is because some BrE publishers prefer ~*ize* to ~*ise*. This means that either ending can be used in BrE, as long as it is used consistently. In AmE, however, only ~*ize* can be used.

Summary
1. Spelling in English can be difficult because words are not always spelt the way they sound.
2. To pluralize a noun, you usually add ~*s*, although there are certain minor irregularities.
3. The most common differences between BrE and AmE are *ise/ize*, *or/our*, *re/er* and *ogue/og*.

D Activation

1. **Complete and comprehend.**

   Look at the passage below. Match each misspelt word a–g with one of the numbered types of mistakes (1–6) from Part C. Then write the word correctly.

The **goverment**[a] should **comitt**[b] to more **meddical**[c] expenditure. In particular, I think they should make spending on health for **childs**[d] a priority. Although they have **past**[e] many **peaces**[f] of legislation, this specific issue has been ignored by all **partys**.[g]

Word	Mistake type	Correction
a.	1	government
b.		
c.		
d.		
e.		
f.		
g.		

2. **Check your understanding.**

   a. **In each pair of words, tick the version which is spelt correctly.**

1.	which ☐	wich ☐		7.	height ☐	hight ☐
2.	paralell ☐	parallel ☐		8.	coming ☐	cuming ☐
3.	diffrence ☐	difference ☐		9.	suprise ☐	surprise ☐
4.	finally ☐	finaly ☐		10.	practicle ☐	practical ☐
5.	experience ☐	expearience ☐		11.	intrest ☐	interest ☐
6.	probly ☐	probably ☐		12.	meant ☐	ment ☐

   b. **Write BrE (British English) or AmE (American English) next to the following words.**

neighbour	BrE	catalogue		emphasise		liter	
honor		criticize		theatre		monolog	

3. **Create your own.**

   Write the word for each definition. Pay careful attention to the spelling in each case. The first few letters are provided in each case.

Place to read books (*lib…*)	library	One more than 39 (*f…*)	
A thousand years (*mil…*)		From another country (*for…*)	
Male child (*s…*)		Seven days (*w…*)	
Belonging to them (*th…*)		Talk about (*dis…*)	
Divided, apart from (*sep…*)		Obtain, get (*ach…*)	

How can prefixes and suffixes help your academic English?

'Every new beginning comes from some other beginning's end.'

attributed to **Seneca (4 BCE–65 CE)**
Roman philosopher, statesman and playwright

A Reflection

Prefixes and suffixes are groups of letters at the start and end of words which can help you to understand them. Match these prefixes and suffixes to their meanings.

Prefix	Meaning
ante~	against
anti~	distant
omni~	before
re~	half
semi~	again
tele~	all

Suffix	Meaning
~arch(y)	love or addiction
~fusion	like/love
~holic	adjective
~ive	mixture
~phile	place
~where	rule, leadership

Note down any other prefixes and suffixes you know, and their meanings.

Prefixes	Suffixes
bio~ (life)	

B Contextualization

Look at the highlighted words in the following sentences. Based on your understanding of the prefixes and suffixes above, write a brief definition of what each word means.

Sentence	Definition of word
1. Have you read her autobiography?	
2. I need to revise my essay. It's not finished.	
3. He recovered after his blood transfusion.	
4. My brother is a workaholic.	
5. My boss is omnipotent. Whatever he says happens.	

C Explanation

How can understanding prefixes and suffixes help me?

Having a good understanding of **PREFIXES** and **SUFFIXES** can be a very good 'shortcut' to developing your academic English. Many academic words contain prefixes and suffixes. (Academic words often come originally from the Greek and Latin languages.) Two ways in which understanding prefixes and suffixes can improve your academic English are as follows.

1. If you come across an unfamiliar word in reading or listening, you may be able to guess its meaning based on your understanding of its prefix or suffix.
2. You can develop your vocabulary very quickly if you know how to modify words using prefixes and suffixes, e.g., *mon**arch**/mon**archy**/monarch**ist**/monarch**ical***.

What suffixes are commonly used in academic English?

One of the main functions of suffixes is to create different **WORD CLASSES**. As discussed in ▶Step 2, the suffix is often a good indicator of the word class.

- **NOUNS**: *~er* (*manager*), *~(t/s)ion* (*invention/decision*), *~(a/e)nce* (*brilliance/consequence*)
- **VERBS**: *~ate* (*indicate*), *~en* (*lengthen*), *~fy* (*fortify*), *~ise/~ize* (*criticise/criticize*)
- **ADJECTIVES**: *~al* (*vital*), *~ent* (*convenient*), *~ful* (*cheerful*), *~ous* (*jealous*)
- **ADVERBS**: *~ly* (*slowly*)

A list of commonly used suffixes in academic English appears in the table below.

Suffix (meaning)	Example word (definition)
~arch(y) (rule, leadership)	*monarchy* (rule of a king/queen)
~cracy (government)	*democracy* (rule of the people)
~dom/~ful/~hood (state or status)	*freedom* (state of being free)
~fusion (mixture)	*confusion* (lack of clarity)
~graph(y) (writing, study)	*geography* (study of the earth)
~holic (love or addiction)	*alcoholic* (addicted to alcohol)
~illion (large numbers)	*million* (1,000,000)
~ism (ideology or religion)	*Marxism* (ideology based on the ideas of Karl Marx)
~less (lacking)	*useless* (without a use)
~let (diminutive form)	*droplet* (small drop)
~meter/~metry (measurement)	*thermometer* (device for measuring heat)
~logy (study)	*zoology* (study of animals)
~phile (like, love)	*Anglophile* (lover of England)
~phobia (fear)	*claustrophobia* (fear of small spaces)
~tain (hold, keep)	*contain* (keep with, keep together)
~th (ordinal number)	*tenth* (10th)
~wards (direction)	*forwards* (the direction in front of you)
~where (place)	*nowhere* (no place)

What prefixes are commonly used in academic English?

Two of the functions which prefixes have are (i) making a word **NEGATIVE** (▶Step 34), as in *dis~* (*disappear*), *il~* (*illegal*), *im~* (*immature*), *in~* (*inability*), *ir~* (*irresponsible*) and *un~* (*undo*); and (ii) referring to numbers, as in *mono~* (= 1, *monograph*), *bi~* (= 2, *bicycle*), *tri~* (= 3, *triangle*), *dec~* (= 10, *decade*), *cent~* (= 100, *century*), *kilo~* (= 1,000, *kilometre*) and *mega~* (=1,000,000, *megawatt*).

A list of commonly used prefixes in academic English appears in the table below.

Prefix (meaning)	Example word (definition)
a~/ab~/an~ (not, without)	*absence* (not being somewhere)
alt~ (another, different)	*alternative* (different option)
ante~/pre~ (before)	*antenatal/prenatal* (before birth)
anti~ (against)	*antisocial* (not sociable)
bio~ (life)	*biology* (study of living things)
co~/con~ (with, together)	*convention* (meeting of a group of people)
demo~ (people)	*democracy* (rule of the people)
ex~ (former, previous)	*ex-president* (former president)
extra~/hyper~ (beyond or more than usual)	*extraordinary* (interesting, amazing)
inter~ (between)	*international* (between countries)
intra~ (within)	*intravenous* (inside a vein)
maxi~ (big, most)	*maximum* (largest value)
mega~ (large, huge)	*megalomania* (obsession with exercising power)
mini~ (small, least)	*minimum* (smallest value)
multi~ (many, several)	*multilingual* (speaking several languages)
omni~ (all)	*omnipotent* (all powerful)
out~ (beyond)	*outperform* (perform better than)
post~ (after)	*posthumous* (after death)
pro~ (in favour of)	*propose* (suggest something)
re~ (again)	*rewrite* (write again)
semi~ (half)	*semicircle* (half a circle)
sub~ (under, beneath)	*submarine* (underwater boat)
super~ (above, beyond)	*superabundance* (more than enough)
tele~ (distant)	*telephone* (device for talking from long distance)
trans~ (across)	*transfer* (send across)
uni~ (one, the same)	*uniform* (identical clothing worn by a group)

Summary

1. Prefixes and suffixes are commonly found in academic words.
2. Knowing prefixes and suffixes can help you to predict the meaning of unfamiliar words.
3. Suffixes can be useful for changing the class of a word.

D Activation

1. **Complete and comprehend.**

   Summarize the reasons why understanding prefixes and suffixes will improve your academic English.

2. **Check your understanding.**

   a. **What do the following prefixes and suffixes refer to?**

Prefix	Meaning
co~/con~	
intra~	
pro~	
uni~	

Suffix	Meaning
~dom	
~holic	
~illion	
~phobia	

   b. **Write definitions of the following words, based on your understanding of the prefixes and suffixes.**

autocracy	
megalopolis	
retain	

   c. **Use a dictionary to find three words containing each prefix.**

Prefix	Example words
anti~	anticlockwise,
demo~	
inter~	
post~	
sub~	

3. **Create your own.**

   Choose five words from the table above and write a sentence using each one.

a.	
b.	
c.	
d.	
e.	

How should I use nouns in academic English?

STEP 47

'One of the glories of English simplicity is the possibility of using the same word as noun and verb.'

Edward Sapir (1884–1939)
American linguist and anthropologist

A Reflection

Fifteen of the following nouns are more commonly used in academic English than in general English. Which are they?

advantage analogy balloon chair circumstance data evaluation function hotel hypothesis impact issue kilogram likelihood method perspective reason relevance system window

B Contextualization

Read the pairs of sentences below. In each case, decide which sentence sounds more academic.

1. **a.** One of the department's priorities was to create a new computer system.
   b. The creation of a new computer system was a priority for the department.
2. **a.** The development of the algorithm by the university has led to an explanation of the phenomenon by its creators.
   b. The university has been developing an algorithm which has led to its creators being able to explain the phenomenon.
3. **a.** The question of whether the hypothesis is relevant is important.
   b. The relevance of the hypothesis is an important question.
4. **a.** The circumstances were not known, which meant a lot of confusion was created.
   b. The unknown circumstances created considerable confusion.
5. **a.** The census data showed that the number of English speakers has increased.
   b. The data which came from the census showed that the number of people who speak English has increased.

C Explanation

What is nominalization and why is it important in academic writing?

NOMINALIZATION is the name of the process which turns grammatical **PHRASES** of various types into **NOUN PHRASES.** Learning to use nominalization will help you to eliminate **REDUNDANT LANGUAGE**, making your writing more focused. Most often, the process transforms verb phrases into noun phrases.

The sentences from Part B which are more academic contain nominalized phrases (in bold).

1.b. **The creation of a new computer system** was **a priority for the department**.
2.a. **The development of the algorithm by the university** has led to **an explanation of the phenomenon by its creators**.
3.b. **The relevance of the hypothesis** is **an important question**.
4.b. **The unknown circumstances** created **considerable confusion**.
5.a. **The census data** showed that **the number of English speakers** has increased.

What should I know about plurals in academic English?

As outlined in ▶Step 45, there are a number of nouns in English whose plurals are **IRREGULAR.** Many such nouns are more common in academic English than in general English. Some examples are given in the table below. Note that some nouns have two acceptable plural forms: one irregular and one regular.

Singular	Plural	Singular	Plural
analysis	analyses	formula	formulae/formulas
appendix	appendices/appendixes	hypothesis	hypotheses
basis	bases	index	indices/indexes
crisis	crises	medium	media/mediums
criterion	criteria	parenthesis	parentheses
curriculum	curricula/curriculums	phenomenon	phenomena
datum	data	species	species
diagnosis	diagnoses	stimulus	stimuli
focus	foci/focuses	thesis	theses

What are binomials?

BINOMIALS are pairs of nouns which commonly occur together in the format *X and Y.* Whilst they do appear in general English (*fish and chips*, *salt and pepper*), they are far more frequent in academic English. Frequently used binomials include: *aims and objectives, education and training, goods and services, growth and development, health and safety, input and output, justice and equality, knowledge and skills, law and order, males and females, materials and methods, policy and resources, research and development, strengths and weaknesses, theory and practice, trial and error.*

How do I know whether the nouns I am using are academic?

One problem which many learners face is not knowing which words are appropriate to use in written English. For academic writing, it can be especially difficult to know which words to use, since students are expected to be able to use vocabulary which does not usually appear in other written texts. The simplest way of identifying whether or not a particular noun is used in academic writing is to identify the frequency with which it is used in the texts you are reading. If the books and articles which you are using for your research use the word frequently, it is likely to be an appropriate academic word for your subject, and you should use it where relevant. A more sophisticated way, however, is to use a word list.

How can I use word lists to develop my vocabulary?

One extremely useful way of checking how frequently a particular word is used is to use a word list. Probably the most accurate and most commonly used academic word list is the **ACADEMIC WORD LIST (AWL)**, which can be accessed at www.victoria.ac.nz/lals/resources/academic word list. The AWL is a group of nearly 1,000 words which are commonly used in academic writing. The list includes words which are used in a wide range of academic texts, but which do not appear frequently in general English. Using the nouns on this list will enable you to sound more professional in your essays and presentations. Learning how to use the words on this list can be a good way of improving your academic language.

The overwhelming majority of the words on the AWL, such as *category*, *factor* and *outcome*, can be used in many different disciplines. Some, however, are used more specifically in particular subject areas: *deviate* is mostly used in mathematics and scientific disciplines, for example.

Substituting academic nouns for general nouns

1. Go through your essays and underline the nouns which you think are not academic. The person marking your essay may have already identified some of these words, or your tutor may be able to advise you. For example, you might have written the following sentence: *There is a match between people born in London and people who have positive views about immigration.* You might identify that *match* is not an academic noun.
2. Look up these words in a thesaurus, and identify synonyms which you think are more academic. A good online thesaurus is www.thesaurus.com. You might find, for example, that *correlation* is a synonym for *match*.
3. If you are unfamiliar with the words you find, it is important to look them up in a concordance, which will give you examples of words used in context. A good online academic concordance is the.sketchengine.co.uk. For example, if you did not know exactly how to use *correlation*, you could find hundreds of examples of this word in use in academic essays.

Summary

1. Nouns are very common in academic English. Nominalization is the name of the process which maximizes the quantity of noun phrases used in a text.
2. Some common academic nouns have irregular plurals.
3. The AWL identifies nouns which are frequently used in academic English, such as *analysis*, *medium* and *perspective*.

D Activation

1. **Complete and comprehend.**

   Write a brief summary of nominalization and how it can improve your academic English.

2. **Check your understanding.**

   a. **Complete each sentence with an appropriate noun from the box.**

parallels	consequence	organizations	aim	classifications	experiments

   1. The ____________________ of this paper is to argue that globalization is good.
   2. Several ____________________ failed to yield the expected results.
   3. A number of ____________________ can be drawn between the two examples.
   4. Several ____________________ have been involved in the research process.

   b. **Complete each sentence using an appropriate plural form from page 192.**

   1. Please refer to the ____________________ at the back of the book to see the data in more detail.
   2. There are several ____________________ which you must fulfil to get a good mark.
   3. You should put non-essential information in ____________________.
   4. I work in several different ____________________, including photography and painting.

3. **Create your own.**

   Choose five nouns from the box below. Look up their meanings in a dictionary, and then write a sentence including each word.

analogy	consensus	doctrine	exclusion	implication
intervention	procedure	restriction	tendency	validity

   a. ____________________

   b. ____________________

   c. ____________________

   d. ____________________

   e. ____________________

How should I use verbs in academic English?

'Misquotation is the pride and privilege of the learned.'

Hesketh Pearson (1887–1964)
English actor and biographer

A Reflection

Fifteen of the following verbs appear more commonly in academic English than in general English. Which are they?

buy cite consider do emphasize evaluate help
investigate induce isolate locate operate perform
precede quote reinforce say speak transform yield

B Contextualization

The following passage is the introduction to an essay entitled 'To what extent is the world now globalized?' Read the passage and highlight all the verb forms you can find.

It is often argued that globalization is an unstoppable force which it is impossible to restrict. Indeed, this point was made by the former Secretary-General of the United Nations, Kofi Annan. A lot of research indicates that globalization now affects even very remote parts of the world. Smith (2012), for example, claims that the most undeveloped parts of the world have closer relationships with the developed world than ever before. This hypothesis is supported by statistical data from many countries. This paper argues that there are now very few places in the world where globalization has not penetrated. Firstly, I demonstrate the degree of integration throughout the world. Secondly, I say why this is a good thing. Thirdly, I consider relevant counterarguments.

Which verb form and voice (active or passive) are used here more commonly than in general English?

Verb form: ______________________________

Voice: ______________________________

C Explanation

Which verb forms are most common in academic English?

The present simple is by far the most commonly used verb form in academic English. If you are unsure which verb form to use, the present simple should be your default option. Specific occasions when the present simple can be used are as follows.

1. **Making general statements and giving general facts**
   ... globalization is ... impossible to restrict.
2. **Reporting what other people have said**
   Smith (2012), for example, claims that ...
3. **Giving evidence to support your position**
   A lot of research indicates that globalization ...
4. **Presenting a THESIS STATEMENT**
   This paper argues that ...
5. **Presenting an outline**
   Firstly, I demonstrate ... I say ... I consider ...

Which voice is most common in academic English?

As outlined in ▶Step 15, the **ACTIVE VOICE** is far more common than the **PASSIVE VOICE** in general English. This is true in academic English, too. However, the frequency of the passive is higher in academic than in general English. There are three main reasons for this.

1. **In academic English, long noun phrases are often used (▶Steps 9 and 10).**
   When a long **NOUN PHRASE** is used as the subject of a sentence in the active voice, the large group of words at the beginning of the sentence can make it unbalanced and difficult to understand. Using the passive voice means that the noun phrase can appear later in the sentence.
   Indeed, this point was made by the former Secretary-General of the United Nations, Kofi Annan.
   not: *The former Secretary-General of the United Nations, Kofi Annan, made this point.*
2. **In academic English, the *what* is often more important than the *who*.**
   In the active voice, the *who* is often in the subject position and the *what* in the object position. Using the passive voice means this emphasis can be reversed.
   This hypothesis is supported by statistical data from many countries.
   not: *Statistical data from many countries support this hypothesis.*
3. **In academic English, it is sometimes not important to state who is responsible for a particular action.**
   It is often argued that globalization is an unstoppable force ...
   not: *Many argue that globalization is an unstoppable force ...*

What reporting verbs are commonly used in academic English?

There is an important group of verbs which are commonly used in academic English called **REPORTING VERBS**. The function of these verbs is to talk about what others have written or said about a subject. Commonly used reporting verbs include *state*, *argue*, *demonstrate* and *suggest*. There are three reasons for using such verbs in academic English.

1. They show that you have read, analyzed and synthesized a range of sources, indicating you have a broad understanding of the subject area.
2. They show that you have considered your sources critically, i.e., in an analytical way, rather than just descriptively.
3. They show that you are academically responsible: that you are not plagiarizing, and that you are trying to represent others' views fairly.

It is important to note that reporting verbs can show weak, neutral or strong positions. Examples can be seen in the table below. The verbs are given in the 3rd person singular form of the present simple, the most common form they take in academic writing.

Function	Weaker position	Neutral position	Stronger position
Agreement	*acknowledges, concedes*	*accepts, adds, agrees*	*affirms, supports*
Disagreement	*doubts, questions*	*disagrees*	*challenges, dismisses, refutes, rejects*
Opinion	*conjectures, expresses, proposes*	*believes, claims, comments, concludes, contends, surmises*	*asserts, advocates, emphasizes, establishes, insists, postulates, proves*
Suggestion	*alleges, implies*	*proposes*	*endorses, recommends*

Other verbs used to report what others have said or written include: *alerts, analyzes, asks, attributes, calculates, clarifies, compares, deduces, debates, defines, describes, discusses, explains, identifies, interprets, lists, mentions, orders, predicts, quotes, reports, stresses.*

Reporting verbs to avoid

- *Say, mention, come up with, reckon, guess* and *feel* are all considered informal and should be avoided.
- *Point out* is sometimes used, but it is a phrasal verb, and many people would consider it informal.
- *Write* is vague and unsophisticated; many alternatives exist.
- *State* is a perfectly acceptable reporting verb, but is often overused. Variety is important, as well as accuracy.

Summary

1. The present simple is by far the most commonly used verb form in academic English. If you are unsure which verb form to use, the present simple is the best option.
2. The passive voice is more common in academic English than in general English.
3. Learn verbs from the AWL to sound more academic.

D Activation

1. **Complete and comprehend.**

   The present simple is the most commonly used verb form in academic English. Identify the five main uses given in Part C.

   a. ______________________________

   b. ______________________________

   c. ______________________________

   d. ______________________________

   e. ______________________________

2. **Check your understanding.**

   a. **Rewrite the sentences with the verbs in the passive.**

      1. Many scholars have already discussed these arguments.

         ____

      2. Many famous politicians from all over the world quote Shakespeare.

         ____

      3. We assume that each of the data sets has been properly analyzed.

         ____

   b. **Complete each sentence with the appropriate form of a verb from the box.**

submit	examine	differ	analyze

      1. The data ______________ thoroughly.
      2. This paper ______________ the link between the First and Second World Wars.
      3. My essay ______________. I cannot change it now!
      4. The argument in this paper ______________ from that of Smith (2012) in several key respects.

3. **Create your own.**

   Look back at the five main uses of the present simple identified in Exercise 1. Write an example sentence for each.

   a. ______________________________

   b. ______________________________

   c. ______________________________

   d. ______________________________

   e. ______________________________

What other constructions are commonly used in academic English?

'What is written without effort is in general read without pleasure.'

Samuel Johnson (1709–1784)
English poet, critic and lexicographer

A Reflection

Match the academic phrases 1–5 with their grammatical constructions a–e.

1. Given that …	**a.** *It* + present perfect passive + *that* relative clause
2. It is likely that …	**b.** *It* + modal verb + passive infinitive + relative clause
3. As a result of …	**c.** *It is* + adjective + *that* relative clause / infinitive
4. It has been found that …	**d.** Preposition (+ article) + noun + *of*
5. It can be seen that …	**e.** Past participle + *that* relative clause

B Contextualization

Read the academic passage below. Find a further example of each of the five grammatical constructions listed above.

It has been suggested that climate change is the biggest issue facing the world. Certainly, it is clear that the relationship between people and their environment is delicate. In terms of evidence which demonstrates that people are responsible for climate change, scientists talk about melting glaciers and deforestation. It could be argued that too much damage has already been done. However, provided that governments work quickly, permanent damage to the environment can still be avoided.

Structure	Example
a. *It* + present perfect passive + *that* relative clause	It has been suggested that …
b. *It* + modal verb + passive infinitive + relative clause	
c. *It is* + adjective + *that* relative clause / infinitive	
d. Preposition (+ article) + noun + *of*	
e. Past participle + *that* relative clause	

C Explanation

Why is it important to think of language as phrases and not just individual words?

Hopefully, by this stage, you have realized that to use grammar well, you need to think at more than just the word level. This is particularly true in academic English, where there are many special **PHRASES** which are commonly used. Knowing how these phrases are constructed means that you will know which words to change in order to create new phrases.

What are ten common grammatical constructions used in academic English?

It is important to emphasize that good academic grammar does not have to be complicated. In fact, it is often simple and easy to understand. A good way to ensure that your academic grammar is both accurate and appropriate to the context is to use the constructions identified below. To gain a better understanding of how each of the example phrases is used, search for them online (e.g., on Google Scholar) and look at them in context. Ten common constructions are given below, along with two or three example usages in each case.

1. **Article + noun + preposition**

   Note: make these phrases more complex by adding **ADJECTIVES** before the noun.

   - **The key reason for** the high failure rate was that people did not revise.
   - **The number of** participants in the survey was extremely high.
   - **One use of** the equation is as follows.

   Similar phrases include *the role of*, *the end/beginning of*, *the relationship between* and *the results of*.

2. ***it* + past simple/present perfect passive + *that* relative clause**

   - **It has been suggested that** climate change is the biggest issue facing the world.
   - **It has been found that** people with good English skills get paid more.
   - **It has been seen that** an increasing number of people have smartphones.

3. ***it* + modal verb + passive infinitive + *that* relative clause**

   This kind of construction is commonly used for **HEDGING**.

   - **It could be argued that** too much damage has already been done.
   - **It might be suggested that** there are better ways to approach this problem.
   - **It can be seen that** millions of people still suffer from this disease.

4. ***it is* + adjective + *that* relative clause**

   - **... it is clear that** the relationship between people and their environment is delicate.
   - **It is possible that** the methodology was incorrect.

5. ***~ing* form + preposition**

   - **Turning to** the issue of economic liberalization, we can see three main trends.
   - **Focusing on** the suggestions made by the committee, the important points are the following.

6. ***~ing* form + noun**

- **Considering the response** by the government, the present policy is unlikely to change.
- **Accepting this conclusion** is impossible.

7. **Preposition (+ article) + noun + *of***

- **In terms of** evidence which demonstrates that people are responsible for climate change …
- **As a result of** these changes, improvements will follow.
- **In the context of** sub-Saharan Africa, this was significant.

Other such phrases include *on the basis of, at the beginning/end of* and *in the case of.*

8. **Preposition (+ article) + noun + other preposition**

Whilst this kind of phrase most commonly ends with *of* (see 7), other prepositions are also possible.

- **In order to** develop, you need to do more training.
- The two groups were similar **with respect to** number, age and sex.
- There are many criticisms to be made **in relation to** this presentation.

9. **Past participle + *that* relative clause**

- … **provided that** governments work quickly, permanent damage to the environment can still be avoided.
- **Given that** the results were disappointing, the experiment was repeated.
- **Granted that** this has never been done before, we still judge the risk to be minimal.

10. **Miscellaneous lexical bundles**

- **One of the most important** reasons for this is …
- **Part/Some/Most of the** data could not be used.
- **There is a** solution, but I cannot identify it.

How can I use the internet to check whether my academic phrases are commonly used?

When you write a multi-word phrase, you may not be confident that it really exists. And if you get just one small part of a phrase wrong, it may not make sense to your reader. In order to check whether your phrase really does exist, you could type it into a search engine in quotation marks and see how many hits it receives. The higher the number of hits, the more likely it is to be a real phrase. Equally, if the search engine returns only a few hundred hits, you can conclude that the phrase is probably not a common English phrase.

Summary

1. By thinking about academic phrases as 'chunks' rather than isolated words, you are less likely to make mistakes.
2. Learn the key constructions and substitute words within them to make more phrases.
3. Check your phrases online to see how many other people have used them, and in what context.

D Activation

1. Complete and comprehend.

Write down some phrases which have the following structures.

Article + noun + preposition	**~*ing* form + preposition**
~*ing* form + noun	**Miscellaneous lexical bundles**

2. Check your understanding.

Complete each sentence with an appropriate phrase from the box.

it is possible that	given that	on the basis of	the results

a. She got the job ______________________ her experience.

b. ______________________ the findings by Smith (2012) are inaccurate.

c. ______________________ this is not his area of expertise, it is surprising that he did not consult with anyone about his methodology.

d. I would be interested to see ______________________ this study.

3. Create your own.

Choose five phrases from Part C which you are unfamiliar with and look them up in order to gain a better understanding of how they are used. Then write five sentences, showing each phrase being used in context.

a.	
b.	
c.	
d.	
e.	

What are the key points about grammar to remember?

STEP 50

'Go on till you come to the end; then stop.'

Lewis Carroll (1832–1898)
English writer and mathematician

A Reflection

Which of the following statements about using grammar are true and which are false? If you do not understand key words, look them up in the *Glossary* at the back of the book.

Statement	True	False
There are some differences between academic grammar and the grammar of general English.		
Your mother tongue has no influence on the way you use grammar.		
Functional words show the relationships between content words such as nouns and verbs.		
You should try to identify the specific areas in which you have grammatical problems, and try to improve them.		
Native speakers never make mistakes in their grammar.		

B Contextualization

Complete the gaps in the sentences below with appropriate words from the box. You will not need to use every word.

active	clauses	conjunctions	content	negative
object	passive	phrases	punctuation	questions
sentences	structure	subject	verb	

1. The normal word order of English is ______________-______________-______________.
2. There are two voices in English: the ______________ and the ______________.
3. Words can be combined to form ______________, which in turn can be combined to make ___________, which in turn can be combined to make ______________.
4. Sentences can be joined together using ______________.
5. Prepositions and articles are examples of ______________ words, while nouns and verbs are examples of ______________ words.

C Explanation

An A–Z guide to grammar

The following list is an A–Z of key points about grammar raised in this book. Where relevant, references are given to steps where these points are discussed in more detail.

Academic grammar can be different to the grammar of general English
For example, **NOUNS** and **NOUN PHRASES** are more frequent in academic English. Whilst the **PRESENT SIMPLE** is quite commonly used in general English, it is extremely common in academic English (▶Steps 46–49).

Building blocks fit together to make sentences
One rule to remember is: words make **PHRASES**, phrases make **CLAUSES**, and clauses make **SENTENCES** (▶Steps 26–29).

Confidence – practise to develop it
The best way to develop the confidence to use grammar effectively is to use it regularly.

Determiners are sometimes forgotten about, but they are very important
At least one **DETERMINER**, such as an **ARTICLE**, **QUANTIFIER**, **DEMONSTRATIVE** or **POSSESSIVE**, appears in almost every English sentence. Despite their importance in clarifying meaning, and their frequency in English, they are a commonly misunderstood part of speech (▶Step 23).

Ensure you are clear about the differences between formal and informal grammar
Formal and informal grammar use different **GENRES** (▶Step 5).

Function: always know what you are trying to say
Before you know what kind of grammar to use, you need to know what you are trying to say. The grammatical choices you make should be directly influenced by the substance and tone of what you want to convey.

Grammar should be appropriate to the context
Grammar is not something abstract – it is an integral part of communication. When making choices about grammar, think about the effect on your reader or listener.

High-frequency grammar is a good place to focus your attention
To build your confidence, and to be more effective in using grammar, it makes sense to focus on grammatical structures which are used very frequently, e.g., commonly used **VERB FORMS**.

Identify the areas where you have problems and try to improve
You probably know (or at least suspect) the grammatical areas in which you are weak. Instead of ignoring them, try to do something about it!

Join clauses and sentences together with conjunctions
Using **SIGNPOSTING LANGUAGE** and **LINKING WORDS** can improve the **COHERENCE** and **COHESION** of your speaking and writing (▶Step 21).

Keep a record of grammatical mistakes you regularly make
If you do this, you will know the areas you need to work on.

Learn about punctuation to ensure that your writing is clear
Punctuation has an important role to play in shaping your writing (▶Steps 41–45).

Mistakes are natural – try not to worry about them
When you learnt your native language as a child, you made many mistakes. To develop the range and accuracy of your grammar, you should try to speak and write as much as possible.

No!
Negative words tend to be very short, and when reading they may sometimes be missed. However, they are important because they completely change the meaning of a sentence (▶Step 34).

Only use emphatic grammar if you really want to emphasize something
Many grammatical mistakes arise from trying to be too complicated (▶Step 39).

Possibility and probability – know what you think
Consider whether you need to make your statement stronger (using an **INTENSIFIER**) or weaker (using **HEDGING LANGUAGE**) (▶Step 31).

Questions, questions ...
There are many different ways of asking questions in English. It is important to know them, and when it is possible to use each of them (▶Steps 26–29).

Remember that native speakers of English make mistakes too
Don't worry if you sometimes make grammatical mistakes. Whilst you should try to ensure your grammar is as accurate as possible, the most important thing is to be understood.

Structure words and content words are the two categories of word class
STRUCTURE WORDS (prepositions, determiners, pronouns and conjunctions) show the relationships between **CONTENT WORDS** (nouns, verbs, adjectives and adverbs) (▶Step 2).

Think of words in groups, not individually
Your grammar is likely to be more accurate and idiomatic if you think about it in terms of whole phrases, where possible.

Use the appropriate sentence type for the situation
There are four sentence types in English: **DECLARATIVE** (the most common), **IMPERATIVE**, **INTERROGATIVE** and **EXCLAMATIVE**. Choose the type which is appropriate for your purpose (▶Step 29).

Voice can be active or passive
There are two voices in English: **ACTIVE** and **PASSIVE**. The active is more common than the passive; the passive is used more in academic writing than in general English (▶Step 15).

Word order is a problem for many learners of English
The normal **WORD ORDER** in English is **SUBJECT-VERB-OBJECT**. The majority of sentences should follow this general structure (▶Step 4).

'X-rated' grammar – avoid!
Do not use complicated grammatical forms which you think sound good, but which you do not really understand. The most important thing is for your spoken and written English to be clear.

Your native language can cause problems
As such, ensure you try to identify the kinds of mistakes you commonly make, and make a conscious effort to avoid them (▶Step 4).

Zzzzzzzzz ...
At times, grammar may seem boring and unnecessary. However, if you want to become a skilled user of English, it is a necessary tool!

Summary
1. Although grammar is important, it does not need to be perfect for you to be understood.
2. It is important that you know what areas of grammar you find difficult, and where you need to improve.
3. The more you practise, the more you will improve!

D Activation

1. **Complete and comprehend.**
   What does each group of terms have in common?

a. Declarative, imperative, interrogative, exclamative	
b. Words, phrases, clauses	
c. Articles, demonstratives, quantifiers, possessives	

2. **Check your understanding.**
   Answer the questions in your own words.

a. How can understanding your own language better help your English?	
b. Why should you try to think in groups of words, rather than thinking of them individually?	
c. Why should you avoid unnecessarily complicated grammar?	
d. Why is it ok to make mistakes in your grammar?	

3. **Create your own.**
   Write down five ways in which you can continue to improve your grammar.

a.	
b.	
c.	
d.	
e.	

Answers

Step 1

1. Complete and comprehend.
Students' own answers.

2. Check your understanding.
a. 5 **b.** 1 **c.** 2 **d.** 3 **e.** 4

3. Create your own.
b. Full stops are needed at the end of a sentence. This is important.
c. The use of positive forms makes your English clearer.
d. It is confusing to use a long noun phrase at the start of a sentence.
e. Do not use informal grammar in written English.

Step 2

1. Complete and comprehend.
a.
See Part C.
b.
1. adjective **2.** preposition **3.** conjunction **4.** pronoun **5.** adverb **6.** verb

2. Check your understanding.

Word	Class(es)
computer	noun
justify	verb
fasten	verb
fast	adjective, adverb

Word	Class(es)
development	noun
around	adverb, preposition, adjective
while	noun, conjunction
some	adjective, pronoun

3. Create your own.
a. compute **b.** colourful **c.** cleaner **d.** speciality, specialize **e.** refusal **f.** miserable
g. obviously **h.** clearly

Step 3

1. Complete and comprehend.
a. 4 **b.** 5 **c.** 1 **d.** 2 **e.** 3

2. Check your understanding.
a. 4 **b.** 5 **c.** 1 **d.** 2 **e.** 3

3. Create your own.
Example answers:
a. Could you answer the phone, as it's ringing?
b. Answer your phone. It's ringing!
c. She answered her phone as soon as it rang.

Step 4

1. Complete and comprehend.

- **a.** subject-verb-object, passive
- **b.** *~s*, *~ed*
- **c.** irregular, *be/have/do/say/make/go/take/come/see/get*
- **d.** five, *eat*, *eats*, *ate*, *eaten*, *eating*

2. Check your understanding.

- **b.** Misused article – *I went to London last year.*
- **c.** Treating an irregular verb like a regular verb – *He fell over in the street.*
- **d.** Inappropriate question form – *Do you like playing football?*
- **e.** Preposition used incorrectly – *I am helping my mother.*

3. Create your own.

Students' own answers.

Step 5

1. Complete and comprehend.

See Part C.

2. Check your understanding.

- **b.** informal – spoken
- **c.** formal – written
- **d.** formal – spoken

3. Create your own.

- **b.** She will definitely like it.
- **c.** Hi, this is what I think about what you said.
- **d.** I'm going to look at Europe in my talk today.

Step 6

1. Complete and comprehend.

- **a.** False. Nouns are content words and an open class.
- **b.** True.
- **c.** False. They can have many senses.
- **d.** True.
- **e.** False. They have a capital letter at the beginning of a sentence, but generally not otherwise. Proper nouns are always capitalized.

2. Check your understanding.

- **a.** Possible answers: *children* (more than one child), *childhood* (the state of being a child), *childminder* (a person whose job is to look after children).
- **b.** Possible answers: group, scenery, part of a tennis match.
- **c.** *modesty*, *patience*, *formality*, *carelessness*
- **d.** Possible answers: *time*, *room*, *noise*. See ▶Step 8.

3. Create your own.
- **b.** The rich are getting richer.
- **c.** I spoke to the receptionist.
- **d.** He had a serious illness.

Step 7

1. Complete and comprehend.

a.

See Part C.

b.

Subject pronoun	Object pronoun	Possessive pronoun	Reflexive pronoun
I	me	mine	myself
you	you	yours	yourself, yourselves
he	him	his	himself
she	her	hers	herself
it	it	its	itself
we	us	ours	ourselves
they	them	theirs	themselves

2. Check your understanding.

a. it **b.** she **c.** him **d.** mine **e.** ourselves

3. Create your own.

Example answer:

The World Cup is a football tournament **which** is played every four years. **It** was first played in 1930. Brazil are the most successful side, having won **it** five times. Italy have won **it** four times. The fact **they** have won nine times in total is amazing, since other countries have only won **it** 11 times in total.

Step 8

1. Complete and comprehend.
- **a.** In many languages, these nouns would be countable, but not in English.
- **b.** These are all nouns which can be used in a countable or uncountable way.
- **c.** *Coffee* was used to show how sometimes countable phrases are left out by native speakers.

2. Check your understanding.

I like **many** different foods from all over the world, although I prefer the food of **some** countries more than others. In particular, I like Italian food, especially pasta. There are two **types of** pasta which I really love: spaghetti and fusilli. When I don't have **lots of** work to do, I like to cook, although my wife thinks I use too much salt – but I only put in **two or three teaspoons of** it. That's **not much**.

3. Create your own.

Example answers:

a.

1. How much equipment is in your gym?

2. Could you give me some paper, please?

b.

1. She drank five glasses of water.

2. How many litres of air can you hold in your lungs?

Step 9

1. Complete and comprehend.

See Part C.

2. Check your understanding.

b. past participle + gerund + noun

c. present participle + adjective + noun

d. possessive noun + present participle + noun

e. possessive phrase + adverb + past participle + noun

3. Create your own.

a happy married couple
a beautiful gold clock
a bicycle's back wheel
a badly injured football player

Step 10

1. Complete and comprehend.

a. *Which/that* are used to refer to **things**. ***That*** is more common than ***which***.

b. *Where*, *when* and *why* can be used in relative clauses. They refer respectively to **places**, **times** and **reasons**.

c. When using an infinitive after a noun, it may be in the active or **passive** voice.

d. If your noun phrases are too **long**, they will be difficult to follow and understand. Make them **complex**, but not complicated.

2. Check your understanding.

a.

1. in the corner

2. different

3. of the cinema

4. whose books are on the table

5. to help me learn English

6. written by my father

b.

1. noun + prepositional phrase

2. noun + adjective

3. noun + *of* + noun

4. noun + relative clause

5. noun + infinitive

6. noun + past participle

3. Create your own.
Students' own answers.

Step 11

1. Complete and comprehend.

a.

1. past, present, future

2. continuous, simple, perfect, perfect continuous

b.

Base form	Present simple 3rd person singular	Past simple	Past participle	Present participle
call	calls	called	called	calling
give	gives	gave	given	giving
want	wants	wanted	wanted	wanting
use	uses	used	used	using
try	tries	tried	tried	trying
tell	tells	told	told	telling

2. Check your understanding.

Sentence	Type of mistake
He ~~think~~ **thinks** about football all the time.	Lack of agreement – missing 3rd person *~s*
You ~~were~~ **will be** travelling all day tomorrow, so go to bed now.	Wrong tense used – future rather than past needed
I ~~am being~~ **am** forty years old.	Wrong aspect used – simple rather than continuous needed

3. Create your own.
Example answers:
Positive: She is going later today.
Negative: She is not going until tomorrow.
Question: Is she going later?
Negative question: Why is she not going until tomorrow?

Step 12

1. Complete and comprehend.
See Part C and the *Glossary* at the back of the book.

2. Check your understanding.

a.

Verb	Regular	Irregular	Transitive	Intransitive
eat		✔	✔	✔
go		✔		✔
look	✔			✔
run		✔	✔	✔
die	✔			✔

b.

My friend Alan **has been learning** English for five years. Although he **likes** learning English, he **prefers** watching TV. He **(definitely) doesn't work / isn't working** hard enough. As a result, I think he **may fail / will fail** his exams next year.

3. Create your own.

Example answers:

b. She can come later.
c. They have been coming here for many years.
d. I dislike people telling me what to do.
e. I dreamt about chocolate last night.

Step 13

1. Complete and comprehend.

See Part C and the *Glossary* at the back of the book.

2. Check your understanding.

b. past perfect **c.** future continuous **d.** present perfect continuous **e.** future perfect

3. Create your own.

Students' own answers.

Step 14

1. Complete and comprehend.

See Part C.

2. Check your understanding.

a. The first sentence talks about a complete action: Sue lived in London in the past, but she does not live there any more – she lives somewhere else. In the second sentence, the action is incomplete: Sue began living in London in the past, and she still lives there now.
b. The first sentence is talking generally about a future event; the second sentence is making a prediction that before a certain point in the future, they will have arrived.
c. In the first sentence, the two events occurred at the same time; in the second sentence, the studying took place before the move.

3. **Create your own.**
   a. am travelling (present continuous)
   b. will be finished (future continuous)
   c. was sitting (past continuous), jumped (past simple)
   d. leaves (present simple), will have got back (future perfect) / will get back (future simple)

Step 15

1. **Complete and comprehend.**
   See Part C.

2. **Check your understanding.**
   a. passive **b.** active **c.** passive **d.** passive **e.** passive

3. **Create your own.**
   Example sentences:
   a. Picasso **was born** in 1881.
   b. Cubism **was invented** by Picasso.
   c. He **was married** twice.
   d. Much of his early life **was spent** in Paris.
   e. His paintings **are found** in many galleries around the world.

Step 16

1. **Complete and comprehend.**
   a. nouns and pronouns **b.** never **c.** comparative **d.** *large*

2. **Check your understanding.**
   a.
   Nouns: *central, daily, skilful, sunny*
   Verbs: *comfortable, creative, expectant, permitted/permissible, urgent*
   b.
   ~al relating to
   ~esque like, similar to
   ~ful full of
   ~ish like
   ~less without

3. **Create your own.**
   Students' own answers.

Step 17

1. **Complete and comprehend.**
   a. all of the above **b.** generally **c.** important

2. **Check your understanding.**
   a.
   2. I strongly agree with you about this issue.
   3. The cost was about $100.
   4. You have to apply independently.

b.
2. surprisingly **3.** clearly/definitely **4.** recently

3. Create your own.
Students' own answers.

Step 18

1. Complete and comprehend.
See table on page 76.

2. Check your understanding.
a. False **b.** True **c.** True **d.** False

3. Create your own.
Example answers:
b. The United States of America is richer than India.
c. London is the largest city in the United Kingdom.
d. My best friend is cleverer than me.
e. Football is the most popular sport in the world.

Step 19

1. Complete and comprehend.
Initial position: *ideally, consequently, similarly*
Mid position: *seldom, definitely, obviously*
End position: *lazily, weekly, inside, tonight, backwards*

2. Check your understanding.
a. **Luckily**, we had enough money to get a taxi.
b. We are getting a new carpet **upstairs**.
c. I am **probably** going to the party tonight.
d. They telephoned me **yesterday**.
e. I **rarely** visit them anymore.

3. Create your own.
Students' own answers.

Step 20

1. Complete and comprehend.
a. The difference between gradeable and ungradeable adjectives is **that the latter cannot be preceded by words like *very* or *quite***.
b. A nominal adjective is **an adjective which can be used to talk about a whole class or group of people**.
c. Hyphens should be used in adjective phrases when **the two components cannot be separated**.

2. Check your understanding.
a. He's a ~~very~~ unique singer.
b. It was ~~completely~~ boiling!

c. There are ~~much~~ **many** reasons for this.
d. (No correction needed.)
e. That book was ~~frightened~~ **frightening** – terrifying, in fact.

3. Create your own.
a.
2. I think the rich should pay more in taxes.
3. The British like to watch football.
4. The government should provide more support to the blind and the deaf.
b.
Students' own answers.

Step 21

1. Complete and comprehend.
See Part C.

2. Check your understanding.
The Chinese language has the most native speakers in the world, **although** English has the most total speakers (c. 1.5 billion). **For this reason**, English is the common international language of business. Several other languages, **such as** French and Japanese, **also** have more than 100 million speakers. **Whereas** the former is spoken by many people as a second language, the overwhelming majority (99 per cent) speak the latter as a first language.

3. Create your own.
Example answer:
Walt Disney is famous for making cartoons **such as** *Dumbo*, *Snow White* and *The Jungle Book*. **As well as** winning 22 Oscars for his films, he **also** won four honorary Oscars. He created many famous characters, **such as** Donald Duck, Goofy and Mickey Mouse. **Although** he was not an actor, he provided the first voice for Mickey Mouse. **With regards to** his non-TV/film interests, he opened Disneyland theme park in California in 1955. **Subsequently**, Disney World was opened in Florida in 1971. Walt Disney died in 1966, aged 65, **due to** lung cancer. **In conclusion**, he had an enormous influence on **both** media **and** leisure.

Step 22

1. Complete and comprehend.
a. The three main categories of prepositions are **place** and **position** (e.g., *at*, *under*), **direction** and **movement** (e.g., *across*, *towards*) and **time** (e.g., *since*, *after*).
b. Prepositions are a closed class of words. This means that **no more will be created**.
c. If you are unsure which prepositions to use, you should **make an intelligent guess**.
d. To avoid confusion, don't use **too many** prepositions in a sentence.

2. Check your understanding.
My favourite object is a vase given **to** me **by** my mother **in** 1998, **on** my 18th birthday. She gave it **to** me **with** a beautiful card she made herself. I have had the vase **for (over)** 15 years. It is made mostly **of / from** glass. I keep it **on** a shelf **in** my bedroom, **next to / by / near / with** a photograph **of** my family. **Before / When** I die, I will leave it **for** my daughter.

3. Create your own.
Students' own answers.

Step 23

1. Complete and comprehend.
See Part C.

2. Check your understanding.
a. much **b.** some / a lot of **c.** both **d.** that / your

3. Create your own.
- **b.** Mistake: order of information – determiners should precede noun phrases.
  Correction: *Did you buy* ***the big*** *house?*
- **c.** Mistake: an article is needed; the meaning is different with no article.
  Correction: *She has* ***a*** *few grey hairs. She's getting old!*
- **d.** Mistake: the present continuous indicates that the action is ongoing – so the ice cream must be nearby. The demonstrative is therefore wrong.
  Correction: *I'm really enjoying* ***this*** *ice cream.*

Step 24

1. Complete and comprehend.
See Part C and the *Glossary* at the back of the book.

2. Check your understanding.
a. 4 **b.** 2 **c.** 1 **d.** 5 **e.** 3

3. Create your own.
New York is **a** very interesting city. In fact, it is probably **the** most interesting city I have ever visited. Although it's not **the** biggest city in **the** world, it does feel like it sometimes! **The** Empire State Building is **an** important symbol of **the** city, as is **the** Statue of Liberty. **An** interesting fact about **the** Statue of Liberty is that it was **a** present from France, back in 1886.

Step 25

1. Complete and comprehend.
a.
1. determiner **2.** proper **3.** countable **4.** sounds
b.
1. False. **Many** geographical features require the definite article.
2. False. Uncountable nouns **never** take an indefinite article.
3. True.
4. False. **Initialisms** generally require *the*, **but** acronyms do not.
5. True.

2. Check your understanding.
Correct versions are as follows:
- **a.** **Trust** is very important, particularly **the trust** between parents and **children**.
- **b.** UNESCO and **UNICEF** are part of the UN.
- **c.** The last time you were late, we missed **the film**.
- **d.** **Dogs** are amazing animals.
- **e.** Is he still in **bed**? We're going to be late if he doesn't get up.

3. Create your own.
The BBC is **a** major international media organization based in **the** UK. It has **Ø** many thousands of employees who work in its **Ø** London headquarters. It was founded in **Ø** 1922. Critics of **the** organization say that it should not be given **Ø** money by **the** British government. Supporters say it provides **a** very good service.

Step 26

1. Complete and comprehend.
a. See Step 4. **b.** See Step 19. **c.** See Step 19. **d.** See Step 7.

2. Check your understanding.
See table on page 12.

3. Create your own.
b. I went to the shops yesterday.
c. They met at the café next to the museum.
d. Terry was working when his flatmate returned.
e. The black dog ran off and got its ball.

Step 27

1. Complete and comprehend.
b. subject pronoun + auxiliary verb + main verb
c. preposition + possessive adjective + uncountable noun
d. adverb + past participle
e. qualifier (adverb) + adverb

2. Check your understanding.
b. [My parents] [have always supported] [me and my brother].
c. [Your birthday present] [is going to be] [a holiday in Los Angeles].
d. [I used to work] [in a factory] [next to a river].

3. Create your own.
Example answers:
b. they were going, she was talking, we were running
c. with her friend, to their home, at her insistence
d. brightly lit, densely populated, well-prepared
e. somewhat happily, fairly well, very easily

Step 28

1. Complete and comprehend.
Independent clauses consist of at least a **subject + verb**. They represent a thought or idea which is **complete**. As such, they **make sense** independently of other clauses.
Dependent clauses consist of at least a **dependent marker word + subject + verb**. They represent a thought or idea which is **incomplete**. As such, they **do not make sense** without an independent clause.

2. Check your understanding.
Dependent clauses: a, b, f, g, h
Independent clauses: c, d, e, i, j

3. Create your own.

- **b.** This is a book whose author is very well known. (i, f)
- **c.** Buzz Aldrin, who was born in 1930, was the second person on the moon. (e, g)
- **d.** Could you pass me the towel that's got my name on it? (j, b)
- **e.** That's the man whom I worked with last year. (c, h)

Step 29

1. Complete and comprehend.

See table on page 121.

2. Check your understanding.

Simple: b, d
Compound: e
Complex: a, c
Complex–compound: f

3. Create your own.

Simple: I went to the park with my dog.
Compound: My train was delayed, so I was late for my meeting.
Complex: The students are working hard because they have an exam.
Complex–compound: Since I love watching films, I suggested we go to the cinema, but my friends didn't want to.

Step 30

1. Complete and comprehend.

Example answers:

- **b.** Use either a coordinating or a subordinating conjunction to join the sentences, depending on the relationship between them.
- **c.** Include a subject or verb if either is missing. If there is a dependent clause, make sure there is also an independent clause.
- **d.** Ensure that sentences are clearly separated by placing a full stop (or other punctuation) between them. Alternatively, join the sentences using a coordinating or subordinating conjunction.
- **e.** Ensure that information follows a familiar–unfamiliar (known–unknown) pattern.
- **f.** Ensure that it is clear what nouns any pronouns refer to, particularly in long sentences.
- **g.** Try to use parallel structures within the same sentence where you can.
- **h.** When using modifiers, ensure that the subject of the sentence matches the information in the modifier.

2. Check your understanding.

a. 3 **b.** 5 **c.** 4 **d.** 6

3. Create your own.

Example answers:

- **a.** My father likes playing basketball, whereas my mother likes playing tennis.
- **b.** Bill Clinton used to be President of the USA. He was one of the most powerful people in the world.
- **c.** I went to the beach, the hotel and the gym. We then went to the restaurant for dinner.
- **d.** Helen had to leave, so she told Rachel. *or* Helen asked Rachel to leave.

Step 31

1. Complete and comprehend.

a. advice **b.** regret **c.** possibility **d.** fact

2. Check your understanding.

a. must **b.** can **c.** couldn't **d.** may / might **e.** might have / could have

3. Create your own.

a.

Example answers:

1. I'd get healthier. (2nd)
2. I'd get fired. (2nd)
3. I'd be able to speak English. (mixed A)
4. I'll be tired tomorrow. (1st)

b.

Students' own answers.

Step 32

1. Complete and comprehend.

a. preposition, adverb **b.** common, less **c.** more than **d.** object, separable **e.** follow

2. Check your understanding.

b. The case **brought about** a change in the law.
c. She **did without** any help from her parents.
d. The doctors **carried out** the operation last night.
e. He really **looks up to** his elder sister.

3. Create your own.

Students' own answers.

Step 33

1. Complete and comprehend.

a.

See Part C.

b.

2. present perfect **3.** present simple, present perfect **4.** present continuous
5. present simple

2. Check your understanding.

b. after **c.** as soon as / once **d.** Until **e.** Before

3. Create your own.

Example answers:

b. *7 o'clock / half past eight / this morning*
c. *ten o'clock / lunchtime*
d. *Christmas / Diwali / the weekend*
e. length of time (*ten years / 18 months*), year (*2005/2014*)
f. *used to*

Step 34

1. Complete and comprehend.

a. and **b.**
See Part C.

2. Check your understanding.

a. no **b.** never **c.** nothing **d.** nobody / no one **e.** neither **f.** not / never
g. None / Neither

3. Create your own.

b. It is impossible to leave after 11 o'clock.
c. There is nowhere left to visit in this town.
d. He was so nervous, he was barely / hardly able to speak.
e. They know nothing.

Step 35

1. Complete and comprehend.

Verb form	Declarative sentence	Interrogative sentence
Present simple	He's often very impatient.	Is he often very impatient?
Past continuous	**You were discussing** Thursday's lecture.	Were you discussing Thursday's lecture?
Present perfect	His brother's decided to study English.	**Has his brother decided** to study English?
Present continuous	She's suggesting his argument is flawed.	**Is she suggesting** his argument is flawed?
Past simple	You **developed** some new ideas.	**Did you** develop some new ideas?
Present perfect continuous	She has been working very hard this year.	**Has she been working** very hard this year?

2. Check your understanding.

b. What is the capital of China?
c. Why do you think he said that?
d. Do you understand the answer?
e. Did she fix her computer?
f. That's not the answer, is it?

3. Create your own.

Example questions:
b. When did she begin learning English?
c. Is the train going to be on time?
d. Where did she live before moving to London?
e. Why did she change her clothes?
f. This train is going to be delayed, isn't it?

Step 36

1. Complete and comprehend.
a. 2 **b.** 1 **c.** 2 **d.** 2

2. Check your understanding.
a. passes **b.** was achieved **c.** is

3. Create your own.
Students' own answers.

Step 37

1. Complete and comprehend.
See Part C.

2. Check your understanding.
a. went, ate **b.** accordingly **c.** them **d.** The building / It

3. Create your own.
Example answer:
Last year, I went on holiday with my parents and brother to New York. We had not been on holiday together for many years. New York is an interesting city; it has hundreds of great places to visit. These include museums, zoos and galleries. On our first day, before going to Central Park Zoo, we went to the Metropolitan Museum of Art.

Step 38

1. Complete and comprehend.
b. Wrong noun – should be *coordination*.
c. Wrong modal verb – change *should* to *may* or *might*.
d. Wrong preposition – should be *at*.

2. Check your understanding.
a. *since*
b. *the*
c. Any appropriate verb in the past simple, e.g., *visited*, *saw*, *phoned*
d. immigrants

3. Create your own.
Students' own answers.

Step 39

1. Complete and comprehend.
See Part C.

2. Check your understanding.
a. It is Robert who I admire the most.
b. What I enjoy most of all is going out to dinner with my friends.
c. That's the best cake I've ever eaten!
d. My parents did enjoy going to London.

3. Create your own.
Students' own answers.

Step 40

1. Complete and comprehend.
See Part A.

2. Check your understanding.
Sally **has lived** in London **for** three years. **Her** house is **a** small flat above a train station. It **has** five rooms. **It has** two bedrooms, a lounge, a kitchen and a bathroom. There **is** a lot of **furniture** in the rooms. **The** best thing about the house is the view of London **from** the window.

3. Create your own.
Example answers:
- **b.** Yesterday I met your friend Tom, who is a doctor.
- **c.** You should buy a computer that can store more information.
- **d.** I went to the doctors' yesterday.

Step 41

1. Complete and comprehend.
Note: the answers here are only suggested. You can express the same ideas with different words.
- **b.** … because *well-known* is an adjective phrase.
- **c.** … because the word *waves* is being used in a slightly unusual way here.
- **d.** … to define the phrase which comes before (*de jure*).
- **e.** … to indicate possession.
- **f.** … to provide additional information about the previous noun phrase, using a non-defining relative clause.
- **g.** … to indicate an alternative (= *and/or*).

2. Check your understanding.
- **a.** My mother is a teacher.
- **b.** Do you still speak to your ex-husband?
- **c.** The British Broadcasting Corporation (BBC) is a large TV company in the UK.
- **d.** She asked, 'Have you seen my father's glasses?'

3. Create your own.
In 1893, New Zealand became the first county to grant universal suffrage (a vote for every citizen); nine years later, the same occurred in Australia. In the UK, things took slightly longer. A movement called the Suffragettes, led by Emmeline Pankhurst, was founded in 1903. The Suffragettes' main demand was simple: equal political rights. This was finally achieved in 1928.

Step 42

1. Complete and comprehend. and **2. Check your understanding.**

Margaret Thatcher's first ministry, **[2]** which took place between 1979 and 1983, **[2]** was very controversial. Three key events of this ministry were economic reforms, **[6]** the restriction of trade unions' power, **[6]** and going to war against Argentina. Interestingly, **[5]** many people think that Thatcher only won the 1983 general election because she won this war. However, **[7]** others argue that her economic reforms were necessary, **[8]** and this is what won her the election. Since she won the election so convincingly, **[3]** her decisions in her second ministry were even more radical.

3. Create your own.

a.

Example answer:

In general, Margaret Thatcher's economic policy can be described as being about freedom. She believed in monetarism, an economic system where the government has little influence. Three of the main benefits of monetarism are low inflation, greater efficiency and less borrowing. However, it also caused unemployment to rise to over 3 million during her time in office. Although many people lost their jobs, Thatcher still believed that her economic policy was right.

b.

Students' own answers.

Step 43

1. Complete and comprehend.

Usage

- They are both followed by **lower**-case letters.
- Can be useful **for dividing up long sentences**.

Function

- Semicolons show **close** relationships between sentences.
- Colons can be used to introduce many different types of statement or text, e.g., **explanation, summary, definition, list** or **series.**

Grammar

- Semicolons must be followed by an **independent** clause.
- Colons can be followed by a **dependent or independent clause**.

In essays

- The colon has two specific uses in academic writing: for **in-text** references and when introducing **long** quotations.

2. Check your understanding.

a. Incorrect. *I'll meet you at 12:30.*
b. Correct, as it is a definition.
c. Incorrect. *New York is the largest city in the USA, but it is not the capital city.*
d. Incorrect. *I have lots of pets: two dogs, three cats and a snake!*

3. Create your own.

a. I have four exams tomorrow: Maths, English, History and Geography.
b. I have to leave now; otherwise, I will miss my train.
c. My diet isn't going very well: for breakfast, I ate eggs, bacon and chips; for lunch, I had a hamburger and chips; and for dinner, I ate another hamburger, more chips and some ice cream.

Step 44

1. Complete and comprehend.

a. ✔ **b.** ? **c.** ? **d.** ✗ **e.** ✗

2. Check your understanding.

a. broke down
b. income tax
c. pre-existing is much more likely, although preexisting is also possible.
d. re-covered
e. best known
f. kilometres

3. Create your own.

b. Ex-president George W. Bush was at the event.
c. Three-quarters of the class passed the exam.
d. She is my sister-in-law.
e. I don't know much about pre-20th Century history.

Step 45

1. Complete and comprehend.

Word	Mistake type	Correction
b.	4	commit
c.	4	medical
d.	5	children
e.	3	passed
f.	3	pieces
g.	5	parties

2. Check your understanding.

a.
1. which **2.** parallel **3.** difference **4.** finally **5.** experience **6.** probably **7.** height **8.** coming **9.** surprise **10.** practical **11.** interest **12.** meant

b.
BrE: catalogue, emphasise, theatre
AmE: honor, criticize, liter, monolog

3. Create your own.

millennium / son / theirs / separate / forty / foreign / week / discuss / achieve

Step 46

1. Complete and comprehend.
See Part C.

2. Check your understanding.

a.
See Part C.

b.
autocracy: rule of one person
megalopolis: large city
retain: keep hold of

c.
Examples: *demonstration*, *intergenerational*, *post-dated*, *subsequent*

3. Create your own.
Students' own answers.

Step 47

1. Complete and comprehend.
See Part C.

2. Check your understanding.

a.
1. aim **2.** experiments **3.** parallels **4.** organizations

b.
1. appendices/appendixes **2.** criteria **3.** parentheses **4.** media

3. Create your own.
Students' own answers.

Step 48

1. Complete and comprehend.
See Part C.

2. Check your understanding.

a.
1. These arguments have already been discussed by many scholars.
2. Shakespeare is quoted by many famous politicians from all over the world.
3. It is assumed that each of the data sets has been properly analyzed.

b.
1. was analyzed **2.** examines **3.** has been submitted **4.** differs

3. Create your own.
Students' own answers.

Step 49

1. Complete and comprehend.
See Part C.

2. Check your understanding.
a. on the basis of **b.** It is possible that **c.** Given that **d.** the results of

3. Create your own.
Students' own answers.

Step 50

1. Complete and comprehend.
- **a.** They are types of sentences.
- **b.** These are the basic building blocks of sentences.
- **c.** These are all determiners.

2. Check your understanding.
- **a.** It can help you identify why you make specific mistakes.
- **b.** You will minimize your mistakes and sound more like a native speaker.
- **c.** You are much more likely to make mistakes, and your effort will often be wasted, since simple grammar is usually just as effective.
- **d.** That's how the language learning process works.

3. Create your own.
Students' own answers.

Glossary

ABBREVIATION
The shortened form of a word or phrase. Two common kinds of abbreviation are **ACRONYMS** and **INITIALISMS**.

ABSOLUTE ADJECTIVE
A type of **UNGRADEABLE ADJECTIVE**. Absolute adjectives refer to states which cannot exist partially; they either exist or do not. Examples include *dead*, *unique*, *mortal* and *pregnant*.

ABSTRACT NOUN
A **NOUN** that refers to a concept or general quality, not a physical object. Examples include *love*, *beauty* and *democracy*. Contrasts with **CONCRETE NOUN**.

ACADEMIC WORD LIST (AWL)
A corpus-based list of words which commonly appear in academic writing.

ACRONYM
An **ABBREVIATION**, formed from the initial letters of a group of words, which is said as a whole word. Examples include *scuba*, *radar* and *UNESCO*. Do not confuse with **INITIALISMS**, where each letter is read individually.

ACTIVE VOICE
See **VOICE**.

ADJECTIVE
A **WORD CLASS** whose function is to describe **NOUNS** and **PRONOUNS**.

ADJECTIVE PHRASE
An **ADJECTIVE** composed of two or more words. Often one of the component words is an adjective (*very happy*) but sometimes neither is (*tennis-loving*).

ADVERB
A **WORD CLASS** whose function is to describe **VERBS**, **ADJECTIVES** and other adverbs. Adverbs are commonly used to add information about place, time, manner, degree and frequency. Often, they have the **SUFFIX** *~ly*, as in *quickly*, *absolutely*, *generally*.

ADVERB PHRASE
An **ADVERB** composed of two or more words.

AGENT
See **SUBJECT**.

AGREEMENT
When a word changes form due to its relationship with other words in a sentence or text. Words must be in agreement when they belong to the same grammatical category, such as number, person or **GENDER**. For example, in *Emily writes very well*, the subject (*Emily*) agrees with the 3rd person singular verb (*writes*). If *write* is used without the *~s* **SUFFIX**, the subject and verb do not agree.

AMERICAN ENGLISH (AmE)
The variety of English spoken and written in the USA. In writing, the differences with **BRITISH ENGLISH** are relatively small. There are some spelling differences, for example:
- *~or* (AmE) vs *~our* (BrE) (*favor* vs *favour*)
- *~er* (AmE) vs *~re* (BrE) (*center* vs *centre*)

APOSTROPHE
A **PUNCTUATION** mark (') which indicates possession (*Tom's bag*) or letters which have been left out in a **CONTRACTION** (*They're leaving*).

ARTICLE
A type of **DETERMINER** which provides more information about a **NOUN** or **NOUN PHRASE**. There are two kinds of article: **DEFINITE** (*the*) and **INDEFINITE** (*a*, *an*).

ASPECT
The aspect of a **VERB** shows whether an action is finished or unfinished. There are four aspects: **CONTINUOUS**, **SIMPLE**, **PERFECT** and **PERFECT CONTINUOUS**.

ATTRIBUTIVE-ONLY ADJECTIVE
An **ADJECTIVE** which can only come before the nouns it describes. Contrasts with **PREDICATIVE-ONLY ADJECTIVE**.

AUXILIARY VERB
A verb which modifies the **MAIN VERB** by changing the **TENSE**, **VOICE** or sentence type, or providing additional information. The most frequently used auxiliary verbs in English are *be*, *have*, *do* and the **MODAL VERBS**.

BARE INFINITIVE
The **INFINITIVE** form of a **VERB** without *to*, e.g., *Can you **make** a cake?*

BASE FORM
See **BARE INFINITIVE**.

BINOMIAL
Two words in the same **WORD CLASS** which are which are commonly used together in the form *X and Y*, e.g., *health and safety*, *research and development*.

BRACKETS
PUNCTUATION marks (( )) which are used to give a definition or indicate that information is non-essential.

BRITISH ENGLISH (BrE)
The variety of English spoken and written in the UK.

BUTTERFLY EFFECT
The idea that one tiny event can have a huge effect.

CAPITAL LETTER
An upper-case letter (*B*, *F*, *P*). Contrasts with lower-case letters (*b*, *f*, *p*). Capital letters are used to begin **SENTENCES** and **PROPER NOUNS**, as well as in titles and most **ACRONYMS**.

CLASSIFYING ADJECTIVE
A type of **UNGRADEABLE ADJECTIVE**. Classifying adjectives divide **NOUNS** into particular groups or types, e.g., *wooden*, *digital*.

CLAUSE
A group of words which is composed of at least a **VERB** and a **SUBJECT**.

CLEFT SENTENCE
A type of **SENTENCE** which is used to focus the reader on specific information, or for special emphasis. Commonly used cleft constructions include:

- *it* + *be* form + phrase + **RELATIVE CLAUSE**
  It was Freud who invented psychoanalysis.
- *what* clause + *be* form + phrase
  What we need is higher pay.

CLOSED WORD CLASS
Also known as **FUNCTIONAL** or **STRUCTURE** grammar words. This group includes the **WORD CLASSES** of **PREPOSITION**, **CONJUNCTION**, **DETERMINER** and **PRONOUN**. These are called closed word classes because no new words can be added to them. These words show the relationships between words in the **OPEN WORD CLASS**.

COHERENCE
The logical organization of a piece of writing.

COHESION
A text has cohesion if it is lucid and easy to follow. Cohesion is created by the relationships between parts of a **SENTENCE** or text which help the reader to follow the meaning. Cohesion may be grammatical (e.g., parallel verb structures) or lexical (e.g., **LINKING WORDS**).

COLLECTIVE NOUN
A **NOUN** which refers to a group of people or things, e.g., *team*, *organization*.

COLLOCATION
Two or more words which frequently appear together, e.g., *heavy smoker*. Using collocations is an effective way of sounding more like a **NATIVE SPEAKER**.

COLON
A **PUNCTUATION** mark (:) which introduces lists, definitions and explanations. It should not be confused with the **SEMICOLON** (;).

COMMA
A **PUNCTUATION** mark (,) which clarifies the meaning of a sentence by dividing it into smaller units.

COMMON NOUN
A general class of person, place or thing, e.g., *part*, *government*, *head*. The most frequently used type of **NOUN**.

COMPARATIVE
The form of an **ADJECTIVE** or **ADVERB** which indicates a greater degree, amount or quality of something in one thing than in another, e.g., *larger*, *worse*. Should not be confused with the **SUPERLATIVE** form.

COMPLEMENT
A word or phrase (often an **ADJECTIVE**) which comes in the **OBJECT** position in a sentence and which describes the **SUBJECT**, e.g., *That cake smells **lovely**.*

COMPLEX SENTENCE
A **SENTENCE** which contains one **INDEPENDENT CLAUSE** and one or more **DEPENDENT CLAUSES**.

COMPLEX–COMPOUND SENTENCE
A **SENTENCE** which contains at least two **INDEPENDENT CLAUSES** and at least one **DEPENDENT CLAUSE**.

COMPOUND NOUN
A combination of two or more words to form a single **NOUN**, e.g., *bus stop*.

COMPOUND SENTENCE
A sentence which contains two or more **INDEPENDENT CLAUSES**.

CONCRETE NOUN
A **NOUN** which exists physically and can be seen, heard, felt, smelt or tasted, e.g., *table*, *cat*. Contrasts with **ABSTRACT NOUN**.

CONDITIONAL SENTENCE
A sentence which includes a condition clause and a result clause. Condition clauses are often introduced by words such as *if*, *unless*, *when*.

CONJUGATION
Changing the **BASE FORM** of a **VERB** by **INFLECTION**, to show information such as person, number, **TENSE**, **ASPECT** or **VOICE**.

CONJUNCTION
A **WORD CLASS** which links **WORDS**, **PHRASES** or **CLAUSES** together. Common conjunctions include *and*, *or*, *but*.

CONNECTOR
See **CONJUNCTION**.

CONSONANT LETTER
All the letters which are not **VOWEL LETTERS** are consonant letters, e.g., *b, c, d, f*. They represent **CONSONANT SOUNDS**.

CONSONANT SOUND
A spoken sound made by completely or partly stopping the flow of air through the mouth. Consonant sounds are represented in text by the **CONSONANT LETTERS**. Contrasts with **VOWEL SOUND**.

CONTENT WORDS
See **OPEN WORD CLASS**.

CONTINUOUS ASPECT
The **ASPECT** of a **VERB** which is generally used to refer to states or events which are unfinished or incomplete. Contrasts with the **SIMPLE ASPECT**.

CONTRACTION
A shortened form of a word or phrase, generally using an **APOSTROPHE**. For example, *it's* is a contraction of *it is*.

COORDINATING CONJUNCTION
A **CONJUNCTION** which links two **INDEPENDENT CLAUSES** together. Common examples include *and*, *but*, *for*, *or*. Contrasts with **SUBORDINATING CONJUNCTION**.

COPULAR VERB
A **VERB** that links a **SUBJECT** to a **COMPLEMENT**, e.g., *That cake **smells** lovely.*

COUNTABLE NOUN
A noun which can be made **PLURAL**, e.g., *table*, *historian*, *concept*. Contrasts with **UNCOUNTABLE NOUN**.

DASH
A **PUNCTUATION** mark (–) which shows a break in thought. It can often be used in a similar way to a **COMMA**, **COLON** or **BRACKETS**. It should not be confused with a **HYPHEN** (-).

DECLARATIVE SENTENCE
A type of **SENTENCE**, the purpose of which is to make a statement or relate a fact.

DEFINING RELATIVE CLAUSE
A type of **RELATIVE CLAUSE** where the information introduced by the **RELATIVE PRONOUN** defines or identifies the **NOUN** which comes before, e.g., *I didn't like the last novel **that she wrote**.* Contrasts with **NON-DEFINING RELATIVE CLAUSE**.

DEFINITE ARTICLE
The word *the*. The definite article is a **DETERMINER** which is generally used before **NOUNS** which both the speaker and the listener know the identity of. Contrasts with the **INDEFINITE ARTICLE**.

DEMONSTRATIVE
A type of **DETERMINER** used to specify whether something is near or far in distance or time. The demonstratives are *this*, *that*, *these* and *those*. Demonstratives can also be used as **PRONOUNS**.

DEPENDENT CLAUSE
A **CLAUSE** which is not a complete **SENTENCE**. A dependent clause must be related to an **INDEPENDENT CLAUSE** with a **DEPENDENT MARKER WORD** to form a sentence.

DEPENDENT MARKER WORD (DMW)
A word which introduces a **DEPENDENT CLAUSE**. There are two types of dependent marker words: **SUBORDINATING CONJUNCTIONS** and **RELATIVE PRONOUNS**.

DETERMINER
A **WORD CLASS** used before a **NOUN** to indicate something specific about it. Determiners include **ARTICLES** (*a*, *an*, *the*), **DEMONSTRATIVES** (e.g., *that*, *those*), **POSSESSIVES** (e.g., *my*, *your*) and **QUANTIFIERS** (e.g., *enough*, *either*).

DIRECT OBJECT
In a **SENTENCE**, the direct object is the **NOUN** or **NOUN PHRASE** that is acted upon, i.e., which receives the action of the **TRANSITIVE VERB**. See also **INDIRECT OBJECT**.

DISTRIBUTIVE
A **DETERMINER** which refers to individual components of a group, not the group as a whole. It refers to specific parts of a general class. Examples include *each* and *every*.

DYNAMIC VERB
A **VERB** which can appear in the **CONTINUOUS ASPECT**, because it can be used to describe temporary or unfinished activity. Contrasts with **STATIVE VERB**.

ELLIPSIS
A **PUNCTUATION** mark (…) which denotes missing information. It is often used in quotations.

EXCLAMATION MARK
A **PUNCTUATION** mark (!) which is used to show surprise or for emphasis.

EXCLAMATIVE SENTENCE
A type of **SENTENCE**, the purpose of which is to talk about interesting, surprising or amazing things.

EXTREME ADJECTIVE
A type of **UNGRADEABLE ADJECTIVE**. Extreme adjectives refer to the fullest possible extent of the meaning of another adjective. Examples include *boiling* and *amazing*.

FORMAL ENGLISH
The type of English which is used in academic writing, for instance. In formal English, informal **CONTRACTIONS** and **PHRASAL VERBS** should be avoided, and slang words should not be used.

FOSSILIZATION
The process by which a grammatical mistake becomes very deeply embedded in a group's way of speaking English.

FULL STOP
A **PUNCTUATION** mark (.) which marks the end of a **SENTENCE**.

FUNCTIONAL WORDS
See **CLOSED WORD CLASS**.

FUTURE TENSE
The **TENSE** which is used to show that actions take place in – or are connected to – the future.

GENDER
The grammatical category which divides **NOUNS** into masculine, feminine and neuter. In modern English, most nouns do not have a gender.

GENRE
A type of text which contains various distinctive characteristics. Genres of text include novels, emails, dictionaries, instruction manuals and academic papers.

GERUND
The use of a **VERB** as a **NOUN** in its *~ing* form, e.g., *I enjoy* ***writing***.

GRADEABLE ADJECTIVE
An **ADJECTIVE** which can be **GRADED.** Contrasts with **UNGRADEABLE ADJECTIVE.**

GRADED
An **ADJECTIVE** is graded when it is preceded by an **ADVERB** like *very* or *quite* which describes the extent of its meaning. For example, in the phrase *extremely difficult* the adjective *difficult* is graded by the adverb *extremely.* Some adjectives cannot be graded – see **UNGRADEABLE ADJECTIVE.**

HEAD WORD
The main word in a phrase – the central information. For example, in the phrase *the black dog in the garden*, *dog* is the head word.

HEDGING LANGUAGE
Language which reduces the strength or directness of a claim. Common hedging language includes **ADVERBS** such as *probably* and *possibly,* **MODAL VERBS** such as *could* and *might* and other verbs such as *seem* and *appear.* Hedging language is commonly used in academic writing.

HETEROGRAPH
A word which sounds the same as another, but which has a different spelling and meaning, e.g., *their/they're.*

HYPHEN
A **PUNCTUATION** mark (-) which joins two words or two **SYLLABLES** together. It should not be confused with a **DASH** (–).

IMPERATIVE SENTENCE
A type of **SENTENCE**, the purpose of which is to tell somebody what to do.

INDEFINITE ARTICLE
The words *a* and *an.* The indefinite article is a **DETERMINER** which is used to introduce a noun when there is not a shared understanding of its identity, or where its identity does not matter. *A* is used before a **CONSONANT SOUND** and *an* before a **VOWEL SOUND.** Contrasts with the **DEFINITE ARTICLE.**

INDEFINITE PRONOUN
A **PRONOUN** which refers to non-specific people or things, e.g., *nothing*, *everyone*, *anything.*

INDEPENDENT CLAUSE
A **CLAUSE** which can be used on its own as a sentence. Contrasts with **DEPENDENT CLAUSE.**

INDIRECT OBJECT
The **NOUN** or **NOUN PHRASE** which refers to the person or thing that an action is done for. In the sentence *I sent Julia a letter,* for example, *a letter* is the **DIRECT OBJECT** (the thing that is acted on by the verb), and *Julia* is the indirect object. **INTRANSITIVE VERBS** can only act on indirect objects – never direct objects.

INFINITIVE
The *to* form of the **VERB**, e.g., *to make.* The infinitive is used in its **BARE** form to make the first and second person present simple: *Can you **make** a cake?* There are four further kinds of infinitive in English sentences: the perfect (*to have* + past participle), the continuous (*to be* + present participle), the perfect continuous (*to have been* + present participle) and the passive (*to be* + past participle).

INFLECTION
A change in a word which represents a specific grammatical function. The main cases of inflection in English are the changes made to verbs to show person and **TENSE** and the use of *~s* to form plurals. Some languages are much more heavily inflected.

INITIALISM
An **ABBREVIATION**, formed from the initial letters of a group of words, where each letter is said individually, e.g., *BBC*, *WHO*, *WWF.* Do not confuse with **ACRONYMS**, which are read as a single word.

INTENSIFIER
A type of **MODIFIER** which strengthens or increases the term which it relates to. Common intensifiers include the **ADVERBS** *really* and *very.*

INTERROGATIVE SENTENCE
A type of **SENTENCE**, the purpose of which is to ask questions or request information.

INTRANSITIVE VERB
A verb which is not followed by a **DIRECT OBJECT** (though it may be followed by an **INDIRECT OBJECT**). Contrasts with **TRANSITIVE VERB.** Many verbs can be used both transitively and intransitively. For example, *drink* is transitive in *Do you drink alcohol?* but intransitive in *I don't drink*.

IRREGULAR VERB
A verb which is not **REGULAR.** Many of the most frequently used verbs in English are irregular, for example, *be*, *have*, *go*.

LEXICAL WORD CLASS
See **OPEN WORD CLASS.**

LINKING WORD
A word which joins parts of a text together, thereby improving the text's **COHESION** and **COHERENCE.** Linking words are usually **ADVERBS** or **CONJUNCTIONS.** Linking words may join **CLAUSES** or **SENTENCES.**

MAIN VERB
The **VERB** in a **SENTENCE** which carries the main meaning. Contrasts with **AUXILIARY** and **MODAL VERBS.**

MID POSITION
One of the positions in which an **ADVERB** can appear in a sentence. Mid position can mean either between the **SUBJECT** and the **VERB**, or immediately after *be* when used as a **MAIN VERB.**

MODAL VERB
A type of **AUXILIARY VERB** which indicates the speaker's attitude towards a **MAIN VERB.** Modal verbs often express possibility, probability or necessity. Common modal verbs include *might*, *could*, *must*.

MODALITY
See **MODAL VERB.**

MODIFIER
A word, **PHRASE** or **CLAUSE** that acts like an **ADJECTIVE** or **ADVERB** to change or qualify the meaning of other words.

MOTHER TONGUE
A language which you learn to speak from early childhood.

MOTHER TONGUE INFLUENCE
The effect your **MOTHER TONGUE** has on the way you learn another language. Often this influence is negative, although it can be positive.

NATIVE SPEAKER
Someone who speaks a language as a **MOTHER TONGUE.**

NEGATIVE
A **PHRASE**, **CLAUSE** or **SENTENCE** containing a negative word such as *no*, *not*, *never*, *none* or *nothing*.

NOMINAL ADJECTIVE
An **ADJECTIVE** which can be used as a **NOUN PHRASE** to refer to a whole class or group of people, e.g., *the rich*, *the French*.

NOMINALIZATION
The process of changing phrases (of various types) into **NOUN PHRASES.** Nominalization is used especially in academic writing.

NON-DEFINING RELATIVE CLAUSE
A type of **RELATIVE CLAUSE** where the information introduced by the **RELATIVE PRONOUN** is not essential to understanding the identity of the noun which comes before, e.g., *Alice, **who lives in London,** travelled by train.* Contrasts with **DEFINING RELATIVE CLAUSE.**

NOUN
A **WORD CLASS** whose job is to refer to people, places or objects.

NOUN PHRASE
A **PHRASE** in which the main word is a **NOUN**. A noun phrase is created by adding information to the noun using **PREMODIFICATION** or **POSTMODIFICATION.**

OBJECT
The part of a **SENTENCE** which is acted upon by the **VERB.** For example, in the sentence *The boy kicked the ball*, the noun phrase *the ball* is the object. Objects can be **DIRECT** or **INDIRECT.**

OBLIQUE
A **PUNCTUATION** mark (/) which shows an alternative. Also known as a **SLASH.**

OPEN WORD CLASS
Also known as lexical or **CONTENT WORDS**. This group includes the **WORD CLASSES** of **NOUN**, **VERB**, **ADJECTIVE** and **ADVERB**. New words can be added to these classes as the language develops. Contrasts with **CLOSED WORD CLASS**.

PART OF SPEECH
See **WORD CLASS**.

PARTICIPLE
Refers to the **PAST PARTICIPLE** (~*ed*) and **PRESENT PARTICIPLE** (~*ing*) ways of expressing verbs, which are used in some **VERB FORMS**.

PARTICLE
A **PREPOSITION** or an **ADVERB** which can be combined with a **VERB** to make a **PHRASAL VERB**.

PASSIVE VOICE
See **VOICE**.

PAST PARTICIPLE
The **CONJUGATION** of a **VERB** which is used in verb forms such as the present perfect and the past perfect.

PAST TENSE
The **TENSE** which is used to show that actions take place in – or are connected to – the past.

PERFECT ASPECT
The **ASPECT** of a **VERB** which is used to indicate states or events which are finished before a point in time. The present perfect, for example, is used to talk about things which happened before the present: *She has visited London before.*

PERFECT CONTINUOUS ASPECT
The **ASPECT** of a **VERB** which is used to indicate states or events which are unfinished before a point in time. A sentence in the present perfect continuous is: *I have been writing my essay for an hour.*

PHRASAL VERB
A **VERB** composed of a **MAIN VERB** and one or more **PARTICLES** (usually **PREPOSITIONS**). Common examples include *look up* and *look into*. Formal speaking and writing tends not to use phrasal verbs, using one-word verbs such as *search* and *investigate* instead.

PHRASE
A group of words which constitute a single grammatical unit. Phrases can be combined to form **CLAUSES**.

PLURAL
More than one, many. Contrasts with **SINGULAR**.

POSSESSIVE
A word used to indicate ownership. There are two main groups of possessives: **PRONOUNS** (*mine, yours, his, hers, its, ours, theirs*) and **DETERMINERS** (*my, your, his, her, its, our, their*).

POSTMODIFICATION
Creating a **NOUN PHRASE** by adding information (such as a **RELATIVE CLAUSE**) after a **NOUN**. Contrasts with **PREMODIFICATION**.

POSTMODIFY
See **POSTMODIFICATION**.

PREDETERMINER
A word which can be used before a **DETERMINER**, e.g., *I lost* ***both*** *my bank cards.*

PREDICATIVE-ONLY ADJECTIVE
An **ADJECTIVE** which can only come after the nouns it describes. Contrasts with **ATTRIBUTIVE-ONLY ADJECTIVE**.

PREFIX
A group of letters which has a particular function or meaning and which appears at the beginning of words. Common prefixes include *post~* (= *after*), *re~* (= *again*), *semi~* (= *half*). See also **SUFFIX**.

PREMODIFICATION
Creating a **NOUN PHRASE** by adding information (such as an **ADJECTIVE**) before a **NOUN**. Contrasts with **POSTMODIFICATION**.

PREMODIFY
See **PREMODIFICATION**.

PREPOSITION
A **WORD CLASS** which appears before **NOUNS** and **PRONOUNS** to show place, position, time, method or movement.

PREPOSITIONAL PHRASE
A **PHRASE** which has one or more **PREPOSITIONS** as its **HEAD WORD**.

PREPOSITIONAL VERB
A type of **PHRASAL VERB** made up of a **MAIN VERB** and one or more **PREPOSITIONS**, e.g., *She* ***talked about*** *her project.*

PRESENT PARTICIPLE
The **CONJUGATION** of a verb which is used in **VERB FORMS** in the **CONTINUOUS ASPECT.** It is created by adding *~ing* to the **BASE FORM**, e.g., *looking*, *walking*.

PRESENT TENSE
The **TENSE** which is used to show that actions take place in – or are connected to – the present.

PRONOUN
A **WORD CLASS** which is used to replace a **NOUN**, e.g., *she*, *her*, *hers*.

PROPER NOUN
The name of a person, place or thing, e.g., *London*, *Queen Elizabeth II*, *Buckingham Palace*.

PUNCTUATION
The use of symbols to divide up and clarify the meaning of texts. Common punctuation marks include the **COMMA, FULL STOP, COLON, SEMICOLON, APOSTROPHE, HYPHEN, DASH, OBLIQUE, QUESTION MARK, EXCLAMATION MARK** and **ELLIPSIS**, along with **QUOTATION MARKS** and **BRACKETS.**

QUALIFIER
A word, often an **ADVERB**, which increases or decreases the meaning of another adverb.

QUANTIFIER
A kind of **DETERMINER** which says something about the quantity of the **NOUN** it precedes, e.g., *any*, *some*.

QUESTION MARK
A **PUNCTUATION** mark (?) which indicates that a question is being asked.

QUESTION TAG
A **PHRASE** composed of an **AUXILIARY VERB** and a **PRONOUN** which turns a statement into a question, e.g., *She's coming later,* ***isn't she****?*

QUESTION WORD
A word used to introduce questions. The question words are *who*, *whom* and *whose* (for people), *when* (time), *what* (thing), *why* (reason), *where* (place), *which* (choice, alternative) and *how* (method).

QUOTATION MARKS
PUNCTUATION marks (' ' or " ") which show the exact words somebody has said or written.

REDUNDANT LANGUAGE
Language which it is not necessary to use, e.g., saying *despite the fact that* instead of *although*, or saying *general consensus of opinion* when *consensus* is sufficient.

REGULAR VERB
A **VERB** with an *~ed* **PAST** and **PAST PARTICIPLE** form. For example, the past and past participle form of *look* is *looked.* **IRREGULAR VERBS** are verbs which do not follow this pattern.

RELATIVE CLAUSE
A type of **DEPENDENT CLAUSE**, introduced by a **RELATIVE PRONOUN**, which provides additional information about a **NOUN PHRASE.** Relative clauses can be **DEFINING** or **NON-DEFINING.**

RELATIVE PRONOUN
A **PRONOUN** which introduces a **RELATIVE CLAUSE.** The relative pronouns used in English are *who*, *whom*, *which*, *whose*, *that*, *what*, *where*, *when*, *why.*

REPORTING VERB
A **VERB** which is used to describe what other writers have said, e.g., *argue*, *demonstrate*, *indicate*, *suggest*. Reporting verbs are common in academic writing.

RHETORICAL QUESTION
A question to which no answer is expected, e.g., in the context of a lecture, *What are the reasons for this?* Its main function is to emphasize a particular point. Rhetorical questions are more common in spoken than in written English.

RISING TONE
Where the pitch of your voice becomes higher at the end of a sentence. Contrasts with falling tone – where your voice becomes lower at the end of the sentence.

ROOT
The root of a word is a group of letters that it has in common with words in other **CLASSES**. Words with the same root have closely related meanings, e.g., *sign* (**NOUN**), *signify* (**VERB**), *significant* (**ADJECTIVE**), *significantly* (**ADVERB**).

SEMICOLON
A **PUNCTUATION** mark (;) which is used to separate two **INDEPENDENT CLAUSES**. It shows the clauses have a close relationship. It should not be confused with the **COLON** (:).

SENSE
The way in which something can be understood or interpreted. Some words can be used in more than one sense.

SENTENCE
A statement, question or instruction which makes sense by itself, starting with a **CAPITAL LETTER** and ending with a **FULL STOP**, **QUESTION MARK** or **EXCLAMATION MARK**. Generally, a sentence must contain a **SUBJECT** and a **VERB**.

SIBILANT
A phoneme which has a hissing sound, e.g., /s/ (***s**end*), /ʃ/ (***sh**op*).

SIGNPOSTING LANGUAGE
Words or phrases which improve the **COHERENCE** of a text by indicating the relevance of a section within the overall structure, e.g., *as mentioned above*, *first of all*, *this said*.

SIMPLE ASPECT
The **ASPECT** of a **VERB** which is used to refer to states and events which are finished or complete. Contrasts with the **CONTINUOUS ASPECT**.

SIMPLE SENTENCE
A **SENTENCE** which contains one **INDEPENDENT CLAUSE**.

SINGULAR
One, single. Contrasts with **PLURAL**.

SLASH
See **OBLIQUE**.

STATIVE VERB
A **VERB** which cannot usually appear in the **CONTINUOUS ASPECT**. Common stative verbs include those which describe thoughts and emotions, such as *agree*, *believe*, *hate*. Contrasts with **DYNAMIC VERB**.

STRONG FORM
The vowel sounds in some common English words are pronounced in two different ways, called the strong form and the weak form. The strong form is used when the word is being emphasized. For example, *can* would usually be used in its weak form (/kən/) in *Can you help me?* but in its strong form (/kæn/) in *Yes, I can*.

STYLE
The type of language which is appropriate in particular situations. The style may change depending on the level of formality expected.

SUBJECT
The part of the **SENTENCE** which is doing or enacting the **VERB**. For example, in *James disagreed with Brian*, the subject is *James*.

SUBJECT-VERB-OBJECT (SVO)
The most common **WORD ORDER** in English sentences, as well as in those of many other languages, e.g., Chinese, Russian, Thai.

SUBORDINATING CONJUNCTION
A **CONJUNCTION** which links a **DEPENDENT CLAUSE** to an **INDEPENDENT CLAUSE**. Common examples include *although*, *because*, *until*, *while*. Contrasts with **COORDINATING CONJUNCTION**.

SUFFIX
A group of letters which has a particular function or meaning and which appears at the end of words. Common suffixes include *~ness*, *~ly*, *~ive*. See also **PREFIX**.

SUPERLATIVE
The form of an **ADJECTIVE** or **ADVERB** which indicates that no object has a higher degree, amount or quality of something, e.g., *largest*, *coldest*, *worst*, *most interesting*. Should not be confused with the **COMPARATIVE** form.

SYLLABLE
A group of letters containing one vowel sound. For example, the word *understand* contains three syllables: */un/-/der/-/stand/.*

SYNONYM
A word which has a very similar meaning to another word. For example, synonyms of *happy* include *cheerful*, *pleased* and *content*.

SYNTAX
The rules which govern the grammar of **SENTENCES**.

TENSE
The tense of a verb shows whether an action takes place in, or is connected to, the **PRESENT**, **PAST** or **FUTURE**.

THESIS STATEMENT
The sentence in an academic essay which summarizes the central argument. It is usually found in the introduction.

TIME WORDS
Words which indicate the time at which something occurs, e.g., *yesterday*, *tomorrow*, *three days ago*, *before*. Looking at the time words can help you to work out which **VERB FORM** is being used.

TOPIC SENTENCE
A sentence in a piece of academic writing which provides an overview of the whole paragraph. The topic sentence is usually the first sentence in the paragraph.

TRANSITIVE VERB
A **VERB** which is followed by a **DIRECT OBJECT**. Contrasts with **INTRANSITIVE VERB.** Many verbs can be used both transitively and intransitively. For example, *drink* is transitive in *Do you drink alcohol?* but intransitive in *I don't drink*.

UNCOUNTABLE NOUN
A noun which cannot be made **PLURAL**, e.g., *air*, *water*, *legislation*, *academia*. Contrasts with **COUNTABLE NOUN.**

UNGRADEABLE ADJECTIVE
An adjective which cannot be **GRADED.** Types of ungradeable adjective include **ABSOLUTE ADJECTIVES, CLASSIFYING ADJECTIVES** and **EXTREME ADJECTIVES.** Contrasts with **GRADEABLE ADJECTIVE.**

VERB
The **WORD CLASS** which shows action, existence or occurrence.

VERB FORM
The use of a **VERB** with a particular **TENSE** and **ASPECT.** Since there are three tenses and four aspects in English, there are 12 verb forms in total.

VERB PHRASE
A **PHRASE** whose **HEAD WORD** is a **VERB.**

VOICE
There are two voices in English: the **ACTIVE** and the **PASSIVE.** The active is by far the more common, but in academic English, the passive is used frequently as well. Sentences which are in the active voice follow the **SUBJECT-VERB-OBJECT** word order. Passive sentences follow an object-verb-(subject) order.

VOWEL LETTER
The vowel letters are *a*, *e*, *i*, *o*, *u*. They represent **VOWEL SOUNDS.**

VOWEL SOUND
A spoken sound made with a constant flow of air through the vocal tract. Vowel sounds are represented in text by the **VOWEL LETTERS.** Contrasts with **CONSONANT SOUND.**

WEAK FORM
See **STRONG FORM.**

WORD CLASS
A group of words which have the same grammatical properties. The main word classes in English are **NOUNS, VERBS, ADJECTIVES, ADVERBS, PREPOSITIONS, CONJUNCTIONS, DETERMINERS** and **PRONOUNS.**

WORD ORDER
The order in which words appear in a **SENTENCE.** The most common word order in English sentences is **SUBJECT-VERB-OBJECT (SVO).** Generally, **PREPOSITIONS** precede **NOUNS,** and **AUXILIARY VERBS** come before **MAIN VERBS.**

NOTES

NOTES

"an extremely useful book … answers all those questions other textbooks leave unanswered"

Lecturer in EFL, University of the West of Scotland

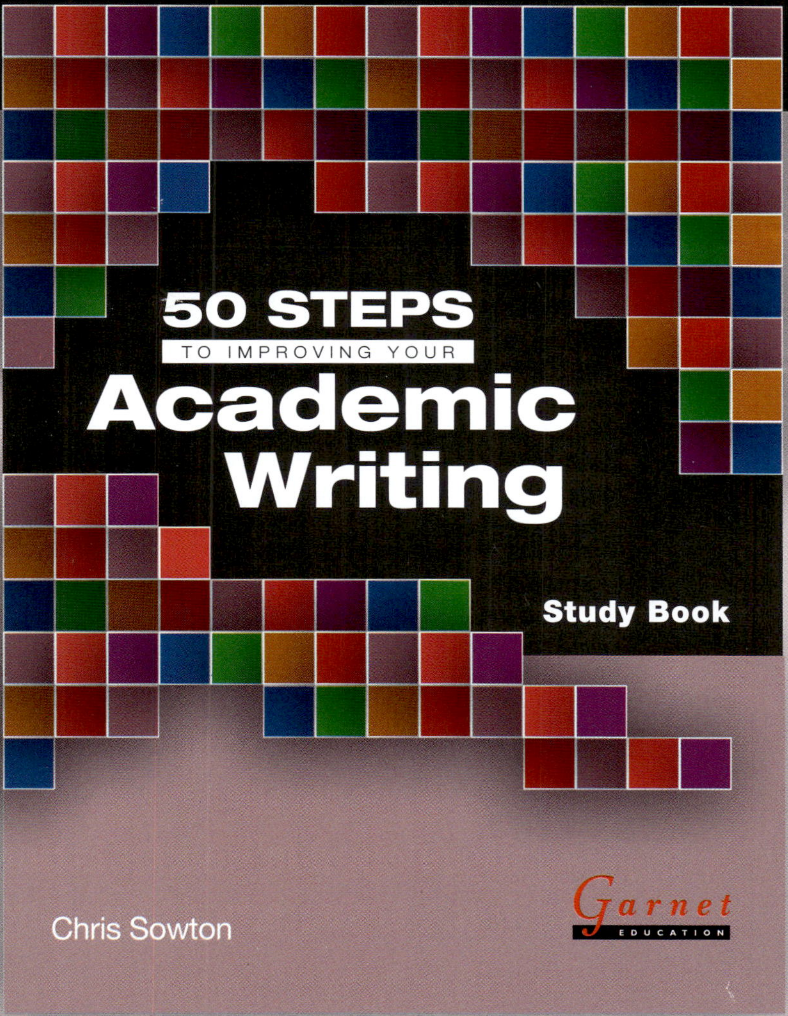

Garnet EDUCATION